Uddhav Gita

In English rhyme

Munindra Misra

https://MunindraBooks.blogspot.com/

Uddhav Gita

In English Rhyme

Published by:

AJG PUBLICATION HOUSE

GURUGRAM, INDIA

eMail: ajgpublication@gmail.com

First edition: 2025, January

ISBN Number: 978-81-19264-83-4

UDDHAV GITA

From: Shrimad Bhagwat Maha Puran

Dedicated to:

Pt. Kanhaiya Lal Misra

Contents

UDDHAV GITA....1
Source: Shrimad-Bhagwat MahaPuran, 1
6 Yadu Dynasty Retires 2
English Rhyme....2
Sanskrit Text 6....4
7 Lord Krishna Instructs 10
English Rhyme....10
Sanskrit Text 7....20
8 The Pingala Story 28
English Rhyme....28
Sanskrit Text 8....35
9 Material Detachment 40
English Rhyme....40
Sanskrit Text 9....45
10 Fruitive Activity 49
English Rhyme....49
Sanskrit Text 10....55
11 Conditioned & Liberated Entities 59
English Rhyme....59
Sanskrit Text 11....65
12 Beyond Renunciation, Knowledge 70
English Rhyme....70
Sanskrit Text 12....75
13 Hamsa Gita 78
English Rhyme....78
Sanskrit Text 13....89
14 The Yoga Scheme 94
English Rhyme....94
Sanskrit Text 14....101
15 Yoga Perfections 106
English Rhyme....106
Sanskrit Text 15....113
16 Lord's Wealth 117
English Rhyme....117
Sanskrit Text 16....125
17 Varnashram System 130
English Rhyme....130
Sanskrit Text 17....137
18 Varnashram Dharma 143

English Rhyme...143
Sanskrit Text 18...149
19 Spiritual Knowledge Perfection 154
English Rhyme...154
Sanskrit Text 19...161
20 Devotion, Knowledge, Detachment 166
English Rhyme...166
Sanskrit Text 20...172
21 Vedic Gita 176
English Rhyme...176
Sanskrit Text 21...182
22 Material Creation Elements 187
English Rhyme...187
Sanskrit Text 22...196
23 Avanti Brahman Gita 202
English Rhyme...202
Sanskrit Text 23...211
24 Sankhya Philosophy 218
English Rhyme...218
Sanskrit Text 24...223
25 Three Nature Modes & Beyond 226
English Rhyme...226
Sanskrit Text 25...231
26 Aila Gita 235
English Rhyme...235
Sanskrit Text 26...240
27 Kriya Yoga Gita 244
English Rhyme...244
Sanskrit Text 27...253
28 Gyan Yoga Gita 259
English Rhyme...259
Sanskrit Text 28...267
29 Bhakti Yoga Gita 272
English Rhyme...272
Sanskrit Text 29...280
30. Yadu Dynasty Disappears 286
Author...287

FAILURE – LIFE CYCLE - SALVATION

The Life – an endless cycle eternally,
To rectify 'Self', striving continually,
Maya – an illusion of things worldly,
Shed this illusion and so become free.

Failures just the stepping stones be,
Do not despair, they are lessons only,
A child falls trying to walk initially,
Falls – stepping stones to success be.

Each life is a continued opportunity,
To shed darkness and gain light truly,
With Karma, knowledge, devotion only,
To achieve salvation, reach Divinity,

UDDHAV GITA

Source: Shrimad-Bhagwat MahaPuran,

Book 11.06-29 (Chapters 6 to 29)

Krishna spoke to Uddhav, His voice so sweet,
Before His departure, in a moment so fleet.

Uddhav, perplexed, couldn't comprehend,
Why Krishna let the Yadava's end.

Uddhav, a devotee, a friend so dear,
Couldn't fathom why Krishna didn't interfere.

Brahma, the creator, and celestials above,
Implored Krishna to return to His divine love.

Krishna explained, with a heavy heart,
Why the Yadavas had to depart.

"Kept in check by me, like the ocean's shore,
Without their end, humanity will be no more."

Uddhav, saddened, approached Krishna's side,
Begged Him to take him along the ride.

In reply, Krishna, with wisdom so great,
Expounded the Uddhav Gita, to illuminate his fate.

These were instructions, from Krishna to Uddhav,
A farewell message, like a salve.

For those who've studied The Bhagwat-Gita with zest,
This was Krishna's final request.

6 Yadu Dynasty Retires

English Rhyme

My dear King, Uddhav's faith never did swing,
A follower of Krishna, to His feet he would cling.

Seeing Yadavas' departure, and omens causing fright,
He approached the Lord, in the quiet of the night.

"O my Lord," said Uddhav, with a voice so soft,
"Your glories we chant, and Your name we loft.

You'll withdraw Your dynasty, it seems so clear,
Your pastimes will end, that time is near.

O Lord Kesava, my master dear,
Your lotus feet, I hold so near.

I cannot bear to see You go,
Take me with You, this I implore.

O dear Krishna, Your pastimes are a treat,
A melody for the ears, so incredibly sweet.

Tasting such pastimes, all else does fade,
In Your divine service, our lives are made.

Garlands and ornaments, Your remnants we wear,
Your illusory energy, no longer a snare.

Naked sages, their minds at peace,
Attain the Brahman, where struggles cease.

O greatest of mystics, Your devotees we be,
Wandering souls, in this vast cosmic sea.

By hearing Your glories, we cross the worldly night,
In Your remembrance, we find the light.

Your amorous pastimes, with the gopis so fair,
Your bold smile, and Your debonair flair.

Your pastimes, O Lord, are a bewitching sight,
Mirroring the mundane, yet filled with divine light.

Sukadeva Gosvami, to King Pariksit did say,
Krishna, the son of Devaki, began to convey,
His words to Uddhav, His servant so true,
A conversation divine, between the chosen few."

Sanskrit Text 6

अथ षष्ठोऽध्यायः।

श्रीशुकः उवाच।
अथ ब्रह्मा आत्मजैः देवैः प्रजेशैः आवृतः अभ्यगात्।
भवः च भूतभव्यैइशः ययौ भूतगणैः वृतः॥१॥

इन्द्रः मरुद्भिः भगवान् आदित्याः वसवः अश्विनौ।
ऋभवः अङ्गिरसः रुद्राः विश्वे साध्याः च देवताः॥२॥

गन्धर्वाप्सरसः नागाः सिद्धचारणगुह्यकाः।
ऋषयः पितरः च एव सविद्याधरकिन्नराः॥३॥

द्वारकाम् उपसञ्जग्मुः सर्वे कृष्णआदिदृक्षवः।
वपुषा येन भगवान् नरलोकमनोरमः।
यशः वितेने लोकेषु सर्वलोकमलापहम्॥४॥

तस्यां विभ्राजमानायां समृद्धायां महर्धिभिः।
व्यचक्षत अवितृप्ताक्षाः कृष्णम् अद्भुतदर्शनम्॥५॥

स्वर्गोद्यानोअपगैः माल्यैः छादयन्तः यदु उत्तमम्।
गीर्भिः चित्रपदार्थाभिः तुष्टुवुः जगत् ईश्वरम्॥६॥

देवाः ऊचुः।
नताः स्म ते नाथ पदारविन्दं बुद्धीन्द्रियप्राणमनोवचोभिः।
यत् चिन्त्यते अन्तर्हृदि भावयुक्तैः मुमुक्षुभिः कर्ममय ऊरुपाशात्॥७॥

त्वं मायया त्रिगुणया आत्मनि दुर्विभाव्यं व्यक्तं सृजसि अवसि लुम्पसि
तत् गुणस्थः।
न एतैः भवान् अजित कर्मभिः अज्यते वै यत् स्वे सुखे अव्यवहिते
अभिरतः अनवद्यः॥८॥

शुद्धिः नृणां न तु तथा ईड्य दुराशयानां
विद्याश्रुताध्ययनदानतपक्रियाभिः।
सत्त्वआत्मनाम् ऋषभ ते यशसि प्रवृद्ध सत् श्रद्धया श्रवणसम्भृतया यथा स्यात्॥९॥

स्यात् नः तव अङ्घ्रिः अशुभाशयधूमकेतुः क्षेमाय यः मुनिभिः आर्द्रहृदौह्यमानः।
यः सात्वतैः समविभूतयः आत्मवद्भिः व्यूहे अर्चितः सवनशः स्वः अतिक्रमाय॥१०॥

यः चिन्त्यते प्रयतपाणिभिः अध्वराग्नौ त्रय्या निरुक्तविधिना ईश हविः गृहीत्वा।
अध्यात्मयोगः उत योगिभिः आत्ममायां जिज्ञासुभिः परमभागवतैः परीष्टः॥११॥

पर्युष्ट्या तव विभो वनमालया इयं संस्पर्धिनी भगवती प्रतिपत्निवत् श्रीः।
यः सुप्रणीतम् अमुयार्हणम् आदत् अन्नः भूयात् सदा अङ्घ्रिः अशुभआशयधूमकेतुः॥१२॥

केतुः त्रिविक्रमयुतः त्रिपत् पताकः यः ते भयाभयकरः असुरदेवचम्वोः।
स्वर्गाय साधुषु खलु एषु इतराय भूमन् पादः पुनातु भगवन् भजताम् अघं नः॥१३॥

नस्योतगावः इव यस्य वशे भवन्ति ब्रह्मआदयः अनुभृतः मिथुरर्द्यमानाः।
कालस्य ते प्रकृतिपूरुषयओः परस्य शं नः तनोतु चरणः पुरुषोत्तमस्या॥१४॥

अस्य असि हेतुः उदयस्थितिसंयमानां अव्यक्तजीवमहताम् अपि कालम् आहुः।
सः अयं त्रिणाभिः अखिल अपचये प्रवृत्तः कालः गभीररयः उत्तमपूरुषः

त्वम्॥१५॥

त्वत्तः पुमान् समधिगम्य यया स्ववीर्य धत्ते महान्तम् इव गर्भम् अमोघवीर्यः।
सः अयं तया अनुगतः आत्मनः आण्डकोशं हैमं ससर्ज बहिः आवरणैः उपेतम्॥१६॥

तत्तस्थुषः च जगतः च भवान् अधीशः यत् मायया उत्थगुणविक्रियया उपनीतान्।
अर्थान् जुषन् अपि हृषीकपते न लिप्तः ये अन्ये स्वतः परिहृतात् अपि बिभ्यति स्म॥१७॥

स्माया अवलोकलवदर्शितभावहारि भ्रूमण्डलप्रहितसौरतमन्त्रशौण्डैः।
पत्न्यः तु षोडशसहस्रम् अनङ्गबाणैः यस्य इन्द्रियं विमथितुं करणैः विभ्व्यः॥१८॥

विभ्व्यः तव अमृतकथा उदवहाः त्रिलोक्याः पादौ अनेजसरितः शमलानि हन्तुम्।
आनुश्रवं श्रुतिभिः अङ्घ्रिजम् अङ्गसङ्गैः तीर्थद्वयं शुचिषदस्तः उपस्पृशन्ति॥१९॥

बादरायणिः उवाच।
इति अभिष्टूय विबुधैः सेशः शतधृतिः हरिम्।
अभ्यभाषत गोविन्दं प्रणम्य अम्बरम् आश्रितः॥२०॥

ब्रह्म उवाच।
भूमेः भार अवताराय पुरा विज्ञापितः प्रभो।
त्वम् अस्माभिः अशेषआत्मन् तत् तथा एव उपपादितम्॥२१॥

धर्मः च स्थापितः सत्सु सत्यसन्धेषु वै त्वया।
कीर्तिः च दिक्षु विक्षिप्ता सर्वलोकमलआपहा॥२२॥

अवतीर्य यदोः वंशे बिभ्रत् रूपम् अनुत्तमम्।
कर्माणि उद्दामवृत्तानि हिताय जगतः अकृथाः॥२३॥

यानि ते चरितानि ईश मनुष्याः साधवः कलौ।
शृण्वन्तः कीर्तयन्तः च तरिष्यन्ति अञ्जसा तमः॥२४॥

यदुवंशे अवतीर्णस्य भवतः पुरुषोत्तम।
शरत् शतं व्यतीयाय पञ्चविंश अधिकं प्रभोः॥२५॥

न अधुना ते अखिल आधार देवकार्य अवशेषितम्।
कुलं च विप्रशापेन नष्टप्रायम् अभूत् इदम्॥२६॥

ततः स्वधाम परमं विशस्व यदि मन्यसे।
सलोकान् लोकपालान् नः पाहि वैकुण्ठकिङ्करान्॥२७॥

श्री भगवान् उवाच।
अवधारितम् एतत् मे यदात्थ विबुधेश्वर।
कृतं वः कार्यम् अखिलं भूमेः भारः अवतारितः॥२८॥

तत् इदं यादवकुलं वीर्यशौर्यश्रियोद्धतम्।
लोकं जिघृक्षत् रुद्धं मे वेलया इव महार्णवः॥२९॥

यदि असंहृत्य दृप्तानां यदुनां विपुलं कुलम्।
गन्तास्मि अनेन लोकः अयम् उद्वेलेन विनङ्क्ष्यति॥३०॥

इदानीं नाशः आरब्धः कुलस्य द्विजशापतः।
यास्यामि भवनं ब्रह्मन् न एतत् अन्ते तव आनघ॥३१॥

श्री शुकः उवाच।
इति उक्तः लोकनाथेन स्वयम्भूः प्रणिपत्य तम्।
सह देवगणैः देवः स्वधाम समपद्यत॥३२॥

अथ तस्यां महोत्पातान् द्वारवत्यां समुत्थितान्।
विलोक्य भगवान् आह यदुवृद्धान् समागतान्॥३३॥

श्री भगवान् उवाच।
एते वै सुमहोत्पाताः व्युत्तिष्ठन्ति इह सर्वतः।
शापः च नः कुलस्य आसीत् ब्राह्मणेभ्यः दुरत्ययः॥३४॥

न वस्तव्यम् इह अस्माभिः जिजीविषुभिः आर्यकाः।
प्रभासं सुमहत् पुण्यं यास्यामः अद्य एव मा चिरम्॥३५॥

यत्र स्नात्वा दक्षशापात् गृहीतः यक्ष्मणोडुराट्।
विमुक्तः किल्बिषात् सद्यः भेजे भूयः कलोदयम्॥३६॥

वयं च तस्मिन् आप्लुत्य तर्पयित्वा पितॄन्सुरान्।
भोजयित्वा उशिजः विप्रान् नानागुणवता अन्धसा॥३७॥

तेषु दानानि पात्रेषु श्रद्धया उप्त्वा महान्ति वै।
वृजिनानि तरिष्यामः दानैः नौभिः इव अर्णवम्॥३८॥

श्री शुकः उवाच।
एवं भगवता आदिष्टाः यादवाः कुलनन्दन।
गन्तुं कृतधियः तीर्थं स्यन्दनान् समयूयुजन्॥३९॥

तत् निरीक्ष्य उद्धवः राजन् श्रुत्वा भगवता उदितम्।
दृष्ट्वा अरिष्टानि घोराणि नित्यं कृष्णम् अनुव्रतः॥४०॥

विविक्तः उपसङ्गम्य जगताम् ईश्वरेश्वरम्।
प्रणम्य शिरसा पादौ प्राञ्जलिः तम् अभाषत॥४१॥

उद्धवः उवाच।
देवदेवेश योगेश पुण्यश्रवणकीर्तन।
संहृत्य एतत् कुलं नूनं लोकं सन्त्यक्ष्यते भवान्।
विप्रशापं समर्थः अपि प्रत्यहन् न यदि ईश्वरः॥४२॥

न अहं तव अङ्घ्रिकमलं क्षणार्धम् अपि केशव।
त्यक्तुं समुत्सहे नाथ स्वधाम नय माम् अपि॥४३॥

तव विक्रीडितं कृष्ण नृणां परममङ्गलम्।
कर्णपीयूषम् आस्वाद्य त्यजति अन्यस्पृहां जनः॥४४॥

शय्यआसनाटनस्थानस्नानक्रीडाशनआदिषु।
कथं त्वां प्रियम् आत्मानं वयं भक्ताः त्यजेमहि॥४५॥

त्वया उपभुक्तस्रक्गन्धवासः अलङ्कारचर्चिताः।
उच्छिष्टभोजिनः दासाः तव मायां जयेमहि॥४६॥

वाताशनाः यः ऋषयः श्रमणा ऊर्ध्वमन्थिनः।
ब्रह्मआख्यं धाम ते यान्ति शान्ताः संन्यासिनः अमलाः॥४७॥

वयं तु इह महायोगिन् भ्रमन्तः कर्मवर्त्मसु।
त्वत् वार्तया तरिष्यामः तावकैः दुस्तरं तमः॥४८॥

स्मरन्तः कीर्तयन्तः ते कृतानि गदितानि च।
गतिउत्स्मितैइक्षणक्ष्वेलि यत् नृलोकविडम्बनम्॥४९॥

श्री शुकः उवाच।
एवं विज्ञापितः राजन् भगवान् देवकीसुतः।
एकान्तिनं प्रियं भृत्यम् उद्धवं समभाषत॥५०॥

इति श्रीमद्भागवते महापुराणे पारमहंस्यां
संहितायामेकादशस्कन्धे देवस्तुत्युद्ध्वविज्ञापनं नाम
षष्ठोऽध्यायः॥६॥

7 Lord Krishna Instructs

English Rhyme

The Lord said with a voice so heavenly,
"Fortunate Uddhav, you reveal accurately,
My desire to withdraw the Yadu dynasty,
Brahma, Shiv pray for my return, finally.

On Brahma's prayers, to the world I came solely,
As Baladeva, with my portion plenary.

Performed many deeds, on gods' plea,
Completed my mission, now I declare freely.

Due to Brahmins' curse, the Yadu dynasty,
Will perish in self-fight, a sight unsightly.

On the seventh day from today, precisely,
Ocean will rise, inundating Dwarika city.

Saintly Uddhav, in the near future, practically,
I will abandon this earth, depart ethereally.

Then, overwhelmed by age of Kali,
The earth will be bereft of all piety.

Dear Uddhav, remain not on earth, surely,
Once I've abandoned this world, finally.

In Kali-yuga, people lost in sinful activities,
So, stay not here, you, my sinless devotee.

Give up all attachment, fix your mind on me,
Observe all things with equal vision, be free.

Wander throughout the earth, spread spirituality,
In verses, Krishna's words hold the key.

The material universe, an illusory reality,
Perceived through senses, a creation of Maya, truly.

All objects of material senses are temporary,
One whose consciousness is bewildered, sees disparity.

Bring all your senses under control, subdue the mind,
See the world within the self, and the self in the divine.

Endowed with Vedic knowledge, realize its ultimate kind,
Perceive the pure self, let your mind be refined.

At that time, dear to all beings, you'll find,
Never hampered by any disturbance, peace you'll bind.

Transcending material good and evil, in kind,
Acts in accordance, with a childlike mind.

Well-wisher of all, peaceful and wise,
Sees the Lord within all, never again dies.

Sukadeva said, to the King he ties,
Krishna instructed Uddhav, who to knowledge flies.

Uddhav said, "Dear Lord, you award yoga's fruit,
Your influence distributes its root.

You're the Supreme Atma, there's no dispute,
Explained sannyasa, for my supreme pursuit.

For those attached to sense gratification,
Renunciation is a difficult situation.

I am foolish, in bodily relation,
Thinking 'I am this body', an illusion's creation.

You are the Absolute Truth, the Lord so divine,
Reveal yourself to devotees, in you they align.

No one else can explain knowledge so fine,
Even gods are bewildered, by your illusory line.

Weary of material life, tormented by distress,
I surrender unto you, my perfect mistress.

You are Narayana, free from all mess,
The true friend of all, in Vaikunt you bless.

The Supreme Lord replied, with a voice so grand,
Humans can analyze the world, take a stand.

Through intelligence, they understand,
Sometimes act as their own master, command.

In human form, self-controlled and expert,
Can see me and my potencies, unhurt.

Many kinds of bodies, in this world assert,
But human form is dear, in this concert.

Though I, the Supreme Lord, can't be captured,
In human life, I can be pictured.

Through intelligence, and perception structured,
Search for me, in symptoms conjectured.

In this regard, sages cite a narration,
Between King Yadu and an Avadhuta, a conversation."

Maharaja Yadu observed a Brahmin Avadhuta, young and learned,
Wandering fearlessly, for knowledge he yearned.

Yadu, himself learned, took the opportunity,
Inquired from him, sought his sagacity.

"Dear Brahmin," Yadu said, with a curious mind,
"You're not engaged in religious activity, yet wisdom you find.

How did you acquire this intelligence, so refined?
Why travel freely, like a child unconfined?
Humans work hard, religiosity to cultivate,
Seek fame, long life, and opulence to accumulate.

But you, capable and learned, in a state,
Appear stupefied, like a creature of fate.

People burn in lust and greed's fire,
You remain free, rise higher and higher.

Like an elephant in the Ganges, your desire,
Is not burned by the worldly mire.

Brahmin, devoid of material enjoyment, you roam,
Alone, without companions, the earth is your home.

Tell us the cause of your ecstasy's dome,
Why within yourself, you blissfully comb?"
Krishna continued, the tale to unfold,
Of King Yadu, respectful and bold.

The Brahmin, pleased, began to hold,
A discourse of wisdom, ancient and old.

"Dear King," the Brahmin began to narrate,
"Many spiritual masters, I did contemplate.

Gained understanding, now in a liberated state,
I wander the earth, freed from the weight.

I've taken shelter of twenty-four gurus, a host,
Earth, air, sky, water, fire, moon, sun, pigeon, and ghost.

Sea, moth, honeybee, elephant, and honey thief boast,
Deer, fish, Pingala, kurara bird, and child coast.

Young girl, arrow maker, serpent, spider, wasp, the rest,
Studying their activities, I learned the self's quest.

Listen, son of Yayati, tiger among men, the best,
I'll explain what I learned, in this spiritual fest.

A sober person, even when harassed, should see,
Aggressors act under God's decree.

Never be distracted, progress steadily,
This rule from the earth, I learned readily.

A saintly person, from the mountain should learn,
To serve others, for their welfare yearn.

Like the tree, to others he should turn,
Dedicate himself, let selfishness burn.

A learned sage, in simple existence should delight,
Not seek satisfaction in senses' flight.

Care for the body, keep higher knowledge in sight,
Don't deviate from self-realization, hold it tight.

A transcendentalist, though surrounded by material array,
Should not become entangled, come what may.

Transcend material good and evil, don't stray,
Act like the wind, that's the way."

Although an Atma, in various bodies may dwell,
Experiencing their qualities, in this world's shell,
He's never entangled, just as the wind's swell,
Carries aromas, but does not with them gel.

A thoughtful sage, in a material body, might be,
But understands himself as pure spirit Atma, free.

Sees the spirit Atma, in all forms of life, a spree,
Both moving and nonmoving, in them, the Atma he can see.

The sky extends everywhere, a comparison so bright,
Does not mix with anything, nor can be divided, despite.

The spirit Atma, unchanged by material nature's might,
His eternal spiritual nature, never affected by time's flight.

A saintly person, like water, pure and gentle,
Creates a beautiful vibration, so simple.

Purifies all those who contact, a principle,
Just like a holy place, his effect is ample.

Saintly persons, powerful by austerities' execution,
Unshakable consciousness, no material world's seduction.

Accept foodstuffs offered by destiny, no obstruction,
Not affected by contaminated food, like fire's function.

A saintly person, like fire, concealed or revealed,
Burns sinful reactions, when offerings are sealed.

Just as fire in wood, differently appealed,
The Supreme Atma, in life forms, his identity wielded.

Phases of material life, birth to death's call,
Are properties of the body, don't affect the Atma at all.

Just as the moon's phases, don't make it small,
Changes are enforced by time, standing tall.

Flames of a fire, appear and disappear,
Unnoticed by the observer, although near.

Mighty waves of time, cause birth, growth, and tear,
Yet the Atma, cannot perceive time's gear.

Just as the sun, evaporates water, returns it as rain,
A saintly person accepts and returns material objects, plain.

Thus, in accepting and giving up, he does not strain,
In the objects of the senses, he is not detained.

Even when reflected in objects, the sun's light,
Is never divided, nor merges, despite.

Only those with dull brains, might,
Consider the sun in this plight.

Similarly, the Atma, though reflected wide,
In different material bodies, does reside,
Remains undivided, in nonmaterial tide,
Excessive affection, one should put aside.

Once lived a pigeon, in the forest's heart,
With his wife, never did they part.

Built a nest, made a start,
Lived for years, playing their part.

Devoted to duties, their hearts tied,
By sentimental affection, side by side.

Attracted by each other, in love they abide,
Completely bound, in affection they confide.

Naively trusting in the future's song,
Carried out their acts, all day long.

Resting, sitting, walking, where they belong,
Conversing, playing, eating, nothing was wrong.

Whenever she desired, the she-pigeon would say,
Her husband would gratify, come what may.

Thus, he could not control his senses, lay,
In her association, every single day.

Then came the time, the lady pigeon's first,
Experienced her pregnancy, ready to burst.

Delivered eggs in the nest, quenched her thirst,
In the presence of her husband, immersed.

When the time was ripe, baby pigeons were born,
With tender limbs and feathers, a new morn.

Parents became affectionate, no longer forlorn,
Listened to their chirping, from dusk till dawn.

Parent birds joyful, seeing their children's wings,
Their chirping, their movements, the happiness it brings.

Seeing their children happy, their heart sings,
Bound by affection, tied with invisible strings.

One day, the parents went out to feed,
Their young ones, to fulfill their need.

Wandered the forest, sowed the seed,
A hunter saw the young ones, his eyes took heed.

Spread out his net, captured them all,
The parents returned, heard their call.

The lady pigeon saw, began to bawl,
Rushed toward them, forgot her thrall.

Bound by ropes of intense affection, her mind,
Overwhelmed by anguish, left her blind.

Rushed to her children, left herself behind,
Caught in the hunter's net, a bind.

The male pigeon saw, began to lament,
His children and wife, in the net, spent.

More dear than life, their time was spent,
His family ruined, his heart was rent.

My wife and I, an ideal match,
She obeyed me, no catch.

But now, her children lost, home empty,
She's gone to heaven, leaving me in plenty.

Now I am wretched, living alone,
My wife is dead; my children are gone.

Why should I live? My heart is stone,
Life itself is suffering, I moan.

The father pigeon, at his children stared,
Trapped in the net, their death neared.

Struggling to free themselves, they cared,
His mind went blank, into the net he veered.

The cruel hunter, fulfilled his desire,
Captured the pigeon family, set off to retire.

One too attached to family, in the mire,
Suffers greatly, situation dire.

The doors of liberation, open wide,
To one who has human life, on his side.

But if devoted to family life, in stride,
He's like the foolish bird, who fell from the ride.

Sanskrit Text 7

अथ सप्तमोऽध्यायः।

श्री भगवान् उवाच।
यत् आत्थ मां महाभाग तत् चिकीर्षितम् एव मे।
ब्रह्मा भवः लोकपालाः स्वर्वासं मे अभिकाङ्क्षिणः॥१॥

मया निष्पादितं हि अत्र देवकार्यम् अशेषतः।
यदर्थम् अवतीर्णः अहम् अंशेन ब्रह्मणार्थितः॥२॥

कुलं वै शापनिर्दग्धं नङ्क्ष्यति अन्योन्यविग्रहात्।
समुद्रः सप्तमे अहन्येतां पुरीं च प्लावयिष्यति॥३॥

यः हि एव अयं मया त्यक्तः लोकः अयं नष्टमङ्गलः।
भविष्यति अचिरात् साधो कलिनाऽपि निराकृतः॥४॥

न वस्तव्यं त्वया एव इह मया त्यक्ते महीतले।
जनः अधर्मरुचिः भद्रः भविष्यति कलौ युगे॥५॥

त्वं तु सर्वं परित्यज्य स्नेहं स्वजनबन्धुषु।
मयि आवेश्य मनः सम्यक् समदृक् विचरस्व गाम्॥६॥

यत् इदं मनसा वाचा चक्षुर्भ्यां श्रवणआदिभिः।
नश्वरं गृह्यमाणं च विद्धि मायामनोमयम्॥७॥

पुंसः अयुक्तस्य नानार्थः भ्रमः सः गुणदोषभाक्।
कर्माकर्मविकर्म इति गुणदोषधियः भिदा॥८॥

तस्मात् युक्तैन्द्रियग्रामः युक्तचित्तः इदं जगत्।
आत्मनि ईक्षस्व विततम् आत्मानं मयि अधीश्वरे॥९॥

ज्ञानविज्ञानसंयुक्तः आत्मभूतः शरीरिणाम्।
आत्मानुभवतुष्टआत्मा न अन्तरायैः विहन्यसे॥१०॥

दोषबुद्ध्या उभयातीतः निषेधात् न निवर्तते।
गुणबुद्ध्या च विहितं न करोति यथा अर्भकः॥११॥

सर्वभूतसुहृत् शान्तः ज्ञानविज्ञाननिश्चयः।
पश्यन् मदात्मकं विश्वं न विपद्येत वै पुनः॥१२॥

श्री शुकः उवाच।
इति आदिष्टः भगवता महाभागवतः नृप।
उद्धवः प्रणिपत्य आह तत्त्वजिज्ञासुः अच्युतम्॥१३॥

उद्धवः उवाच।
योगेश योगविन्न्यास योगात्म योगसम्भव।
निःश्रेयसाय मे प्रोक्तः त्यागः संन्यासलक्षणः॥१४॥

त्यागः अयं दुष्करः भूमन् कामानां विषयआत्मभिः।
सुतरां त्वयि सर्वआत्मन् न अभक्तैः इति मे मतिः॥१५॥

सः अहं मम अहम् इति मूढमतिः विगाढः त्वत् मायया विरचित आत्मनि सानुबन्धे।
तत् तु अञ्जसा निगदितं भवता यथा अहम् संसाधयामि भगवन् अनुशाधि भृत्यम्॥१६॥

सत्यस्य ते स्वदृशः आत्मनः आत्मनः अन्यम् वक्तारम् ईश विबुधेषु अपि न अनुचक्षे।
सर्वे विमोहितधियः तव मायया इमे ब्रह्मआदयः तनुभृतः बहिः अर्थभावः॥१७॥

तस्मात् भवन्तम् अनवद्यम् अनन्तपारम् सर्वज्ञम् ईश्वरम् अकुण्ठविकुण्ठधिष्णि अयम्।
निर्विण्णधीः अहम् उ ह वृजनाभितप्तः नारायणं नरसखं शरणं प्रपद्ये॥१८॥

श्री भगवान् उवाच।
प्रायेण मनुजा लोके लोकतत्त्वविचक्षणाः।
समुद्धरन्ति हि आत्मानम् आत्मना एव अशुभआशयात्॥१९॥

आत्मनः गुरुः आत्मा एव पुरुषस्य विशेषतः।
यत् प्रत्यक्ष अनुमानाभ्यां श्रेयः असौ अनुविन्दते॥२०॥

पुरुषत्वे च मां धीराः साङ्ख्ययोगविशारदाः।
आविस्तरां प्रपश्यन्ति सर्वशक्ति उपबृंहितम्॥२१॥

एकद्वित्रिचतुष्पादः बहुपादः तथा अपदः।
बह्व्यः सन्ति पुरः सृष्टाः तासां मे पौरुषी प्रिया॥२२॥

अत्र मां मार्गयन्त्यद्धाः युक्ताः हेतुभिः ईश्वरम्।
गृह्यमाणैः गुणैः लिङ्गैः अग्राह्यम् अनुमानतः॥२३॥

अत्र अपि उदाहरन्ति इमम् इतिहासं पुरातनम्।
अवधूतस्य संवादं यदोः अमिततेजसः॥२४॥

अवधूतं द्विजं कञ्चित् चरन्तम् अकुतोभयम्।
कविं निरीक्ष्य तरुणं यदुः पप्रच्छ धर्मवित्॥२५॥

यदुः उवाच।
कुतः बुद्धिः इयं ब्रह्मन् अकर्तुः सुविशारदा।
याम् आसाद्य भवान् लोकं विद्वान् चरति बालवत्॥२६॥

प्रायः धर्मार्थकामेषु विवित्सायां च मानवाः।
हेतुना एव समीहन्ते आयुषः यशसः श्रियः॥२७॥

त्वं तु कल्पः कविः दक्षः सुभगः अमृतभाषणः।
न कर्ता नेहसे किञ्चित् जडौन्मत्तपिशाचवत्॥२८॥

जनेषु दह्यमानेषु कामलोभदवाग्निना।
न तप्यसे अग्निना मुक्तः गङ्गाम्भस्थः इव द्विपः॥२९॥

त्वं हि नः पृच्छतां ब्रह्मन् आत्मनि आनन्दकारणम्।
ब्रूहि स्पर्शविहीनस्य भवतः केवल आत्मनः॥३०॥

श्री भगवान् उवाच।
यदुना एवं महाभागः ब्रह्मण्येन सुमेधसा।
पृष्टः सभाजितः प्राह प्रश्रय अवनतं द्विजः॥३१॥

ब्राह्मणः उवाच।
सन्ति मे गुरवः राजन् बहवः बुद्ध्या उपाश्रिताः।
यतः बुद्धिम् उपादाय मुक्तः अटामि इह तान् श्रुणु॥३२॥

पृथिवी वायुः आकाशम् आपः अग्निः चन्द्रमा रविः।
कपोतः अजगरः सिन्धुः पतङ्गः मधुकृद् गजः॥३३॥

मधुहा हरिणः मीनः पिङ्गला कुररः अर्भकः।
कुमारी शरकृत् सर्पः ऊर्णनाभिः सुपेशकृत्॥३४॥

एते मे गुरवः राजन् चतुर्विंशतिः आश्रिताः।
शिक्षा वृत्तिभिः एतेषाम् अन्वशिक्षम् इह आत्मनः॥३५॥

यतः यत् अनुशिक्षामि यथा वा नाहुषआत्मज।
तत् तथा पुरुषव्याघ्र निबोध कथयामि ते॥३६॥

भूतैः आक्रमाणः अपि धीरः दैववशानुगैः।
तत् विद्वान् न चलेत् मार्गात् अन्वशिक्षं क्षितेः व्रतम्॥३७॥

शश्वत् परार्थसर्वेहः परार्थ एकान्तसम्भवः।
साधुः शिक्षेत भूभृत्तः नगशिष्यः परात्मताम्॥३८॥

प्राणवृत्त्या एव सन्तुष्येत् मुनिः न एव इन्द्रियप्रियैः।
ज्ञानं यथा न नश्येत न अवकीर्येत वाङ्मनः॥३९॥

विषयेषु आविशन् योगी नानाधर्मेषु सर्वतः।
गुणदोषव्यपेत आत्मा न विषज्जेत वायुवत्॥४०॥

पार्थिवेषु इह देहेषु प्रविष्टः तत् गुणआश्रयः।
गुणैः न युज्यते योगी गन्धैः वायुः इव आत्मदृक्॥४१॥

अन्तः हितः च स्थिरजङ्गमेषु ब्रह्म आत्मभावेन समन्वयेन।
व्याप्त्य अवच्छेदम् असङ्गम् आत्मनः मुनिः नभः त्वं विततस्य
भावयेत्॥४२॥

तेजः अबन्नमयैः भावैः मेघ आद्यैः वायुना ईरितैः।
न स्पृश्यते नभः तद्वत् कालसृष्टैः गुणैः पुमान्॥४३॥

स्वच्छः प्रकृतितः स्निग्धः माधुर्यः तीर्थभूः नृणाम्।
मुनिः पुनाति अपां मित्रम् ईक्ष उपस्पर्शकीर्तनैः॥४४॥

तेजस्वी तपसा दीप्तः दुर्धर्षौदरभाजनः।
सर्वभक्षः अपि युक्त आत्मा न आदत्ते मलम् अग्निवत्॥४५॥

क्वचित् शन्नः क्वचित् स्पष्टः उपास्यः श्रेयः इच्छताम्।
भुङ्क्ते सर्वत्र दातृणां दहन् प्राक् उत्तर अशुभम्॥४६॥

स्वमायया सृष्टम् इदं सत् असत् लक्षणं विभुः।
प्रविष्टः ईयते तत् तत् स्वरूपः अग्निः इव एधसि॥४७॥

विसर्गाद्याः श्मशानान्ताः भावाः देहस्य न आत्मनः।
कलानाम् इव चन्द्रस्य कालेन अव्यक्तवर्त्मना॥४८॥

कालेन हि ओघवेगेन भूतानां प्रभव अपि अयौ।
नित्यौ अपि न दृश्येते आत्मनः अग्नेः यथा अर्चिषाम्॥४९॥

गुणैः गुणान् उपादत्ते यथाकालं विमुञ्चति।
न तेषु युज्यते योगी गोभिः गाः इव गोपतिः॥५०॥

बुध्यते स्वेन भेदेन व्यक्तिस्थः इव तत् गतः।
लक्ष्यते स्थूलमतिभिः आत्मा च अवस्थितः अर्कवत्॥५१॥

न अतिस्नेहः प्रसङ्गः वा कर्तव्यः क्व अपि केनचित्।
कुर्वन् विन्देत सन्तापं कपोतः इव दीनधीः॥५२॥

कपोतः कश्चन अरण्ये कृतनीडः वनस्पतौ।
कपोत्या भार्यया सार्धम् उवास कतिचित् समाः॥५३॥

कपोतौ स्नेहगुणितहृदयौ गृहधर्मिणौ।
दृष्टिं दृष्ट्याङ्गम् अङ्गेन बुद्धिं बुद्ध्या बबन्धतुः॥५४॥

शय्याअसनाटनस्थानवार्ताक्रीडाशनआदिकम्।
मिथुनीभूय विस्रब्धौ चेरतुः वनराजिषु॥५५॥

यं यं वाञ्छति सा राजन् तर्पयन्ति अनुकम्पिता।
तं तं समनयत् कामं कृच्छ्रेण अपि अजितैन्द्रियः॥५६॥

कपोती प्रथमं गर्भं गृह्णति कालः आगते।
अण्डानि सुषुवे नीडे स्वपत्युः संनिधौ सती॥५७॥

तेषू काले व्यजायन्त रचितावयवा हरेः।
शक्तिभिः दुर्विभाव्याभिः कोमलाङ्गतनूरुहाः॥५८॥

प्रजाः पुपुषतुः प्रीतौ दम्पती पुत्रवत्सलौ।
शृण्वन्तौ कूजितं तासां निर्वृतौ कलभाषितैः॥५९॥

तासां पतत्रैः सुस्पर्शैः कूजितैः मुग्धचेष्टितैः।
प्रत्युद्गमैः अदीनानां पितरौ मुदम् आपतुः॥६०॥

स्नेहानुबद्धहृदयौ अन्योन्यं विष्णुमायया।
विमोहितौ दीनधियौ शिशून् पुपुषतुः प्रजाः॥६१॥

एकदा जग्मतुः तासाम् अन्नार्थं तौ कुटुम्बिनौ।
परितः कानने तस्मिन् अर्थिनौ चेरतुः चिरम्॥६२॥

दृष्ट्वा तान् लुब्धकः कश्चित् यदृच्छ अतः वनेचरः।
जगृहे जालम् आतत्य चरतः स्वालयान्तिके॥६३॥

कपोतः च कपोती च प्रजापोषे सदा उत्सुकौ।
गतौ पोषणम् आदाय स्वनीडम् उपजग्मतुः॥६४॥

कपोती स्वात्मजान् वीक्ष्य बालकान् जालसंवृतान्।
तान् अभ्यधावत् क्रोशन्ती क्रोशतः भृशदुःखिता॥६५॥

सा असकृत् स्नेहगुणिता दीनचित्ता अजमायया।
स्वयं च अबध्यत शिचा बद्धान् पश्यन्ति अपस्मृतिः॥६६॥

कपोतः च आत्मजान् बद्धान् आत्मनः अपि अधिकान् प्रियान्।
भार्यां च आत्मसमां दीनः विललाप अतिदुःखितः॥६७॥

अहो मे पश्यत अपायम् अल्पपुण्यस्य दुर्मतेः।
अतृप्तस्य अकृतार्थस्य गृहः त्रैवर्गिकः हतः॥६८॥

अनुरूपा अनुकूला च यस्य मे पतिदेवता।
शून्ये गृहे मां सन्त्यज्य पुत्रैः स्वर्याति साधुभिः॥६९॥

सः अहं शून्ये गृहे दीनः मृतदारः मृतप्रजः।
जिजीविषे किमर्थं वा विधुरः दुःखजीवितः॥७०॥

तान् तथा एव आवृतान् शिग्भिः मृत्युग्रस्तान् विचेष्टतः।
स्वयं च कृपणः शिक्षु पश्यन् अपि अबुधः अपतत्॥७१॥

तं लब्ध्वा लुब्धकः क्रूरः कपोतं गृहमेधिनम्।
कपोतकान् कपोतीं च सिद्धार्थः प्रययौ गृहम्॥७२॥

एवं कुटुम्बी अशान्त आत्मा द्वन्द्व आरामः पतत् त्रिवत्।
पुष्णन् कुटुम्बं कृपणः सानुबन्धः अवसीदति॥७३॥

यः प्राप्य मानुषं लोकं मुक्तिद्वारम् अपावृतम्।
गृहेषु खगवत् सक्तः तम् आरूढच्युतं विदुः॥७४॥

इति श्रीमद्भागवते महापुराणे पारमहंस्यां
संहितायामेकादशस्कन्धे श्रीकृष्णोद्धवसंवादे
यद्वधूतेतिहासे सप्तमोऽध्यायः॥७॥

8 The Pingala Story

English Rhyme

The saintly Brahmin said, "King, hear this,
In heaven or hell, unhappiness or bliss,
Is experienced automatically, in life's abyss,
Seek not material happiness, give it a miss.

Like the python, give up material attempts,
Accept food that comes, in all extents.

Delicious or tasteless, ample or scant,
By God's arrangement, fast if food is absent.

Remain peaceful and patient, a saintly narration,
Materially inactive, maintain without creation.

Even with full strength, avoid temptation,
Remain alert to self-interest, that's the foundation.

A saintly sage, happy and pleasing outside,
Internally grave, in knowledge he'll confide.

Immeasurable, unlimited, in him we confide,
Like tranquil waters, in him we abide.

During the rainy season, rivers rush to the sea,
In dry summer, they reduce their spree.

Yet the ocean remains, does not flee,
So does the devotee, in poverty or glee.

Failed to control senses, attraction is near,
A woman's form, created by the Supreme seer.

Enticing words, coquettish smile, sensuous gear,
Captures the mind, falls into darkness, I fear.

A foolish person, aroused at the sight,
Of a lusty woman, in golden light.

Loses all intelligence, in the night,
Destroyed like the moth, in the fire's might.

A saintly person, accepts enough food,
To keep body and Atma in good mood.

From door to door, in a humble brood,
Like the honeybee, he includes.

Takes nectar from all flowers, big and small,
An intelligent human, learns from all.

From all religious scriptures, he'll install,
The essence, he'll recall.

A saintly person, should not think,
To store food for later, in a blink.

Use his own hands as his plate, in sync,
His belly, his storage, the link.

A saintly mendicant, should not collect,
Foodstuffs to eat later, he should reject.

Like the honeybee, he should reflect,
That which is collected, will him affect."

A saintly person, pure and noble,
Should not touch a young girl, it's a trouble.

Not even let his foot touch a doll of wood,
Lest he be captured by illusion, misunderstood.

A man of intelligent discrimination, wise and bright,
Should not exploit a woman's form, it's not right.

Just as an elephant, by she-elephants, is killed,
A man can be destroyed, if lust is not stilled.

A greedy person, with struggle and pain,
Accumulates wealth, but may not gain.

Like the bee, producing honey, so sweet,
Which is stolen by others, a deceit.

Just as a hunter takes away the honey, so pure,
Saintly mendicants enjoy the wealth, for sure.

The wealth accumulated by householders, with dedication,
Is enjoyed by brahmacharis and sannyasis, without hesitation.

A saintly person, in the forest, so deep,
Should not listen to songs, that material enjoyment reap.

Like the deer, captured by the hunter's sweet song,
One can be misled, if one is not strong.

Attracted to worldly singing, dancing, and delight,
Even the great sage Rsyasrnga lost his sight.

Like a pet animal, under their control,
Lost in the allure of pleasure, paid the toll.

Just as a fish, trapped on the hook,
A foolish person can be taken, just a look.

The desire to enjoy the tongue, so strong,
Can lead one to ruin, it's wrong.

By fasting, learned men, so wise,
Bring all senses under control, a prize.

But the tongue, if not conquered, remains a vice,
Control the tongue, it's a good advice.

In the city of Videha, a tale unfolds,
Of a prostitute named Pingala, the story holds.

Desiring to bring a lover, showing her form,
Studied all the men, in a swarm.

Anxious to get money, in the night,
Thought about all the men, in her sight.

"Oh, this one surely has money, can pay the price,
Would enjoy my company, it would be nice."

In the doorway, Pingala stood, her heart in dismay,
Men came and went, walking by her way.

Her sustenance was prostitution, her hope in vain,
"Maybe this one is rich," she thought, again and again.

With vain hope, she leaned against the door,
Unable to sleep, her heart sore.

Out of anxiety, she walked out to the street,
And sometimes back into her house, in retreat.

As the night wore on, her face dried up,
Filled with anxiety for money, an empty cup.

She felt a great detachment, cutting like a sword,
Happiness arose in her mind, of its own accord.

Just as a human, bereft of spiritual knowledge,
Clings to his false sense of proprietorship, a bondage.

So does a person, without detachment, hold,
To the bondage of the material body, bold.

Pingala said, "See how illusioned I am,
Desiring lusty pleasure from an insignificant man.

I have given up the service of the Lord, most dear,
Neglected him in my heart, in fear.

I have served insignificant men, in folly,
Brought me unhappiness, fear, anxiety, melancholy.

Oh, how I have tortured my own Atma, in vain,
Sold my body to lusty, greedy men, in pain.

This material body is like a house, a shell,
In which I, the Atma, dwell.

The bones are like beams, crossbeams, and pillars,
The whole structure, full of foul distillers.

Certainly, in this city of Videha, I am a fool,
Neglected the Lord, broke every rule.

The Lord, the most dear one, for all living beings,
Is the Supreme Atma, the king of kings.

Therefore, I will now pay the price of surrender,
Purchasing the Lord, no more will I pander.

I will enjoy with him, just like Lakshmi devi,
In his divine love, forever ready."

Men provide pleasure, a fleeting delight,
But all men, even gods, are out of sight.

Temporary creations, time will erase,
What pleasure or happiness, could they embrace?

Stubbornly I hoped, the material world to enjoy,
But detachment in my heart, did deploy.

Making me happy, Vishnu must be pleased,
Somehow, his satisfaction, I must have seized.

Developed detachment, gives up the bondage,
Of material society, friendship, love, a bandage.

Great suffering brings detachment, out of despair,
Indifferent to the material world, no longer care.

Such suffering awoke detachment, in my heart,
How could I be unfortunate, it's a start?
I am fortunate, received the Lord's mercy,
He must be pleased with me, in this journey.

With devotion, I accept the Lord's great benefit,
Sinful desires for sense gratification, I quit.

I take shelter of him, the Lord, so divine,
Completely satisfied, in his mercy, I align.

I will maintain myself, with what comes naturally,
Enjoy life with the Lord, the source of love, actually.

The intelligence of the living entity, stolen away,
Falls into the dark well of material existence, in dismay.

Seized by the deadly serpent of time, in the well,
Who but the Lord could save from this spell?
When the universe is seized by the serpent of time,
The living entity detaches, a condition sublime.

Qualified to be his own protector, he becomes,
Pingala, her mind made up, to her senses succumbs.

Cut off sinful desires, to enjoy lovers,
Situated in perfect peace, she discovers.

Material desire, the cause of unhappiness, greatest,
Freedom from such desire, the cause of happiness, latest.

Cutting off her desire to enjoy so-called lovers,
Pingala very happily, in peace, recovers.

Sanskrit Text 8

अथास्षटमोऽध्यायः।

सुखम् ऐन्द्रियकं राजन् स्वर्गे नरकः एव च।
देहिनः यत् यथा दुःखं तस्मात् न इच्छेत तत् बुधाः॥१॥

ग्रासं सुमृष्टं विरसं महान्तं स्तोकम् एव वा।
यदृच्छया एव अपतितं ग्रसेत् आजगरः अक्रियः॥२॥

शयीत अहानि भूरीणि निराहारः अनुपक्रमः।
यदि न उपनमेत् ग्रासः महाहिः इव दिष्टभुक्॥३॥

ओजः सहोबलयुतं बिभ्रत् देहम् अकर्मकम्।
शयानः वीतनिद्रः च नेहेत इन्द्रियवान् अपि॥४॥

मुनिः प्रसन्नगम्भीरः दुर्विगाह्यः दुरत्ययः।
अनन्तपारः हि अक्षोभ्यः स्तिमित उदः इव अर्णवः॥५॥

समृद्धकामः हीनः वा नारायणपरः मुनिः।
न उत्सर्पेत न शुष्येत सरिद्भिः इव सागरः॥६॥

दृष्ट्वा स्त्रियं देवमायां तत् भावैः अजितेन्द्रियः।
प्रलोभितः पतति अन्धे तमसि अग्नौ पतङ्गवत्॥७॥

योषित् हिरण्य आभरण अम्बरादि द्रव्येषु मायारचितेषु मूढः।
प्रलोभितात्मा हि उपभोगबुद्ध्या पतङ्गवत् नश्यति नष्टदृष्टिः॥८॥

स्तोकं स्तोकं ग्रसेत् ग्रासं देहः वर्तेत यावता।
गृहान् अहिंसत् न आतिष्ठेत् वृत्तिं माधुकरीं मुनिः॥९॥

अणुभ्यः च महद्भ्यः च शास्त्रेभ्यः कुशलः नरः।
सर्वतः सारम् आदद्यात् पुष्पेभ्यः इव षट्पदः॥१०॥

सायन्तनं श्वस्तनं वा न सङ्गृह्णीत भिक्षितम्।
पाणिपात्र उदरामत्रः मक्षिका इव न सङ्ग्रही॥११॥

सायन्तनं श्वस्तनं वा न सङ्गृह्णीत भिक्षुकः।
मक्षिकाः इव सङ्गृह्णन् सह तेन विनश्यति॥१२॥

पद अपि युवतीं भिक्षुः न स्पृशेत् दारवीम् अपि।
स्पृशन् करीव बध्येत करिण्या अङ्गसङ्गतः॥१३॥

न अधिगच्छेत् स्त्रियं प्राज्ञः कर्हिचित् मृत्युम् आत्मनः।
बल अधिकैः स हन्येत गजैः अन्यैः गजः यथा॥१४॥

न देयं न उपभोग्यं च लुब्धैः यत् दुःख सञ्चितम्।
भुङ्क्ते तत् अपि तत् च अन्यः मधुहेव अर्थवित् मधु॥१५॥

सुख दुःख उपार्जितैः वित्तैः आशासानां गृह आशिषः।
मधुहेव अग्रतः भुङ्क्ते यतिः वै गृहमेधिनाम्॥१६॥

ग्राम्यगीतं न श्रृणुयात् यतिः वनचरः क्वचित्।
शिखेत हरिणात् वद्धात् मृगयोः गीतमोहितात्॥१७॥

नृत्यवादित्रगीतानि जुषन् ग्राम्याणि योषिताम्।
आसां क्रीडनकः वश्यः ऋष्यशृङ्गः मृगीसुतः॥१८॥

जिह्वया अतिप्रमाथिन्या जनः रसविमोहितः।
मृत्युम् ऋच्छति असत् बुद्धिः मीनः तु बडिशैः यथा॥१९॥

इन्द्रियाणि जयन्ति आशुः निराहाराः मनीषिणः।
वर्जयित्वा तु रसनं तत् निरन्नस्य वर्धते॥२०॥

तावत् जितेन्द्रियः न स्यात् विजितानि इन्द्रियः पुमान्।
न जयेत् रसनं यावत् जितं सर्वं जिते रसे॥२१॥

पिङ्गला नाम वेश्या आसीत् विदेहनगरे पुरा।
तस्या मे शिक्षितं किञ्चित् निबोध नृपनन्दन॥२२॥

सा स्वैरिण्येकदा कान्तं सङ्केत उपनेष्यती।
अभूत्काले बहिर्द्वारि बिभ्रती रूपमुत्तमम्॥२३॥

मार्ग आगच्छतो वीक्ष्य पुरुषान्पुरुषर्षभ।
तान् शुल्कदान्वित्तवतः कान्तान्मेनेऽर्थकामुका॥२४॥

आगतेष्वपयातेषु सा सङ्केतोपजीवनी।
अप्यन्यो वित्तवान्कोऽपि मामुपैष्यति भूरिदः॥२५॥

एअवं दुराशया ध्वस्तनिद्रा द्वार्यवलम्बती।
निर्गच्छन्ती प्रविशती निशीथं समपद्यत॥२६॥

तस्या वित्ताशया शुष्यद्वक्त्राया दीनचेतसः।
निर्वेदः परमो जज्ञे चिन्ताहेतुः सुखावहः॥२७॥

तस्या निर्विण्णचित्ताया गीतं श्रृणु यथा मम।
निर्वेद आशापाशानां पुरुषस्य यथा ह्यसिः॥२८॥

न हि अङ्गाजातनिर्वेदः देहबन्धं जिहासति।
यथा विज्ञानरहितः मनुजः ममतां नृप॥२९॥

पिङ्गला उवाच।
अहो मे मोहविततिं पश्यत अविजित आत्मनः।
या कान्तात् असतः कामं कामये येन बालिशा॥३०॥

सन्तं समीपे रमणं रतिप्रदं वित्तप्रदं नित्यम् इमं विहाय।
अकामदं दुःखभय आदि शोक मोहप्रदं तुच्छम् अहं भजे अज्ञा॥३१॥

अहो मयात्मा परितापितो वृथा साङ्केत्यवृत्त्याऽतिविगर्ह्यवार्तया।
स्त्रैणान्नराद्याऽर्थतृषोऽनुशोच्या त्क्रीतेन वित्तं रतिमात्मनेच्छती॥३२॥

यदस्थिभिर्निर्मितवंशवंश्य स्थूणं त्वचा रोमनखैः पिनद्धम्।
क्षरन्नवद्वारमगारमेतद् विण्मूत्रपूर्णं मदुपैति कान्या॥३३॥

विदेहानां पुरे ह्यस्मिन्नहमेकैव मूढधीः।
याऽन्यस्मिच्छन्त्यसत्यस्मादात्मदात्काममच्युतात्॥३४॥

सुहृत्प्रेष्ठतमो नाथ आत्मा चायं शरीरिणाम्।
तं विक्रीयात्मनैवाहं रमेऽनेन यथा रमा॥३५॥

कियत्प्रियं ते व्यभजन्कामा ये कामदा नराः।
आद्यन्तवन्तो भार्याया देवा वा कालविद्रुताः॥३६॥

नूनं मे भगवान् प्रीतः विष्णुः केन अपि कर्मणा।
निर्वेदः अयं दुराशाया यत् मे जातः सुखावहः॥३७॥

मैवं स्युर्मन्दभग्यायाः क्लेशा निर्वेदहेतवः।
येनानुबन्धं निहृत्य पुरुषः शममृच्छति॥३८॥

तेन उपकृतम् आदाय शिरसा ग्राम्यसङ्गताः।
त्यक्त्वा दुराशाः शरणं व्रजामि तम् अधीश्वरम्॥३९॥

सन्तुष्टा श्रद्दधत्येतद्यथालाभेन जीवती।
विहराम्यमुनैवाहमात्मना रमणेन वै॥४०॥

संसारकूपे पतितं विषयैर्मुषितेक्षणम्।
ग्रस्तं कालाहिनाऽऽत्मानं कोऽन्यस्त्रातुमधीश्वरः॥४१॥

आत्मा एव हि आत्मनः गोप्ता निर्विद्येत यदाखिलात्।
अप्रमत्तः इदं पश्यत् ग्रस्तं कालाहिना जगत्॥४२॥

ब्राह्मण उवाच।
एअवं व्यवसितमतिर्दुराशां कान्ततर्षजाम्।
छित्वोपशममास्थाय शय्यामुपविवेश सा॥४३॥

आशा हि परमं दुःखं नैराश्यं परमं सुखम्।
यथा संछिद्य कान्ताशां सुखं सुष्वाप पिङ्गला॥४४॥

इति श्रीमद्भागवते महापुराणे पारमहंस्यां
संहितायामेकादशस्कन्धे पिङ्गलोपाख्यानेऽष्टमोऽध्यायः॥८॥

9 Material Detachment

English Rhyme

The wise Brahmin spoke with grace,
"Attachment brings but a mournful face.

Let go of the world, embrace the divine,
In detachment, true happiness you'll find."

A hawk, once strong, now weak and frail,
Gave up his meat, to tell a tale.

In letting go, he found his peace,
In surrender, all fears cease.

In the realm of family and home,
Parents worry, children roam.

But I, a wanderer, free and wild,
Find joy in life, like a child.

Two types of souls in this world are free,
One touched by folly, one by divinity.

Both share a laugh, both share a song,
In their own ways, they both belong.

A young maiden, alone and shy,
Welcomed guests who happened by.

Her bracelets clanged with a noisy riot,
In their silence, she found quiet.

Traveling the earth, far and wide,
I learn from life, with time as my guide.

From a young girl's wisdom, pure and bright,
I learned solitude brings delight.

With yoga's discipline, mind and breath align,
On the Lord's form, the thoughts entwine.

Freed from desire, the mind takes flight,
In the Lord's love, it finds light.

In the realm of the Absolute, where Truth is the guide,
Duality fades, and illusions subside.

Like the arrow maker, lost in his craft,
Unaware of the king who silently passed.

The saintly soul, alone and free,
Wanders the world, in quiet glee.

Speaking but little, moving unseen,
In solitude finds a joy serene.

A home built in sand, a futile quest,
The snake finds shelter in another's nest.

In borrowed spaces, it thrives and grows,
A lesson in life, the wise one knows.

Narayana, the Lord, the cosmic dome,
Creates and withdraws the universe in His home.

In Him resides all, in Him it ends,
In the aftermath, alone He stands.

In the dance of time, in the cosmic play,
He guides the modes, in their sway.

Free from designations, beyond all strife,
In His form, one finds eternal life.

As the spider weaves, and then withdraws,
The Lord displays, and then defrosts.

The cosmic web, a divine art,
Drawn from within His sacred heart.

In love or fear, in hate or delight,
The form one meditates, becomes one's sight.

Like the insect, trapped in the wasp's hive,
Becomes the wasp, in its captive life.

From masters, I learned, from life, I grew,
Now listen, O King, as I share my view.

In the body's wisdom, in its silent speech,
Lies a lesson, that only experience can teach.

The body, a master, teaches me to let go,
In its fleeting existence, wisdom it bestows.

Though it houses knowledge, a vessel so grand,
It's but a transient guest in this temporal land.

A man of the world, in material delight,
Struggles for possessions with all his might.

Yet, like a tree that seeds before its fall,
The body too, answers the karmic call.

A man with many wives, in constant strife,
Reflects the senses that pull us in life.

Tongue, thirst, touch, and more,
Each a relentless tide on a restless shore.

The Supreme Lord, in His divine play,
Crafted countless beings in a splendid array.

Yet, only in humans, He found His delight,
For they alone perceive the Absolute Light.

After cycles of birth, in forms far and wide,
One attains human life, with wisdom as a guide.

This precious chance, one must not waste,
For in this life, the Divine can be embraced.

From masters, I learned, from life, I grew,
In the Lord's realization, I found a view.

Unattached, egoless, I wander this sphere,
In the light of knowledge, everything is clear.

The Absolute Truth, though one and unique,
Is described in many ways by the sages who speak.

From one master, complete knowledge may not unfurl,
For the Truth is a gem with many a pearl.

The Lord spoke, the Brahmin heard,
In his heart, divine love was stirred.

With a farewell, he went on his way,
Just as he came, without any sway.

Uddhav, hearing the Avadhuta's word,
Found his mind to the spiritual lured.

Free from attachment, in tranquility,
His mind found rest in spirituality.

Sanskrit Text 9

अथ नवमोऽध्यायः।
ब्राह्मणः उवाच।
परिग्रहः हि दुःखाय यत् यत् प्रियतमं नृणाम्।
अनन्तं सुखम् आप्नोति तत् विद्वान् यः तु अकिञ्चनः॥१॥

सामिषं कुररं जघ्नुः बलिनः ये निरामिषाः।
तत् आमिषं परित्यज्य सः सुखं समविन्दत॥२॥

न मे मानावमानौ स्तः न चिन्ता गेहपुत्रिणाम्।
आत्मक्रीडः आत्मरतिः विचरामि इह बालवत्॥३॥

द्वौ एव चिन्तया मुक्तौ परम आनन्दः आप्लुतौ।
यः विमुग्धः जडः बालः यः गुणेभ्यः परं गतः॥४॥

क्वचित् कुमारी तु आत्मानं वृणानान् गृहम् आगतान्।
स्वयं तान् अर्हयामास क्वापि यातेषु बन्धुषु॥५॥

तेषम् अभ्यवहारार्थं शालीन् रहसि पार्थिव।
अवघ्नन्त्याः प्रकोष्ठस्थाः चक्रुः शङ्खाः स्वनं महत्॥६॥

सा तत् जुगुप्सितं मत्वा महती व्रीडिता ततः।
बभञ्ज एकैकशः शङ्खान् द्वौ द्वौ पाण्योः अशेषयत्॥७॥

उभयोः अपि अभूत् घोषः हि अवघ्नन्त्याः स्म शङ्खयोः।
तत्र अपि एकं निरभिदत् एकस्मान् न अभवत् ध्वनिः॥८॥

अन्वशिक्षम् इमं तस्याः उपदेशम् अरिन्दम।
लोकान् अनुचरन् एतान् लोकतत्त्वविवित्सया॥९॥

वासे बहूनां कलहः भवेत् वार्ता द्वयोः अपि।
एकः एव चरेत् तस्मात् कुमार्याः इव कङ्कणः॥१०॥

मनः एकत्र संयुज्यात् जितश्वासः जित आसनः।
वैराग्याभ्यासयोगेन ध्रियमाणम् अतन्द्रितः॥११॥

यस्मिन् मनः लब्धपदं यत् एतत् शनैः शनैः मुञ्चति कर्मरेणून्।
सत्त्वेन वृद्धेन रजः तमः च विधूय निर्वाणम् उपैति अनिन्धनम्॥१२॥

तत् एवम् आत्मनि अवरुद्धचित्तः न वेद किञ्चित् बहिः अन्तरं वा।
यथा इषुकारः नृपतिं व्रजन्तम् इषौ गतात्मा न ददर्श पार्श्वे॥१३॥

एकचार्यनिकेतः स्यात् अप्रमत्तः गुहाशयः।
अलक्ष्यमाणः आचारैः मुनिः एकः अल्पभाषणः॥१४॥

गृहारम्भः अतिदुःखाय विफलः च अध्रुवात्मनः।
सर्पः परकृतं वेश्म प्रविश्य सुखम् एधते॥१५॥

एको नारायणो देवः पूर्वसृष्टं स्वमायया।
संहृत्य कालकलया कल्पान्त इदमीश्वरः॥१६॥

एक एवाद्वितीयोऽभूदात्माधारोऽखिलाश्रयः।
कालेनात्मानुभावेन साम्यं नीतासु शक्तिषु।
सत्त्वादिष्वादिपुएरुषः प्रधानपुरुषेश्वरः॥१७॥

परावराणां परम आस्ते कैवल्यसंज्ञितः।
केवलानुभवानन्दसन्दोहो निरुपाधिकः॥१८॥

केवलात्मानुभावेन स्वमायां त्रिगुणात्मिकाम्।
संक्षोभयन्सृजत्यादौ तया सूत्रमरिन्दम॥१९॥

तामाहुस्त्रिगुणव्यक्तिं सृजन्तीं विश्वतोमुखम्।
यस्मिन्प्रोतमिदं विश्वं येन संसरते पुमान्॥२०॥

यथा ऊर्णनाभिः हृदयात् ऊर्णां सन्तत्य वक्त्रतः।
तया विहृत्य भूयस्तां ग्रसति एवं महेश्वरः॥२१॥

यत्र यत्र मनः देही धारयेत् सकलं धिया।
स्नेहात् द्वेषात् भयात् वा अपि याति तत् तत् सरूपताम्॥२२॥

कीटः पेशस्कृतं ध्यायन् कुड्यां तेन प्रवेशितः।
याति तत् स्सत्मतां राजन् पूर्वरूपम् असन्त्यजन्॥२३॥

एवं गुरुभ्यः एतेभ्यः एष मे शिक्षिता मतिः।
स्वात्मा उपशिक्षितां बुद्धिं श्रुणु मे वदतः प्रभो॥२४॥

देहः गुरुः मम विरक्तिविवेकहेतुः बिभ्रत् स्म सत्त्वनिधनं सतत अर्त्युत् अर्कम्।
तत्त्वानि अनेन विमृशामि यथा तथा अपि पारक्यम् इति अवसितः विचरामि असङ्गः॥२५॥

जायाअत्मजार्थपशुभृत्यगृहाप्तवर्गान् पुष्णाति यत् प्रियचिकीर्षया वितन्वन्॥

स्वान्ते सकृच्छ्रम् अवरुद्धधनः सः देहः सृष्ट्वा अस्य बीजम् अवसीदति वृक्षधर्मा॥२६॥

जिह्वा एकतः अमुम् अवकर्षति कर्हि तर्षा शिश्नः अन्यतः त्वक् उदरं श्रवणं कुतश्चित्।
घ्राणः अन्यतः चपलदृक् क्व च कर्मशक्तिः बह्व्यः सपत्न्यः इव गेहपतिं लुनन्ति॥२७॥

सृष्ट्वा पुराणि विविधानि अजया आत्मशक्त्या वृक्षान् सरीसृपपशून्खगदंशमत्स्यान्।
तैः तैः अतुष्टहृदयः पुरुषं विधाय ब्रह्मावलोकधिषणं मुदमाप देवः॥२८॥

लब्ध्वा सुदुर्लभम् इदं बहुसम्भवान्ते मानुष्यमर्थदमनित्यमपीह धीरः।
तूर्णं यतेत न पतेत् अनुमृत्युः यावत् निःश्रेयसाय विषयः खलु सर्वतः स्यात्॥२९॥

एवं सञ्जातवैराग्यः विज्ञानलोक आत्मनि।
विचरामि महीम् एतां मुक्तसङ्गः अनहङ्कृतिः॥३०॥

न हि एकस्मात् गुरोः ज्ञानं सुस्थिरं स्यात् सुपुष्कलम्।
ब्रह्म एतत् अद्वितीयं वै गीयते बहुधा ऋषिभिः॥३१॥

श्रीभगवानुवाच।
इत्युक्त्वा स यदुं विप्रस्तमामन्त्रय गभीरधीः।
वन्दितोऽअभ्यर्थितो राज्ञा ययौ प्रीतो यथागतम्॥३२॥

अवधूतवचः श्रुत्वा पूर्वेषां नः स पूर्वजः।
सर्वसङ्गविनिर्मुक्तः समचित्तो बभूव ह॥३३॥

इति श्रीमद्भागवते महापुराणे पारमहंस्यां
संहितायामेकादशस्कन्धे भगवदुद्धवसंवादे
नवमोऽध्यायः॥९॥

10 Fruitive Activity

English Rhyme

In the Lord's shelter, with mind so pure,
In devotion, one finds a life secure.

Free from desire, in Varnashram's fold,
One finds the path, as by the Lord told.

The Atma, purified, begins to see,
The folly of sense, the false decree.

In dreams and illusions, pleasure we chase,
But they're mere shadows, in life's vast space.

Fixed on the Lord, as life's supreme goal,
One renounces sense, gains spiritual control.

In search of truth, in Atma's light,
One transcends the scriptural rite.

Accepting the Lord, as life's highest aim,
One observes the scriptures, in His holy name.

Approaching the master, peaceful and wise,
One sees the Lord, through enlightened eyes.

The disciple, humble, active, and free,
Renounces all, in divine decree.

With love for the master, and envy for none,
He seeks wisdom, under the spiritual sun.

Seeing self-interest, in every state,
One detaches from worldly trait.

From wife, children, wealth, and land,
In the Lord alone, one takes a stand.

As fire differs from the wood it burns,
The Atma, from the body, wisdom discerns.

The seer and seen, in their unique role,
Play out the drama, in the cosmic scroll.

As fire takes form, from the fuel's state,
The Atma assumes bodies, in a dance so great.

Subtle and gross, in nature's play,
The bodies form, in the Lord's array.

In illusion, we claim, what's not our own,
The body's qualities, in ignorance shown.

Yet, this illusion, by knowledge, is shattered,
In the light of truth, only the Atma mattered.

In the heart's quiet chamber, the Lord resides,
In pure, transcendental existence, He abides.

With knowledge as the lamp, and truth as the key,
One unlocks the illusion, and finally is free.

The guru and disciple, kindling sticks in hand,
Ignite the fire of wisdom, at the guru's command.

The flame of transcendental knowledge, bright and clear,
Burns ignorance to ashes, both to guru and disciple dear.

By hearing from the master, with a heart so pure,
The disciple gains knowledge, of that, we're sure.

This knowledge, like a fire, consumes illusion's might,
Until nothing remains, but the eternal light.

Yet, philosophers may challenge, with a different view,
Seeing the world as eternal, with transformations anew.

Even if one accepts this, with time's relentless tide,
Birth, death, old age, and disease, will not subside.

The worker seeks happiness, in actions he performs,
Yet often finds sorrow, in its many forms.

Controlled by another, in destiny's dance,
How can he expect, to leave it to chance?

In the world's grand theatre, a paradox we find,
Sometimes, the intelligent are unhappy, the fools are kind.

The pursuit of happiness, through actions we make,
Is but a display of ego, a mere shadow, a fake.

Even if one knows, how to find joy, avoid pain,
The mystery of death, still does remain.

For death is a specter, casting a pall,
Over all worldly pleasures, however big or small.

The happiness we seek, in heavenly delight,
Is but a reflection, of our earthly plight.

Both tainted by envy, decay, and strife,
Such is the nature, of the material life.

Performing rituals, with precision and care,
May lead to heaven, but let us beware.

Even this reward, time will erase,
Nothing in this world, can time replace.

So, hear this now, take it to heart,
True happiness comes, when from illusion we part.

In the Lord within, seek your treasure,
And find a joy, that knows no measure.

In the heavenly realms, where the pious reside,
In glowing airplanes, they take their ride.

Glorified by Gandharvas, in clothes so grand,
In the company of goddesses, they make their stand.

On pleasure rides, in the heavenly sphere,
With tinkling bells ringing clear.

In gardens of delight, they find their rest,
Unaware of the piety, they're putting to test.

As long as the fruits of piety last,
They enjoy the heavens, vast and vast.

But when the fruits are finally spent,
Down from heaven, they are sent.

Engaged in sin, with senses untamed,
The human being is shamed.

Full of desire, greedy and mean,
In the exploitation of others, he is seen.

Polluted minds, violent and wild,
Slaughter the innocent, beguiled.

Worshiping spirits, lost in illusion,
They fall into hell, in confusion.

In a body of darkness, they find their fate,
Performing actions, that only create,

A cycle of suffering, pain, and strife,
What happiness is there, in such a life?

From heavenly realms to the hellish deep,
In the form of time, fear does creep.

Even Brahma, with life span so grand,
In the face of time, cannot stand.

The senses stir, in nature's dance,
Creating a world of circumstance.

Bound by the modes, in countless forms,
The Atma weathers life's many storms.

In the play of nature, varied and vast,
The Atma fears the future and past.

In material life, it seeks its pleasure,
Only to find, it's but fleeting treasure.

When nature stirs, and modes interact,
The Atma sees the divine fact.

In time, the Self, the universe wide,
In all these, the Lord does reside.

Uddhav asked, with a humble plea,
"How can the Atma ever be free?

Transcendental, yet bound in strife,
What is the true nature of life?"

"Sometimes conditioned, sometimes free,
What is the Atma's reality?

In life's various roles, in joy and sorrow,
What makes the Atma, today and tomorrow?"

-

Sanskrit Text 10

अथ दशमोऽध्यायः।
श्रीभगवान् उवाच।
मया उदितेषु अवहितः स्वधर्मेषु मदाश्रयः।
वर्णाश्रमकुल आचारम् अकामात्मा समाचरेत्॥१॥

अन्वीक्षेत विशुद्धात्मा देहिनां विषयात्मनाम्।
गुणेषु तत्त्वध्यानेन सर्वारम्भविपर्ययम्॥२॥

सुप्तस्य विषयालोकः ध्यायतः वा मनोरथः।
नानात्मकत्वात् विफलः तथा भेदात्मदीः गुणैः॥३॥

निवृत्तं कर्म सेवेत प्रवृत्तं मत्परः त्यजेत्।
जिज्ञासायां सम्प्रवृत्तः न अद्रियेत् कर्म चोदनाम्॥४॥

यमानभीक्ष्णं सेवेत नियमान् मत्परः क्वचित्।
मदभिज्ञं गुरुं शान्तम् उपासीत मदात्मकम्॥५॥

अमान्यमत्सरः दक्षः निर्ममः दृढसौहृदः।
असत्वरः अर्थजिज्ञासुः अनसूयौः अमोघवाक्॥६॥

जायापत्यगृहक्षेत्रस्वजनद्रविण आदिषु।
उदासीनः समं पश्यन् सर्वेषु अर्थम् इव आत्मनः॥७॥

विलक्षणः स्थूलसूक्ष्मात् देहात् आत्मेक्षिता स्वदृक्।
यथाग्निः दारुणः दाह्यात् दाहकः अन्यः प्रकाशकः॥८॥

निरोध उत्पत्ति अणु बृहन् नानात्वं तत्कृतान् गुणान्।
अन्तः प्रविष्टः आधत्तः एवं देहगुणान् परः॥९॥

यः असौ गुणैः विरचितः देहः अयं पुरुषस्य हि।
संसारः तत् निबन्धः अयं पुंसः विद्यात् छिदात्मनः॥१०॥

तस्मात् जिज्ञासया आत्मानम् आत्मस्थं परम्।
सङ्गम्य निरसेत् एतत् वस्तुबुद्धिं यथाक्रमम्॥११॥

आचार्यः अरणिः आद्यः स्यात् अन्तेवासि उत्तर अरणिः।
तत् सन्धानं प्रवचनं विद्या सन्धिः सुखावहः॥१२॥

वैशारदी सा अतिविशुद्धबुद्धिः धुनोति मायां गुणसम्प्रसूताम्।
गुणान् च सन्दह्य यत् आत्मम् एतत् स्वयं च शाम्यति असमिद् यथा अग्निः॥१३॥

अथ एषां कर्मकर्तॄणां भोक्तॄणां सुखदुःखयोः।
नानात्वम् अथ नित्यत्वं लोककालागम आत्मनाम्॥१४॥

मन्यसे सर्वभावानां संस्था हि औत्पत्तिकी यथा।
तत् तत् आकृतिभेदेन जायते भिद्यते च धीः॥१५॥

एवम् अपि अङ्ग सर्वेषां देहिनां देहयोगतः।
काल अवयवतः सन्ति भावा जन्मादयोः असकृत्॥१६॥

अत्र अपि कर्मणां कर्तुः अस्वातन्त्र्यं च लक्ष्यते।
भोक्तुः च दुःखसुखयोः कः अन्वर्थः विवशं भजेत्॥१७॥

न देहिनां सुखं किञ्चित् विद्यते विदुषाम् अपि।
तथा च दुःखं मूढानां वृथा अहङ्करणं परम्॥१८॥

यदि प्राप्तिं विघातं च जानन्ति सुखदुःखयोः।
ते अपि अद्धा न विदुः योगं मृत्युः न प्रभवेत् यथा॥१९॥

कः अन्वर्थः सुखयति एनं कामः वा मृत्युः अन्तिके।
आघातं नीयमानस्य वध्यसि एव न तुष्टिदः॥२०॥

श्रुतं च दृष्टवत् दुष्टं स्पर्धा असूया अत्ययव्ययैः।
बहु अन्तराय कामत्वात् कृषिवत् च अपि निष्फलम्॥२१॥

अन्तरायैः अविहतः यदि धर्मः स्वनुष्ठितः।
तेनापि निर्जितं स्थानं यथा गच्छति तत् शृणु॥२२॥

इष्ट्वा इह देवताः यज्ञैः स्वर्लोकं याति याज्ञिकः।
भुञ्जीत देववत् तत्र भोगान् दिव्यान् निज अर्जितान्॥२३॥

स्वपुण्य उपचिते शुभ्रे विमानः उपगीयते।
गन्धर्वैः विहरन्मध्ये देवीनां हृद्यवेषधृक्॥२४॥

स्त्रीभिः कामगयानेन किङ्किणीजालमालिना।
क्रीडन् न वेद आत्मपातं सुराक्रीडेषु निर्वृतः॥२५॥

तावत् प्रमोदते स्वर्गे यावत् पुण्यं समाप्यते।
क्षीणपुण्यः पतति अर्वाक् अनिच्छन् कालचालितः॥२६॥

यदि अधर्मरतः सङ्गात् असतां वा अजितेन्द्रियः।
कामात्मा कृपणः लुब्धः स्त्रैणः भूतविहिंसकः॥२७॥

पशून् अविधिना आलभ्य प्रेतभूतगणान् यजन्।
नरकान् अवशः जन्तुः गत्वा याति उल्बणं तमः॥२८॥

कर्माणि दुःख उदर्काणि कुर्वन् देहेन तैः पुनः।
देहम् आभजते तत्र किं सुखं मर्त्यधर्मिणः॥२९॥

लोकानां लोक पालानां मद्भयं कल्पजीविनाम्।
ब्रह्मणः अपि भयं मत्तः द्विपराधपर आयुषः॥३०॥

गुणाः सृजन्ति कर्माणि गुणः अनुसृजते गुणान्।
जीवः तु गुणसंयुक्तः भुङ्क्ते कर्मफलानि असौ॥३१॥

यावत् स्यात् गुणवैषम्यं तावत् नानात्वम् आत्मनः।
नानात्वम् आत्मनः यावत् पारतन्त्र्यं तदा एव हि॥३२॥

यावत् अस्य अस्वतन्त्रत्वं तावत् ईश्वरतः भयम्।
यः एतत् समुपासीरन् ते मुह्यन्ति शुचार्पिताः॥३३॥

कालः आत्मा आगमः लोकः स्वभावः धर्मः एव च।
इति मां बहुधा प्राहुः गुणव्यतिकरे सति॥३४॥

उद्धवः उवाच।
गुणेषु वर्तमानः अपि देहजेषु अनपावृताः।
गुणैः न बध्यते देही बध्यते वा कथं विभो॥३५॥

कथं वर्तेत विहरेत् कैः वा ज्ञायेत लक्षणैः।
किं भुञ्जीत उत विसृजेत् शयीत आसीत याति वा॥३६॥

एतत् अच्युत मे ब्रूहि प्रश्नं प्रश्नविदां वर।
नित्यमुक्तः नित्यबद्धः एकः एव इति मे भ्रमः॥३७॥

इति श्रीमद्भागवते महापुराणे पारमहंस्यां
संहितायामेकादशस्कन्धे भगवदुद्धवसंवादे
दशमोऽध्यायः॥१०॥

11 Conditioned & Liberated Entities

English Rhyme

The Lord spoke to Uddhav, His words so clear,
"Bound or free, have no fear.

For the Atma, in truth, is ever free,
And so am I, in my divine decree.

Just as a dream, with no substance or form,
So is the world, in its norm.

Lamentation, illusion, joy, and strife,
Are but illusions, in the Atma's life.

Knowledge and ignorance, both from me arise,
They bind and liberate, in their guise.

The jiva, part of me, in ignorance does dwell,
But by knowledge, can break the spell.

In the same body, joy and sorrow reside,
For the Lord and Atma, within it, abide.

Two birds in a tree, a tale to tell,
One eats the fruits, the other dwells.

The bird that refrains, is the Lord so bright,
The other, the Atma, lost in the night.

Covered by ignorance, it cannot see,
That like the Lord, it's meant to be free.

Awake from the dream, the wise one knows,
He's not the body, as the illusion shows.

Free from desire, he stands apart,
Engages the senses, but keeps a pure heart.

The fool, however, in ignorance bound,
Thinks he's the doer, in actions found.

But the wise one, in detachment, finds his peace,
In the world, but not of it, he finds release."

The Lord spoke to Uddhav, His words so clear,
"Engage in devotion, hold me dear.

Offer your work, its fruits to me,
In such service, you'll find the key.

One who's kind, to all life's forms,
Who sails through life's many storms.

Who sees himself, not as a proprietor,
But as a humble, loving warrior.

He who's steady, in joy and sorrow,
Who borrows not, today or tomorrow.

Who's free from cares, and from all pains,
In my love, he forever reigns.

One who's equal, to friend and foe,
Who's steady, come weal or woe.

Who renounces all, the good and bad,
Is dear to me, makes me glad.

One who's silent, satisfied with all,
Who cares not, for the big or small.

Who's fixed in knowledge, in devotion strong,
Is dear to me, all life long.

Follow this path, of devotion true,
Engage in faith, make me your view.

Such a one, in every way,
Is very, very dear to me, I say."

The Lord spoke to Uddhav, His words so kind,
"Narrations of my pastimes, in your mind,

Purify the universe, bring auspicious light,
In such devotion, find your might.

One who serves, with pure devotion,
Finds in me, his life's motion.

To my abode, he easily goes,
Revealed by devotees, as the holy river flows.

Uddhav asked, with a humble plea,
"What makes a devotee, in your decree?

What service is worthy, in your sight?
Please guide me, in your light.

You, the Absolute, beyond all measure,
Accept many forms, for your devotees' pleasure.

Transcendental to all, yet close at hand,
In your devotees' hearts, you make your stand.

A saintly person, the Lord explained,
Is merciful, has his senses restrained.

His strength comes from truth, his heart is clear,
Such a one, to me, is very dear.

He works for all, his mind is steady,
From worldly desires, he is already free.

He honors others, seeks no fame,
In Krishna consciousness, he plays the game.

Such a person, learned and wise,
Sees beyond the worldly disguise.

He worships me, renounces the rest,
Such a devotee, I consider the best."

The Lord spoke to Uddhav, His words so true,
"My devotees may not know me, in all I do.

But if they worship with love, pure and bright,
They are the best of devotees, in my sight.

Give up false pride, engage in devotion,
In seeing, touching, and in motion.

Worship my form, offer prayers of love,
Glorify my qualities, like a dove.

Offer to me, all that you gain,
Accept yourself as my servant, without any pain.

Celebrate my birth, my activities too,
In festivals and ceremonies, be true.

Observe the vows, take the initiation,
Support my Deity's installation.

Consider yourself, my humble servant,
Clean the temple, be observant.

Never advertise, your devotional deeds,
Avoid using lamps, for other needs.

Offer to me, what's dear to you,
Such an offering, will make you new.

Worship me in the sun, the fire, the air,
In Brahmins, cows, and Vaishnavas fair.

In water, earth, and all living entities,
Maintain equal vision, free from enmities."

The Lord spoke to Uddhav, His voice so calm,
"Meditate on my form, in your palm.

A conch, a disc, a club, a flower,
Worship me, feel the divine power.

One who performs, with devotion true,
Obtains my service, and knowledge too.

By the quality of service, so fine,
He realizes, the divine.

Dear Uddhav, I am the ultimate shelter,
For the saintly, no helter-skelter.

Without my service, there's no escape,
From material existence, in any shape.

Dear Uddhav, of the Yadu clan,
Hear my words, understand my plan.

I'll reveal to you, the greatest mystery,
Listen closely, to this divine history."

Sanskrit Text 11

अथ एकादशोऽध्यायः।
श्रीभगवान् उवाच।
बद्धः मुक्तः इति व्याख्या गुणतः मे न वस्तुतः ।
गुणस्य मायामूलत्वात् न मे मोक्षः न बन्धनम्॥१॥

शोकमोहौ सुखं दुःखं देहापत्तिः च मायया।
स्वप्नः यथा आत्मनः ख्यातिः संसृतिः न तु वास्तवी॥२॥

विद्या अविद्ये मम तनू विद्धि उद्धव शरीरिणाम्।
मोक्षबन्धकरी आद्ये मायया मे विनिर्मिते॥३॥

एकस्य एव मम अंशस्य जीवस्य एव महामते।
बन्धः अस्य अविद्यया अनादिः विद्यया च तथा इतरः॥४॥

अथ बद्धस्य मुक्तस्य वैलक्षण्यं वदामि ते।
विरुद्धधर्मिणोः तात स्थितयोः एकधर्मिणि॥५॥

सुपर्णौ एतौ सदृशौ सखायौ यदृच्छया एतौ कृतनीडौ च वृक्षे।
एकः तयोः खादति पिप्पलान्नम् अन्यः निरन्नः अपि बलेन भूयान्॥६॥

आत्मानम् अन्यं च सः वेद विद्वान् अपिप्पलादः न तु पिप्पलादः।
यः अविद्यया युक् स तु नित्यबद्धः विद्यामयः यः स तु नित्यमुक्तः॥७॥

देहस्थः अपि न देहस्थः विद्वान् स्वप्नात् यथा उत्थितः।
अदेहस्थः अपि देहस्थः कुमतिः स्वप्नदृक् यथा॥८॥

इन्द्रियैः इन्द्रियार्थेषु गुणैः अपि गुणेषु च।
गृह्यमाणेषु अहङ्कुर्यात् न विद्वान् यः तु अविक्रियः॥९॥

दैवाधीने शरीरे अस्मिन् गुणभाव्येन कर्मणा।
वर्तमानः अबुधः तत्र कर्ता अस्मि इति निबध्यते॥१०॥

एवं विरक्तः शयनः आसनाटनमज्जने।
दर्शनस्पर्शनघ्राणभोजनश्रवणआदिषु॥११॥

न तथा बध्यते विद्वान् तत्र तत्र आदयन् गुणान्।
प्रकृतिस्थः अपि असंसक्तः यथा खं सविता अनिलः॥१२॥

वैशारद्येक्षया असङ्गशितया छिन्नसंशयः।
प्रतिबुद्धः इव स्वप्नात् नानात्वात् विनिवर्तते॥१३॥

यस्य स्युः वीतसङ्कल्पाः प्राणेन्द्रियमनोधियाम्।
वृत्तयः सः विनिर्मुक्तः देहस्थः अपि हि तत् गुणैः॥१४॥

यस्य आत्मा हिंस्यते हिंस्यैः येन किञ्चित् यदृच्छया।
अर्च्यते वा क्वचित् तत्र न व्यतिक्रियते बुधः॥१५॥

न स्तुवीत न निन्देत कुर्वतः साधु असाधु वा।
वदतः गुणदोषाभ्यां वर्जितः समदृक् मुनिः॥१६॥

न कुर्यात् न वदेत् किञ्चित् न ध्यायेत् साधु असाधु वा।
आत्मारामः अनया वृत्त्या विचरेत् जडवत् मुनिः॥१७॥

शब्दब्रह्मणि निष्णातः न निष्णायात् परे यदि।
श्रमः तस्य श्रमफलः हि अधेनुम् इव रक्षतः॥१८॥

गां दुग्धदोहाम् असतीं च भार्याम् देहं पराधीनम् असत्प्रजां च।
वित्तं तु अतीर्थीकृतम् अङ्ग वाचम् हीनां मया रक्षति दुःखदुःखी॥१९॥

यस्यां न मे पावनम् अङ्ग कर्म स्थितिउद्भवप्राण निरोधनम् अस्य।
लीलावतारैइप्सितजन्म वा स्यात् बन्ध्यां गिरं तां बिभृयात् न
धीरः॥२०॥

एवं जिज्ञासया अपोह्य नानात्वभ्रमम् आत्मनि।
उपारमेत विरजं मनः मयि अर्प्य सर्वगे॥२१॥

यदि अनीशः धारयितुं मनः ब्रह्मणि निश्चलम्।
मयि सर्वाणि कर्माणि निरपेक्षः समाचर॥२२॥

श्रद्धालुः मे कथाः शृण्वन् सुभद्रा लोकपावनीः।
गायन् अनुस्मरन् कर्म जन्म च अभिनयन् मुहुः॥२३॥

मदर्थे धर्मकामार्थान् आचरन् मदपाश्रयः।
लभते निश्चलां भक्तिं मयि उद्धव सनातने॥२४॥

सत्सङ्गलब्धया भक्त्या मयि मां सः उपासिता।
सः वै मे दर्शितं सद्भिः अञ्जसा विन्दते पदम्॥२५॥

उद्धव उवाच।
साधुः तव उत्तमश्लोक मतः कीदृग्विधः प्रभो।
भक्तिः त्वयि उपयुज्येत कीदृशी सद्भिः आदृता॥२६॥

एतत् मे पुरुषाध्यक्ष लोकाध्यक्ष जगत् प्रभो।
प्रणताय अनुरक्ताय प्रपन्नाय च कथ्यताम्॥२७॥

त्वं ब्रह्म परमं व्योम पुरुषः प्रकृतेः परः।
अवतीर्णः असि भगवन् स्वेच्छाउपात्तपृथक् वपुः॥२८॥

श्रीभगवान् उवाच।
कृपालुः अकृतद्रोहः तितिक्षुः सर्वदेहिनाम्।
सत्यसारः अनवद्यात्मा समः सर्वोपकारकः॥२९॥

कामैः अहतधीः दान्तः मृदुः शुचिः अकिञ्चनः।
अनीहः मितभुक् शान्तः स्थिरः मत् शरणः मुनिः॥३०॥

अप्रमत्तः गभीरात्मा धृतिमाञ्जितषड्गुणः।
अमानी मानदः कल्पः मैत्रः कारुणिकः कविः॥३१॥

आज्ञाय एवं गुणान् दोषान्मयादिष्टान् अपि स्वकान्।
धर्मान् सन्त्यज्य यः सर्वान् मां भजेत सः सत्तमः॥३२॥

ज्ञात्वा अज्ञात्वा अथ ये वै मां यावान् यः च अस्मि यादृशः।
भजन्ति अनन्यभावेन ते मे भक्ततमाः मताः॥३३॥

मल्लिङ्गमद्भक्तजनदर्शनस्पर्शनार्चनम्।
परिचर्या स्तुतिः प्रह्वगुणकर्म अनुकीर्तनम्॥३४॥

मत्कथाश्रवणे श्रद्धा मत् अनुध्यानम् उद्धव।
सर्वलाभ उपहरणं दास्येन आत्मनिवेदनम्॥३५॥

मज्जन्मकर्मकथनं मम पर्वानुमोदनम्।
गीतताण्डववादित्रगोष्ठीभिः मद्गृह उत्सवः॥३६॥

यात्रा बलिविधानं च सर्ववार्षिकपर्वसु।
वैदिकी तान्त्रिकी दीक्षा मदीयव्रतधारणम्॥३७॥

मम अर्चास्थापने श्रद्धा स्वतः संहत्य च उद्यमः।
उद्यान उपवनाक्रीडपुरमन्दिरकर्मणि।३८॥

संमार्जन उपलेपाभ्यां सेकमण्डलवर्तनैः।
गृहशुश्रूषणं मह्यं दासवद्यदमायया॥३९॥

अमानित्वम् अदम्भित्वं कृतस्य अपरिकीर्तनम्।
अपि दीपावलोकं मे न उपयुञ्ज्यात् निवेदितम्॥४०॥

यत् यत् इष्टतमं लोके यत् च अतिप्रियम् आत्मनः।
तत् तत् निवेदयेत् मह्यं तत् आनन्त्याय कल्पते॥४१॥

सूर्यः अग्निः ब्राह्मणः गावः वैष्णवः खं मरुत् जलम्।
भूः आत्मा सर्वभूतानि भद्र पूजापदानि मे॥४२॥

सूर्ये तु विद्यया त्रय्या हविषाग्नौ यजेत माम्।
आतिथ्येन तु विप्राग्र्यः गोष्वङ्ग यवसादिना॥४३॥

वैष्णवे बन्धुसत्कृत्या हृदि खे ध्याननिष्ठया।
वायौ मुख्यधिया तोये द्रव्यैः तोयपुरस्कृतैः॥४४॥

स्थण्डिले मन्त्रहृदयैः भोगैः आत्मानम् आत्मनि।
क्षेत्रज्ञं सर्वभूतेषु समत्वेन यजेत माम्॥४५॥

धिष्ण्येषु एषु इति मद्रूपं शङ्खचक्रगदाम्बुजैः।
युक्तं चतुर्भुजं शान्तं ध्यायन् अर्चेत् समाहितः॥४६॥

इष्टापूर्तेन माम् एवं यः यजेत समाहितः।
लभते मयि सद्भक्तिं मत्स्मृतिः साधुसेवया॥४७॥

प्रायेण भक्तियोगेन सत्सङ्गेन विना उद्धव।
न उपायः विद्यते सध्र्यङ् प्रायणं हि सताम् अहम्॥४८॥

अथ एतत् परमं गुह्यं श्रुण्वतः यदुनन्दन।
सुगोप्यम् अपि वक्ष्यामि त्वं मे भृत्यः सुहृत् सखा॥४९॥

इति श्रीमद्भागवते महापुराणे पारमहंस्यां
संहितायामेकादशस्कन्धे श्रीकृष्णोद्धवसंवादे
एकादशपूजाविधानयोगो नाम एकादशोऽध्यायः॥११॥

12 Beyond Renunciation, Knowledge

English Rhyme

The Lord spoke with a voice so divine,
"Dear Uddhav, listen to this truth of mine.

By associating with my devotees pure,
One can worldly attachments obscure.

Such purifying association, you see,
Brings even me under the devotee's decree.

One may perform astanga-yoga with zest,
Or engage in philosophical analysis, doing their best.

Nonviolence, piety, and the Vedas' chant,
Penance, renunciation, no desire to enchant.

Sacrifices, wells, trees, and charity,
Severe vows, worship, mantras in parity.

Visit holy places, accept injunctions with grace,
Yet, by these alone, one cannot my presence trace.

In every yuga, many entities find,
My devotees' association kind.

Daityas, Raksasas, birds, and beasts,
Gandharvas, Apsaras, Nagas, to say the least.

Siddhas, Caranas, Guhyakas, and Vidyadharas,
Vaisyas, sudras, women, avatars.

All these beings, high and low,
To my supreme abode, they go.

Vrtrasura, Prahlada Maharaja, and others alike,
Achieved my abode, riding the devotee's bike.

Vrsaparva, Bali Maharaja, Banasura, and Maya,
Vibhisana, Sugriva, Hanuman, Jambavan, they say,

Gajendra, Jatayu, Tuladhara, Dharma-vyadha, and Kubja,
The gopis in Vrindavan, Brahmins' wives, all loved ya.

By association with my devotees, they won,
And thus, my dear Uddhav, my message is done."

The Lord spoke, His voice clear and bright,
"Those I mentioned, in Vedic studies took no delight.

No worship of saints, no vows severe,
Yet by association with me, they held me dear.

In Vrindavan, where love for me is pure,
Gopis, cows, trees, and creatures demure,

Animals, bushes, and Kaliya the snake,
Achieved perfection, for unalloyed love's sake.

Though one may try with all their might,
In yoga, charity, or scholarly insight,

In vows, penances, sacrifices grand,
Still, without love, they cannot understand.

In Vrindavan, love for me is so deep,
That when from them, I was taken in sleep,

By Akrura, to Mathura, away from their sight,
Their happiness vanished, turned into night.

The gopis, my beloved, felt time swiftly flow,
When with me, but in my absence, time slowed.

Each night without me, an eternity it seemed,
A day of Brahma, in their hearts it beamed.

Just as sages in yoga trance unite,
With self-realization, like rivers in the night,

The gopis too, were so engrossed in me,
Of their own bodies, they were free.

Hundreds of thousands of gopis, in number,
Saw me as their lover, in slumber.

Unaware of my position, yet close in relation,
They attained me, the Supreme, by association.

So, dear Uddhav, let the Vedic mantras be,
And the procedures of the Vedas, you see.

Take shelter in me, let go of your fears,
For I am the Lord, who always hears."

Uddhav replied, his voice filled with awe,
"Lord, your words I heard, but still there's a flaw.

My heart is filled with doubt, my mind in a haze,
Your mystic power leaves me in a daze."

The Lord said, "Uddhav, listen to me,
I give life to all, in the heart I be.

With life air and sound, I reside,
Perceived subtly, as the mind's guide.

I control the minds, even of gods like Shiv,
In the Vedas' sounds, I live.

Like fire from wood, rubbed with might,
In the Vedas' vibration, I ignite."

The senses, both working and wise,
Speak, touch, see, taste, hear, and surmise,

Mind, intelligence, consciousness, and ego's guise,
All these, the Lord's materially manifest form comprise.

Seeds in a field, from soil they rise,
Trees, bushes, vegetables, under the skies.

So too, the Lord, beyond cosmic ties,
Gives life to all, in eternal guise.

Just as cloth on threads does rest,
The universe on the Lord's potency is blessed.

The Atma, in material bodies dressed,
Like great trees, our existence they attest.

This tree of existence, complex and grand,
Two seeds, hundreds of roots, on sun's command.

Three lower trunks, five upper stand,
Eleven branches, a nest by two birds planned.

Covered in three barks, two fruits it yields,
One for the lusty, the other for renounced fields.

Understanding this tree, the Vedic truth it wields,
The one Supreme Truth, in many forms revealed.

With steady intelligence, devotion you should rear,
Worship the spiritual master, hold them dear.

With knowledge's axe, make the Atma clear,
On realizing the Lord, let go of fear.

Sanskrit Text 12

अथ द्वादशोऽध्यायः।
श्रीभगवान् उवाच।
न रोधयति मां योगः न रसाङ्ख्यं धर्मः एव च।
न स्वाध्यायः तपः त्यागः न इष्टापूर्तं न दक्षिणा॥१॥

व्रतानि यज्ञः छन्दांसि तीर्थानि नियमाः यमाः।
यथा अवरुन्धे सत्सङ्गः सर्वसङ्ग अपहः हि माम्॥२॥

सत्सङ्गेन हि दैतेया यातुधानः मृगाः खगाः।
गन्धर्व अप्सरसः नागाः सिद्धाः चारणगुह्यकाः॥३॥

विद्याधराः मनुष्येषु वैश्याः शूद्राः स्त्रियः अन्त्यजाः।
रजः तमः प्रकृतयः तस्मिन् तस्मिन् युगे अनघ॥४॥

बहवः मत्पदं प्राप्ताः त्वाष्ट्रकायाधवादयः।
वृषपर्वा बलिः वाणः मयः च अथ विभीषणः॥५॥

सुग्रीवः हनुमान् ऋक्षः गजः गृध्रः वणिक्पथः।
व्याधः कुब्जा व्रजे गोप्यः यज्ञपत्न्यः तथा अपरे॥६॥

ते न अधितश्रुतिगणाः न उपासितमहत्तमाः।
अव्रतातप्ततपसः मत्सङ्गात् माम् उपागताः॥७॥

केवलेन हि भावेन गोप्यः गावः नगाः मृगाः।
ये अन्ये मूढधियः नागाः सिद्धाः माम् ईयुः अञ्जसा॥८॥

यं न योगेन साङ्ख्येन दानव्रततपः अध्वरैः।
व्याख्याः स्वाध्यायसंन्यासैः प्राप्नुयात् यत्नवान् अपि॥९॥

रामेण सार्धं मथुरां प्रणीते श्वाफल्किना मयि अनुरक्तचित्ताः।
विगाढभावेन न मे वियोग तीव्राधयः अन्यं ददृशुः सुखाय॥१०॥

ताः ताः क्षपाः प्रेष्ठतमेन नीताः मया एव वृन्दावनगोचरेण।
क्षणार्धवत् ताः पुनरङ्ग तासां हीना माया कल्पसमा बभूवुः॥११॥

ताः न अविदन् मयि अनुषङ्गबद्ध धियः स्वमात्मानम् अदः तथा इदम्।
यथा समाधौ मुनयः अब्धितोये नद्यः प्रविष्टाः इव नामरूपे॥१२॥

मत्कामा रमणं जारम् अस्वरूपविदः अबलाः।
ब्रह्म मां परमं प्रापुः सङ्गात् शतसहस्रशः॥१३॥

तस्मात् त्वम् उद्धव उत्सृज्य चोदनां प्रतिचोदनाम्।
प्रवृत्तं च निवृत्तं च श्रोतव्यं श्रुतम् एव च॥१४॥

माम् एकम् एव शरणम् आत्मानं सर्वदेहिनाम्।
याहि सर्वात्मभावेन मया स्याः हि अकुतोभयः॥१५॥

उद्धवः उवाच।
संशयः श्रुण्वतः वाचं तव योगेश्वर ईश्वर।
न निवर्ततः आत्मस्थः येन भ्राम्यति मे मनः॥१६॥

श्रीभगवान् उवाच।
सः एष जीवः विवरप्रसूतिः प्राणेन घोषेण गुहां प्रविष्टः।
मनोमयं सूक्ष्मम् उपेत्य रूपं मात्रा स्वरः वर्णः इति स्थविष्ठः॥१७॥

यथा अनलः खे अनिलबन्धुः ऊष्मा बलेन दारुण्यधिमथ्यमानः।
अणुः प्रजातः हविषा समिध्यते तथा एव मे व्यक्तिः इयं हि वाणी॥१८॥

एवं गदिः कर्मगतिः विसर्गः घ्राणः रसः दृक् स्पर्शः श्रुतिः च।
सङ्कल्पविज्ञानम् अथ अभिमानः सूत्रं रजः सत्त्वतमोविकारः॥१९॥

अयं हि जीवः त्रिवृत् अब्जयोनिः अव्यक्तः एकः वयसा सः आद्यः।
विश्लिष्टशक्तिः बहुधा एव भाति बीजानि योनिं प्रतिपद्य यद्वत्॥२०॥

यस्मिन् इदं प्रोतम् अशेषम् ओतं पटः यथा तन्तुवितानसंस्थः।
यः एष संसारतरुः पुराणः कर्मात्मकः पुष्पफले प्रसूते॥२१॥

द्वे अस्य बीजे शतमूलः त्रिनालः पञ्चस्कन्धः पञ्चरसप्रसूतिः।
दश एकशाखः द्विसुपर्णनीडः त्रिवल्कलः द्विफलः अर्कं प्रविष्टः॥२२॥

अदन्ति च एकं फलम् अस्य गृध्रा ग्रामेचराः एकम् अरण्यवासाः।
हंसाः यः एकं बहुरूपम् इज्यैः मायामयं वेद सः वेद वेदम्॥२३॥

एवं गुरु उपासनया एकभक्त्या विद्याकुठारेण शितेन धीरः।
विवृश्च्य जीवाशयम् अप्रमत्तः सम्पद्य च आत्मानम् अथ त्यज
अस्त्रम्॥२४॥

इति श्रीमद्भागवते महापुराणे पारमहंस्यां
संहितायामेकादशस्कन्धे श्रीकृष्णोद्धवसंवादे
द्वादशोऽध्यायः॥१२॥

13 Hamsa Gita

English Rhyme

The Lord said:
Three modes of material nature, namely
Goodness, passion, ignorance clearly,

Pertain to intelligence, not Atma surely,
With development of material goodness.

Thus conquered passion, ignorance be,
By cultivation of uplifting goodness surely,

And one may so free oneself completely,
Even from material goodness absolutely.

When In goodness, religious values be,
Then prominent with devotional to me;

Goodness strengthened by cultivation be,
Of things within, so pious values arise truly.

Religious values, empowered by goodness be,
Destroys impact of passion, ignorance clearly;

When passion and ignorance overcome be,
Their original cause, irreligion, is shed quickly.

According to religious scripture's quality,
Water, linked with kids or people generally,

The particular place, the time and activities,
Birth, meditation, mantras chanting clearly,

And with the rituals, practices purificatory,
Nature modes become prominent differently.

Among ten items I have stated previously,
The sages knowing Vedic knowledge truly,

Recommended those in goodness mood be,
Rejected those in mode of ignorance fully;

And they have shown indifference totally,
To those in the mode of passion in actuality.

Till one's direct knowledge but revived be,
And drives away the identification illusory,

With mind, the body, nature mode three,
One must nurture things in goodness only.

By increasing goodness, one automatically,
Knows, practices religious principles truly,

And by such devoted practice unfailingly,
Transcendental knowledge awakened be.

In a bamboo forest wind at times clearly,
Rub bamboo stalks together repeatedly,

Such frictions do generate a fire blazingly,
Consuming its birth source, that forest fully.

Thus, this engulfing fire is but automatically,
But calmed by its own action subsequently.

By interaction of material nature modes truly,
Subtle, gross material bodies generated be;

If for knowledge is uses the mind and body,
Such enlightenment destroys influence fully,

That of the very modes of nature completely,
Which have been generated by one's body.

Thus, like the fire, the body and mind truly,
Pacifies actions, destroys birth source fully.

Uddhav said:
Dear Krishna, generally humans knowing be,
Material life brings future unhappiness greatly,

Yet still they try to enjoy material life endlessly,
How can knower act as a dog, ass, goat sadly?
The Lord said:
Dear Uddhav, one bereft of intellect falsely,
Identifies self with the mind, material body,

When such false knowledge arises within be,
One's consciousness, material passion surely;

The cause of suffering, pervading the mind be,
Which by nature is placed in goodness clearly.

Then the mind, contaminated by passion only,
Lost in making plans for material progress be.

Thus, lost in material nature modes constantly,
Fool afflicted with endless material desires be.

One who does not control material senses truly,
Under the control of material desires will be;

And is thus bewildered and confused totally,
By the strong waves of passion mode clearly.

Such a person executes material activities,
Though seeing that result beget only misery.

The intelligence of a learned person may be,
Dazed by passion, ignorance modes truly,

He should bring mind under control carefully,
Knowing pollution of nature, unattached be.

One should be attentive, grave and never lazy,
Mastering yoga of breathing and sitting properly,

One should ever practice the fixing mind on Me,
At dawn, noon, sunset, mind be absorbed in Me.

Actual yoga system as taught by my devotees,
Headed by Sanaka Kumar, is simply this truly:

Withdrawing mind from all other objects fully,
One should then appropriately absorb it in Me.

Uddhav said:
Dear Keshav, at what time and form actually,
You instruct yoga to Sanaka, his brothers fully?

The Lord said:
Once, the mental sons of Brahma, namely,
Sages headed by Sanaka, but inquiring be,

From their father of subject matter difficulty,
Of the supreme final goal of yoga in actuality.

Sages headed by Sanaka said:
Lord, people's minds but attracted be,
To the material sense objects naturally,

The sense objects in form of desire truly,
Ever do enter within the mind similarly;

How a person desiring liberation truly,
Wanting to shed sense gratification fully,

Destroy relation of sense objects clearly,
With mind – do explain to us this plainly.

The Lord said:
Brahma himself, is from the Lord's body,
Who is creator of all worldly living entities,

Being best of gods, contemplated seriously,
Question of his sons headed by Sanaka truly.

Brahma's intellect affected by creation activities,
So he did not know this answer categorically.

Wanting this answer which puzzling him be,
He fixed his mind onthe Supreme Lord, Me;

At that time, in my form of Hamsa plainly,
I became visible to Brahma but effortlessly.

The sages, with Brahma in lead, seeing Me,
Asked who am I, worshipping my lotus feet.

To know ultimate yoga system truth eagerly,
Inquired from Me - Do hear that attentively:

Dear Brahmins, if, when asking me who I be,
Believing I an Atma, no variance amidst us be,

As Atmas are ultimately without individuality,
Then how this question possible or proper be?

What the real situation or resting place be,
Of both of yourselves and of me ultimately?

If by asking me "Who are you?" categorically,
You were referring to just the material body,

Then I must point out that all material bodies,
Made from: earth, water, fire, air and ether be.

Thus, you have asked, "Who you five be?"
Reflect all material bodies are one ultimately,

They constituted of same elements essentially,
Thus then your question still meaningless be;

There no deep purpose in distinguishing be,
From one body from another – all same be.

Thus, it appears that in asking my identity,
You speak words, without purpose merely.

Within this world, what perceived does be,
By mind, speech, eyes, other senses is me;

All that I alone and nothing else besides me,
Know this by analyzing these facts logically.

Dear sons, the mind has a natural proclivity,
To enter into material sense objects clearly,

Sense objects enter into the mind similarly,
Both material mind and the sense objects be:

Designations that cover the spirit Atma clearly,
Who is the very part and parcel of whole me.

Who achieves me knowing he not different be,
Realizes that the material mind is lodged truly,

Within sense objects with its gratification only,
Material objects existing in material mind truly.

Understanding my transcendental nature fully,
Gives up material mind and its objects totally.

The waking, sleeping, and deep sleep do be,
Of material modes, intellectual functions three,

Living entity in body with the characteristics be,
Different from these three states, so witness be.

Atma in bondage of material intelligence be,
Engagement in the modes of nature illusory,

But I the fourth stage of the consciousness be,
Past wakefulness, dreaming, deep sleep truly.

Atma should shed material consciousness fully,
And become situated completely wholly in Me,

At that time, the living entity will automatically,
Forsake material sense objects and mind fully

False ego causes bondage of the living entity,
Awards him opposite of what he desires really,

Wise person must shed constant material anxiety,
Be in Lord, who past material consciousness be.

Per my instructions, one should fix mind on me,
But if one continues to see values, goals many,

In life rather than seeing everything within me,
Though apparently awake, one dreaming surely,

That but due to incomplete knowledge does be,
As may dream, one wakened from dream be.

Those states of existence that conceived do be,
Separate from Lord have no existence actually,

They create separation from Truth absolutely,
As seer of dream imagines different activities,

The sense of separateness from Lord's reality,
Living entity falsely performs fruitive activities,

Thinking them to be the cause and in actuality,
Of all future rewards and destinations foolishly.

Awake, living entity enjoys with his senses fully,
Fleeting characteristics of material mind, body,

Dreaming enjoys experiences in mind similarly,
In deep dreamless sleep all in ignorance do be.

By remembering, contemplating succession truly,
Of wakefulness, dreaming and deep sleep fully,

The living entity can understand that he one be,
Through three stages, he the lord of senses be.

Ponder how, by influence of my illusory energy,
Three states of mind, imagined to exist in me,

Having ascertained the truth of Atma definitely,
Utilize the sharpen sword of knowledge clearly,

From directives of sages, Vedic scriptures truly,
To cut ego - the breeding ground of doubts be,

All of you should then worship me devotedly,
I who am situated within the heart certainly.

One should see that the material world surely,
Is a distinct illusion appearing in the mind only,

As material objects with flickering existence be,
Are here today and gone tomorrow completely;

They as streaking red line by a whirling stick be,
Atma in single state of pure consciousness be,

In world seen in varied existence forms many,
The nature dividing Atma's consciousness be,

Wakefulness, dreaming, dreamless sleep be,
All perceptions are maya, and is as dream only.

Knowing temporary nature of material illusory,
One should remain without material desires truly,

By experiencing the happiness of Atma clearly,
One should give up material speaking, activities.

If sometimes one must observe material worldly,
Shed it knowing that it is not the ultimate reality,

By such constant memory up till death of body,
One will not fall into illusion of this world surely.

Just a drunkard notices not what he wearing be,
Self-realized who has achieved eternal identity,

Does not notice whether the temporary body,
Is sitting or standing on the earth but similarly.

Indeed, if by the will of God is finished the body,
Or if by God's will he again obtains a new body,

A self-realized Atma does not notice in actuality,
As a drunken man of that of his dress certainly.

Material body moves in control of supreme destiny,
So, live with senses, vital air till karma in effect be.

A self-realized Atma awakened to absolute reality,
Who highly situated in the perfect stage of yoga be,

Surrenders not to manifestations of material body,
Knowing it just as a body visualized in dream only.

Dear Brahmins, I told knowledge of Sankhya fully,
By which is distinguished matter from spirit truly,

Please know that I the Lord – the Lord Vishnu be,
I appeared before you to clarify your actual duties.

Best of the Brahmins, please do know that I be,
The supreme shelter of the yoga system clearly,

Action, truthful religious principles, fame, beauty,
Power, self-control and the analytic philosophy,.

All transcendental qualities, beyond the nature be,
Detached, well -wisher, dear and Parmatma truly,

Everywhere, and from material entanglement free,
All qualities, free from changes of material qualities,

They but find their shelter, their refuge undoubtedly,
Their object, worship and devotion absolutely in Me.

Dear Uddhav, thus all of the doubts of sages be,
Headed by Sanaka, destroyed by my words fully,

With uplifting love and devotion worshiping me,
They chanted with excellent hymns my glories.

Greatest of sages, headed by Sanaka Rishi,
Thus worshiped and glorified me perfectly,

And as Lord Brahma looked on respectfully,
I returned to my own abode subsequently.

Sanskrit Text 13

अथ त्रयोदशोऽध्यायः।
श्रीभगवान् उवाच।
सत्त्वं रजः तमः इति गुणाः बुद्धेः न च आत्मनः।
सत्त्वेन अन्यतमौ हन्यात् सत्त्वं सत्त्वेन च एव हि॥१॥

सत्त्वात् धर्मः भवेत् वृद्धात् पुंसः मद्भक्तिलक्षणः।
सात्विक उपासया सत्त्वं ततः धर्मः प्रवर्तते॥२॥

धर्मः रजः तमः हन्यात् सत्त्ववृद्धिः अनुत्तमः।
आशु नश्यति तत् मूलः हि अधर्मः उभये हते॥३॥

आगमः अपः प्रजा देशः कालः कर्म च जन्म च।
ध्यानं मन्त्रः अथ संस्कारः दश एते गुणहेतवः॥४॥

तत् तत् सात्विकम् एव एषां यत् यत् वृद्धाः प्रचक्षते।
निन्दन्ति तामसं तत् तत् राजसं तत् उपेक्षितम्॥५॥

सात्त्विकानि एव सेवेत पुमान् सत्त्वविवृद्धये।
ततः धर्मः ततः ज्ञानं यावत् स्मृतिः अपोहनम्॥६॥

वेणुसङ्घर्षजः वह्निः दग्ध्वा शाम्यति तत् वनम्।
एवं गुणव्यत्ययजः देहः शाम्यति तत् क्रियः॥७॥

उद्धवः उवाच।
विदन्ति मर्त्याः प्रायेण विषयान् पदम् आपदाम्।
तथा अपि भुञ्जते कृष्ण तत् कथं श्व खर अजावत्॥८॥

श्रीभगवान् उवाच।
अहम् इति अन्यथाबुद्धिः प्रमत्तस्य यथा हृदि।
उत्सर्पति रजः घोरं ततः वैकारिकं मनः॥९॥

रजोयुक्तस्य मनसः सङ्कल्पः सविकल्पकः।
ततः कामः गुणध्यानात् दुःसहः स्यात् हि दुर्मतेः॥१०॥

करोति कामवशगः कर्माणि अविजितेन्द्रियः।
दुःखोदर्काणि सम्पश्यन् रजोवेगविमोहितः॥११॥

रजः तमोभ्यां यत् अपि विद्वान् विक्षिप्तधीः पुनः।
अतन्द्रितः मनः युञ्जन् दोषदृष्टिः न सज्जते॥१२॥

अप्रमत्तः अनुयुञ्जीतः मनः मयि अर्पयन् शनैः।
अनिर्विण्णः यथाकालं जितश्वासः जितासनः॥१३॥

एतावान् योगः आदिष्टः मत् शिष्यैः सनक आदिभिः।
सर्वतः मनः आकृष्य मय्यद्धा आवेश्यते यथा॥१४॥

उद्धवः उवाच।
यदा त्वं सनक आदिभ्यः येन रूपेण केशव।
योगम् आदिष्टवान् एतत् रूपम् इच्छामि वेदितुम्॥१५॥

श्रीभगवान् उवाच।
पुत्राः हिरण्यगर्भस्य मानसाः सनक आदयः।
पप्रच्छुः पितरं सूक्ष्मां योगस्य ऐकान्तिकीं गतिम्॥१६॥

सनक आदयः ऊचुः।
गुणेषु आविशते चेतः गुणाः चेतसि च प्रभो।
कथम् अन्योन्यसन्त्यागः मुमुक्षोः अतितितीर्षोः॥१७॥

श्रीभगवान् उवाच।
एवं पृष्टः महादेवः स्वयम्भूः भूतभावनः।
ध्यायमानः प्रश्नबीजं न अभ्यपद्यत कर्मधीः॥१८॥

सः माम् अचिन्तयत् देवः प्रश्नपारतितीर्षया।
तस्य अहं हंसरूपेण सकाशम् अगमं तदा॥१९॥

दृष्ट्वा माम् त उपव्रज्य कृत्वा पाद अभिवन्दनम्।
ब्रह्माणम् अग्रतः कृत्वा पप्रच्छुः कः भवान् इति॥२०॥

इति अहं मुनिभिः पृष्टः तत्त्वजिज्ञासुभिः तदा।
यत् अवोचम् अहं तेभ्यः तत् उद्धव निबोध मे॥२१॥

वस्तुनः यदि अनानात्वम् आत्मनः प्रश्नः ईदृशः।
कथं घटेत वः विप्राः वक्तुः वा मे कः आश्रयः॥२२॥

पञ्चात्मकेषु भूतेषु समानेषु च वस्तुतः।
कः भवान् इति वः प्रश्नः वाचारम्भः हि अनर्थकः॥२३॥

मनसा वचसा दृष्ट्या गृह्यते अन्यैः अपि इन्द्रियैः।
अहम् एव न मत्तः अन्यत् इति बुध्यध्वम् अञ्जसा॥२४॥

गुणेषु आविशते चेतः गुणाः चेतसि च प्रजाः।
जीवस्य देहः उभयं गुणाः चेतः मत् आत्मनः॥२५॥

गुणेषु च आविशत् चित्तम् अभीक्ष्णं गुणसेवया।
गुणाः च चित्तप्रभवाः मत् रूपः उभयं त्यजेत्॥२६॥

जाग्रत् स्वप्नः सुषुप्तं च गुणतः बुद्धिवृत्तयः।
तासां विलक्षणः जीवः साक्षित्वेन विनिश्चितः॥२७॥

यः हि संसृतिबन्धः अयम् आत्मनः गुणवृत्तिदः।
मयि तुर्ये स्थितः जह्यात् त्यागः तत् गुणचेतसाम्॥२८॥

अहङ्कारकृतं बन्धम् आत्मनः अर्थविपर्ययम्।
विद्वान् निर्विद्य संसारचिन्तां तुर्ये स्थितः त्यजेत्॥२९॥

यावत् नानार्थधीः पुंसः न निवर्तेत युक्तिभिः।
जागर्ति अपि स्वपन् अज्ञः स्वप्ने जागरणं यथा॥३०॥

असत्त्वात् आत्मनः अन्येषां भावानां तत् कृता भिदा।
गतयः हेतवः च अस्य मृषा स्वप्नदृशः यथा॥३१॥

यो जागरे बहिः अनुक्षणधर्मिणः अर्थान्
भुङ्क्ते समस्तकरणैः हृदि तत् सदृक्षान्।
स्वप्ने सुषुप्तः उपसंहरते सः एकः स्मृति
अन्वयात् त्रिगुणवृत्तिदृक् इन्द्रिय ईशः॥३२॥

एवं विमृश्य गुणतः मनसः त्र्यवस्था
मत् मायया मयि कृता इति निश्चितार्थाः।
संछिद्य हार्दम् अनुमानसत् उक्तितीक्ष्ण
ज्ञानासिना भजतः मा अखिलसंशयाधिम्॥३३॥

ईक्षेत विभ्रमम् इदं मनसः विलासम् दृष्टं
विनष्टम् अतिलोलम् अलातचक्रम्।
विज्ञानम् एकम् उरुधा इव विभाति माया
स्वप्नः त्रिधा गुणविसर्गकृतः विकल्पः॥३४॥

दृष्टिं ततः प्रतिनिवर्त्य निवृत्ततृष्णः
तूष्णीं भवेत् निजसुख अनुभवः निरीहः।
सन्दृश्यते क्व च यदि इदम् अवस्तुबुद्ध्या
त्यक्तं भ्रमाय न भवेत् स्मृतिः आनिपातात्॥३५॥

देहं च नश्वरम् अवस्थितम् उत्थितं वा
सिद्धः न पश्यति यतः अध्यगमत्स्वरूपम्।
दैवात् अपेतम् उत दैवशात् उपेतम् वासः
यथा परिकृतं मदिरामदान्धः॥३६॥

देहः अपि दैववशगः खलु कर्म यावत्
स्वारम्भकं प्रतिसमीक्षतः एव सासुः।
तं अप्रपञ्चम् अधिरूढसमाधियोगः
स्वाप्नं पुनः न भजते प्रतिबुद्धवस्तुः॥३७॥

मया एतत् उक्तं वः विप्राः गुह्यं यत् साङ्ख्ययोगयोः।
जानीतम् आगतं यज्ञं युष्मत् धर्मविवक्षया॥३८॥

अहं योगस्य साङ्ख्यस्य सत्यस्यर्तस्य तेजसः।
परायणं द्विजश्रेष्ठाः श्रियः कीर्तेः दमस्य च॥३९॥

मां भजन्ति गुणाः सर्वे निर्गुणं निरपेक्षकम्।
सुहृदं प्रियम् आत्मानं साम्य असङ्ग आदयः गुणाः॥४०॥

इति मे छिन्नसन्देहाः मुनयः सनक आदयः।
सभाजयित्वा परया भक्त्या अगृणत संस्तवैः॥४१॥

तैः अहं पूजितः सम्यक् संस्तुतः परम ऋषिभिः।
प्रत्येयाय स्वकं धाम पश्यतः परमेष्ठिनः॥४२॥

इति श्रीमद्भागवते महापुराणे पारमहंस्यां
संहितायामेकादशस्कन्धे श्रीकृष्णोद्धवसंवादे
हंसगीतानिरूपणं नाम त्रयोदशोऽध्यायः॥१३॥

14 The Yoga Scheme

English Rhyme

Uddhav asked with a curious mind,
"Krishna, in Vedic texts, what do we find?

Are all processes of equal kind,
Or is there one, supreme, defined?

You've explained devotion, pure and free,
By which one's mind on you can be.

But tell me, Lord, I wish to see,
The essence of this mystery."

Krishna replied with a gentle nod,
"I am the principles, in the Vedas laud.

At creation's dawn, I gave the nod,
To Brahma, the knowledge of God.

Brahma to Manu, the knowledge passed,
And sages like Bhrigu held it fast.

From them came beings, a vast cast,
Gods, demons, humans, a diverse contrast.

Thus, due to desires, varied and wide,
Different paths in life are tried.

Some seek the divine, some deride,
In countless ways, they decide.

Some find joy in piety's grace,
Others in fame, or pleasure's chase.

Truth, control, peace, or power's embrace,
Each has its place in life's race.

Yet, all these fruits are but brief,
Bringing future sorrow, not relief.

Even in joy, there lurks grief,
For such is the material life's motif.

But those who fix their minds on me,
From material desires, they are free.

They share a joy, eternally,
A happiness, beyond sensory glee.

One who desires nothing, finds peace,
Whose senses are controlled, whose wants cease,

Whose mind in me finds release,
Finds happiness that will never decrease.

Such a person, in me is content,
Desires not Brahma's tent,

Nor Indra's abode, nor earthly rent,
Nor yoga's siddhis, nor liberation's event.

Uddhav, dear to me, beyond all measure,
More than Brahma, Shiv, or any treasure.

With my devotees' dust, I seek to cleanse,
The material worlds, their purity immense.

Those free from desire, their minds on me,
Peaceful, merciful, from ego free,

Their consciousness, from sense gratification apart,
In me, they find a joy, the world can't impart.

If a devotee's senses are not fully won,
By material desires, he may be undone.

But with unflinching devotion, he stands tall,
Against sense gratification, he will not fall.

Just as fire turns wood to ash,
Devotion burns sins, in a flash.

My devotees' service, pure and whole,
Brings me under their control.

Not by yoga, philosophy, or renunciation,
Can one obtain my divine station.

Only by service, pure and devout,
Can one drive all contamination out.

Neither religious acts, nor knowledge vast,
Can purify the consciousness, if in the past,

There's no loving service, in the heart's core,
Without such service, one can't explore.

If hairs don't stand, how can the heart melt?
And if it doesn't, how can love be felt?

Without tears of joy, how can one serve?
And without such service, who can observe?

A devotee, whose speech may choke,
Whose heart melts, who may evoke,

Tears and laughter, shame and dance,
Purifies the universe, in a trance.

Just as gold, in fire's embrace,
Sheds impurities, shows its grace,

So the Atma, in devotion's fire,
Is purified, ascends higher.

As ointment heals the diseased eye,
So does chanting my glories purify.

The living entity, once blind, now sees,
My subtle form, with ease.

The mind, on sense objects, is entwined,
But remembering me, peace it finds.

Reject all material elevation's scheme,
Absorb your mind in me, like a dream.

Conscious of the self, eternal and pure,
Give up association, that's the cure.

In solitude, fearlessly reside,
On me, let your mind confide.

Of all the bonds that cause us pain,
From attachments, we strive to abstain,

None greater than the sensual chain,
That ties us to desire's domain.

Uddhav asked, with a heart sincere,
"Krishna, how does one hold you near?

In meditation, what should we revere?
Your form, your nature, make it clear."

Krishna replied, with wisdom profound,
"On a level seat, let your body be found,

Straight and erect, yet comfort-bound,
Hands on lap, eyes on the ground.

Purify the breath, in a rhythmic dance,
Puraka, kumbhaka, recaka, in a trance.

Control the senses, give the mind a chance,
To practice pranayama, in advance.

From the muladhara, let the life air rise,
Like fibers in a lotus, reaching the skies,

To the heart, where the sacred syllable lies,
Om, like a bell, in size.

Fixed in the omkara, let the breath flow,
At sunrise, noon, sunset, let it grow.

In a month, the life air you'll know,
And conquer it, with a steady blow.

Eyes half-closed, fixed on the nose's tip,
Alert and enlivened, let nothing slip.

Meditate on the lotus, let your mind flip,
Eight petals, on an erect stalk's grip.

Sun, moon, and fire, in the lotus whorl,
My form within the fire, let it unfurl.

Perfect, gentle, cheerful, like a pearl,
Four long arms, in a gentle twirl.

A charming neck, a handsome face,
A pure smile, full of grace.

Earrings glowing, a beautiful trace,
A form of a dark cloud, in space.

Garbed in silk, golden and bright,
Srivatsa, goddess of fortune, in sight.

Conch, disc, club, lotus, light,
Garland of flowers, a delightful sight.

Brilliant feet, with bells and bands,
Kaustubha gem, in effulgent strands.

Golden belt, valuable hand bands,
All limbs capturing hearts, like sands.

Face beautified by a merciful glance,
Pulling senses back, in a trance.

Grave, self-controlled, in stance,
On my form, let your mind dance."-

Pull back the consciousness, let it retreat,
From the limbs of the Lord, to the face so sweet.

Meditate on the smile, so wonderfully neat,
In the Lord's face, let your focus meet.

Established in meditation, let the mind fly,
Withdraw the consciousness, fix it in the sky.

Then give up such meditation, let it lie,
In me, become established, let the self tie.

One who has fixed his mind on me,
Should see me within, the Atma free.

And see the Atma within me, the Lord,
The individual Atmas with the Supreme, in accord.

Just as the sun's rays with the sun unite,
So do the Atmas, in the Supreme's light.

When the yogi controls his mind, so bright,
Illusions of the world, take flight.

Sanskrit Text 14

अथ चतुर्दशोऽध्यायः।
उद्धवः उवाच।
वदन्ति कृष्ण श्रेयांसि बहूनि ब्रह्मवादिनः।
तेषां विकल्पप्राधान्यम् उत अहो एकमुख्यता॥१॥

भवत् उदाहृतः स्वामिन् भक्तियोगः अनपेक्षितः।
निरस्य सर्वतः सङ्गं येन त्वयि आविशेत् मनः॥२॥

श्रीभगवान् उवाच।
कालेन नष्टा प्रलये वाणीयं वेदसंज्ञिता।
मया आदौ ब्रह्मणे प्रोक्ता धर्मः यस्यां मदात्मकः॥३॥

तेन प्रोक्ता च पुत्राय मनवे पूर्वजाय सा।
ततः भृगु आदयः अगृह्णन् सप्तब्रह्ममहर्षयः॥४॥

तेभ्यः पितृभ्यः तत् पुत्राः देवदानवगुह्यकाः।
मनुष्याः सिद्धगन्धर्वाः सविद्याधरचारणाः॥५॥

किन्देवाः किन्नराः नागाः रक्षः किंपुरुष आदयः।
बह्व्यः तेषां प्रकृतयः रजःसत्त्वतमोभुवः॥६॥

याभिः भूतानि भिद्यन्ते भूतानां मतयः तथा।
यथाप्रकृति सर्वेषां चित्राः वाचः स्रवन्ति हि॥७॥

एवं प्रकृतिवैचित्र्यात् भिद्यन्ते मतयः नृणाम्।
पारम्पर्येण केषांचित् पाखण्डमतयः अपरे॥८॥

मन्मायामोहितधियः पुरुषाः पुरुषर्षभ।
श्रेयः वदन्ति अनेकान्तं यथाकर्म यथारुचि॥९॥

धर्मम् एके यशः च अन्ये कामं सत्यं दमं शमम्।
अन्ये वदन्ति स्वार्थं वा ऐश्वर्यं त्यागभोजनम्।
केचित् यज्ञतपोदानं व्रतानि नियम अन्यमान्॥१०॥

आदि अन्तवन्तः एव एषां लोकाः कर्मविनिर्मिताः।
दुःख उदर्काः तमोनिष्ठाः क्षुद्र आनन्दाः शुच अर्पिताः॥११॥

मयि अर्पित मनः सभ्य निरपेक्षस्य सर्वतः।
मया आत्मना सुखं यत् तत् कुतः स्यात् विषय आत्मनाम्॥१२॥

अकिंचनस्य दान्तस्य शान्तस्य समचेतसः।
मया सन्तुष्टमनसः सर्वाः सुखमयाः दिशः॥१३॥

न पारमेष्ठ्यं न महेन्द्रधिष्ण्यम् न सार्वभौमं न रसाधिपत्यम्।
न योगसिद्धीः अपुनर्भवं वा मयि अर्पित आत्मा इच्छति मत् विना
अन्यत्॥१४॥

न तथा मे प्रियतमः आत्मयोनिः न शङ्करः।
न च सङ्कर्षणः न श्रीः न एव आत्मा च यथा भवान्॥[१५॥

निरपेक्षं मुनिं शातं निर्वैरं समदर्शनम्।
अनुव्रजामि अहं नित्यं पूयेयेति अङ्घ्रिरेणुभिः॥१६॥

निष्किञ्चना मयि अनुरक्तचेतसः शान्ताः महान्तः
अखिलजीववत्सलाः।
कामैः अनालब्धधियः जुषन्ति यत् तत् नैरपेक्ष्यं न विदुः सुखं
मम॥१७॥

बाध्यमानः अपि मद्भक्तः विषयैः अजितेन्द्रियः।
प्रायः प्रगल्भया भक्त्या विषयैः न अभिभूयते॥१८॥

यथा अग्निः सुसमृद्ध अर्चिः करोति एधांसि भस्मसात्।
तथा मद्विषया भक्तिः उद्धव एनांसि कृत्स्नशः॥१९॥

न साधयति मां योगः न साङ्‌ख्यं धर्मः उद्धव।
न स्वाध्यायः तपः त्यागः यथा भक्तिः मम ऊर्जिता॥२०॥

भक्त्या अहम् एकया ग्राह्यः श्रद्धया आत्मा प्रियः सताम्।
भक्तिः पुनाति मन्निष्ठा श्वपाकान् अपि संभवात्॥२१॥

धर्मः सत्यदया उपेतः विद्या वा तपसान्विता।
मद्भक्त्यापेतम् आत्मानं न सम्यक् प्रपुनाति हि॥२२॥

कथं विना रोमहर्षं द्रवता चेतसा विना।
विनानन्द अश्रुकलया शुध्येत् भक्त्या विनाशयः॥२३॥

वाक् गद्गदा द्रवते यस्य चित्तम् रुदति अभीक्ष्णं हसति क्वचित् च।
विलज्जः उद्गायति नृत्यते च मद्भक्तियुक्तः भुवनं पुनाति॥२४॥

यथा अग्निना हेम मलं जहाति ध्मातं पुनः स्वं भजते च रूपम्।
आत्मा च कर्मानुशयं विधूय मद्भक्तियोगेन भजति अथः माम्॥२५॥

यथा यथा आत्मा परिमृज्यते असौ मत्पुण्यगाथाश्रवण अभिधानैः।
तथा तथा पश्यति वस्तु सूक्ष्मम् चक्षुः यथा एव अञ्जनसंप्रयुक्तम्॥२६॥

विषयान् ध्यायतः चित्तं विषयेषु विषज्जते।
माम् अनुस्मरतः चित्तं मयि एव प्रविलीयते॥२७॥

तस्मात् असत् अभिध्यानं यथा स्वप्नमनोरथम्।
हित्वा मयि समाधत्स्व मनः मद्भावभावितम्॥२८॥

स्त्रीणां स्त्रीसङ्गिनां सङ्गं त्यक्त्वा दूरतः आत्मवान्।
क्षेमे विविक्तः आसीनः चिन्तयेत् माम् अतन्द्रितः॥२९॥

न तथा अस्य भवेत् क्लेशः बन्धः च अन्यप्रसङ्गतः।
योषित् सङ्गात् यथा पुंसः यथा तत् सङ्गिसङ्गतः॥३०॥

उद्धवः उवाच।
यथा त्वाम् अरविन्दाक्ष यादृशं वा यदात्मकम्।
ध्यायेत् मुमुक्षुः एतत् मे ध्यानं मे वक्तुम् अर्हसि॥३१॥

श्रीभगवान् उवाच।
समः आसनः आसीनः समकायः यथासुखम्।
हस्तौ उत्सङ्गः आधाय स्वनासाग्रकृत ईक्षणः।३२॥

प्राणस्य शोधयेत् मार्गं पूरकुम्भकरेचकैः।
विपर्ययेण अपि शनैः अभ्यसेत् निर्जितेन्द्रियः॥३३॥

हृदि अविच्छिन्नम् ओङ्कारं घण्टानादं बिसोर्णवत्।
प्राणेन उदीर्य तत्र अथ पुनः संवेशयेत् स्वरम्॥३४॥

एवं प्रणवसंयुक्तं प्राणम् एव समभ्यसेत्।
दशकृत्वः त्रिषवणं मासात् अर्वाक् जित अनिलः॥३५॥

हृत्पुण्डरीकम् अन्तस्थम् ऊर्ध्वनालम् अधोमुखम्।
ध्यात्वा ऊर्ध्वमुखम् उन्निद्रम् अष्टपत्रं सकर्णिकम्॥३६॥

कर्णिकायां न्यसेत् सूर्यसोमाग्नीन् उत्तरोत्तरम्।
वह्निमध्ये स्मरेत् रूपं मम एतत् ध्यानमङ्गलम्॥३७॥

समं प्रशान्तं सुमुखं दीर्घचारुचतुर्भुजम्।
सुचारुसुन्दरग्रीवं सुकपोलं शुचिस्मितम्॥३८॥

समान कर्ण विन्यस्त स्फुरन् मकर कुण्डलम्।
हेम अम्बरं घनश्यामं श्रीवत्स श्रीनिकेतनम्॥३९॥

शङ्ख चक्र गदा पद्म वनमाला विभूषितम्।
नूपुरैः विलसत् पादं कौस्तुभ प्रभया युतम्॥४०॥

द्युमत् किरीट कटक कटिसूत्र अङ्गद अयुतम्।
सर्वाङ्ग सुन्दरं हृद्यं प्रसाद सुमुख ईक्षणम्॥४१॥

सुकुमारम् अभिध्यायेत् सर्वाङ्गेषु मनः दधत्।
इन्द्रियाणि इन्द्रियेभ्यः मनसा आकृष्य तत् मनः।
बुद्ध्या सारथिना धीरः प्रणयेत् मयि सर्वतः॥४२॥

तत् सर्व व्यापकं चित्तम् आकृष्य एकत्र धारयेत्।
न अन्यानि चिन्तयेत् भूयः सुस्मितं भावयेत् मुखम्॥४३॥

तत्र लब्धपदं चित्तम् आकृष्य व्योम्नि धारयेत्।
तत् च त्यक्त्वा मदारोहः न किञ्चित् अपि चिन्तयेत्॥४४॥

एवं समाहितमतिः माम् एव आत्मानम् आत्मनि।
विचष्टे मयि सर्वात्मत् ज्योतिः ज्योतिषि संयुतम्॥४५॥

ध्यानेन इत्थं सुतीव्रेण युञ्जतः योगिनः मनः।
संयास्यति आशु निर्वाणं द्रव्य ज्ञान क्रिया भ्रमः॥४६॥

इति श्रीमद्भागवते महापुराणे पारमहंस्यां
संहितायामेकादशस्कन्धे श्रीकृष्णोद्धवसंवादे
भक्तिरहस्यावधारणयोगो नाम चतुर्दशोऽध्यायः॥१४॥

15 Yoga Perfections

English Rhyme

The Lord said, "Dear Uddhav, listen well,
On yoga's mystic perfections, I'll tell.

Conquer the senses, steady the mind,
In me, let your thoughts bind.

Uddhav asked, "Acyuta, divine,
How can these perfections be mine?

How many are there, in yoga's shrine?
You, the bestower, make them shine."

The Lord replied, "In yoga's realm,
Eighteen perfections helm.

Eight primary, in me they dwell,
Ten secondary, from goodness swell.

Anima, mahima, laghima, see,
Transform the body, set it free.

Prapti, prakamya-siddhi, find,
Fulfill desires, of every kind.

Isita-siddhi, manipulate maya's play,
Vasita-siddhi, modes of nature sway.

Kamavasayita-siddhi, obtain,
Anything, anywhere, break the chain.

Ten secondary, from nature arise,
Free from hunger, thirst, the body lies.

Hear and see, far away,
Move at mind's speed, in yoga's way.

Assume any form, enter others' guise,
Die when desired, the yogi tries.

Witness gods and Apsaras play,
Fulfill orders, without delay.

Know past, present, future's tide,
Tolerate duality, in stride.

Know others' minds, check fire's glow,
Remain unconquered, let yoga flow.

Worship me, in atomic form,
In subtle elements, let the mind swarm.

Obtain anima, become the least,
In yoga's feast, find inner peace.

Absorb the mind, in mahat-tattva's core,
Meditate on me, explore and soar.

Achieve mahima, become the most,
In yoga's host, a divine post.

I exist in all, the essence pure,
In atomic form, the yogi's lure.

Achieve laghima, become light,
In yoga's flight, reach new height.

With every breath, the soul ignites,
In cosmic dance, the spirit delights.

Fixing his mind in me, the yogi finds,
In the false ego, where goodness binds.

He the senses' proprietor, in all kinds,
For his mind in me, he aligns.

Concentrating all thoughts, in me, the soul,
In the mahat-tattva's role,

Obtains prakamya, the mystic goal,
From me, beyond material control.

Placing consciousness on Visnu, the prime,
The Supreme Lord, sublime.

Obtains control, in time,
Over Atmas, in their prime.

The yogi, in my form, does rest,
Narayana, the fourth, the best.

Obtains vasita, the mystic quest,
Endowed with my nature, blessed.

Fixing his pure mind, in me, the vast,
In my form, the impersonal cast,

Obtains happiness, unsurpassed,
Where desires are fulfilled, fast.

Concentrating on me, the pure,
The Lord of Svetadvipa, sure.

Obtains existence, secure,
From material disturbances, the cure.

The purified entity, in sound vibrations, does sink,
In me, the sky, the life air's link.

Perceives the speaking, in a blink,
Of all entities, on the brink.

Merging sight into the sun, so bright,
And the sun into the eyes, light.

Meditates on me, in sight,
Acquires the power, to see the night.

The yogi, his mind in me, does steep,
Uses the wind, the mind to keep.

Obtains the perfection, deep,
Where the body follows the mind's leap.

The yogi, his mind, a certain way,
Desires a form, without delay.

That form appears, in the fray,
Absorbing the mind, in my play.

The perfect yogi, another's body to enter,
Meditates on himself, the center.

Gives up his body, the tormentor,
Enters the other's, as a renter.

The yogi, svacchanda-mrtyu, the mystic call,
Blocks the anus, with the foot's fall.

Lifts the Atma, through the hall,
Gives up the body, once and for all.

The yogi, in the gods' gardens, to stay,
Meditates on goodness, in my bay.

Heavenly women, in aerial cars, sway,
Approach him, in the day.

The yogi, faith in me, does keep,
Absorbs his mind in me, deep.

Knowing my purpose, does seep,
Achieves his purpose, in a leap.

The one who meditates on me, pure,
Acquires my nature, sure.

His order, like mine, secure,
Cannot be frustrated, endure.

The yogi, his existence, does refine,
By devotion to me, divine.

Obtains knowledge, time's line,
Sees birth and death, of him and thine.

Just as water, the aquatic's shield,
The yogi, in devotion, is sealed.

Fire, sun, water, poison, in the field,
Cannot harm him, his protection revealed.

My devotee, unconquerable, does become,
Meditating on my incarnations, some.

Decorated with Srivatsa, weapons, a sum,
Flags, umbrellas, fans, they hum.

The learned devotee, in meditation deep,
Worships me, rewards he'll reap.

Mystic perfections, in his keep,
In all respects, he'll leap.

The sage, his senses, does defeat,
Breathing, mind, in retreat.

Self-controlled, in meditation's seat,
What perfection can't he meet?

Experts say, in service to the divine,
Mystic perfections, they decline.

Impediments, in the supreme line,
Where all perfection, does shine.

Perfections, by birth, herbs, austerities, chants,
Are achieved by devotion, in all slants.

The actual perfection of yoga, enchants,
By no other means, one enhances.

Dear Uddhav, I am the cause, the protector, the Lord,
Of all mystic perfections, in accord.

Of the yoga system, knowledge, activity, the word,
Of Vedic teachers, by me, they're adored.

Just as elements, in and out, do reside,
I cannot be covered, far and wide.

Within everything, as Parmatma, I hide,
Outside of everything, in feature, I glide.

Sanskrit Text 15

अथ पञ्चदशोऽध्यायः।
श्रीभगवान् उवाच।
जितेन्द्रियस्य युक्तस्य जितश्वासस्य योगिनः
मयि धारयतः चेतः उपतिष्ठन्ति सिद्धयः॥१॥

उद्धवः उवाच।
कया धारणया कास्वित् कथंस्वित् सिद्धिः अच्युत।
कति वा सिद्धयः ब्रूहि योगिनां सिद्धिदः भवान्॥२॥

श्रीभगवान् उवाच।
सिद्धयः अष्टादश प्रोक्ता धारणायोगपारगैः।
तासाम् अष्टौ मत् प्रधानाः दशः एव गुणहेतवः॥३॥

अणिमा महिमा मूर्तेः लघिमा प्राप्तिः इन्द्रियैः।
प्राकाम्यं श्रुतदृष्टेषु शक्तिप्रेरणम् ईशिता॥४॥

गुणेषु असङ्गः वशिता यत् कामः तत् अवस्यति।
एताः मे सिद्धयः सौम्य अष्टौ उत्पत्तिकाः मताः॥५॥

अनूर्मिमत्त्वं देहे अस्मिन् दूरश्रवणदर्शनम्।
मनोजवः कामरूपं परकायप्रवेशनम्॥६॥

स्वच्छन्दमृत्युः देवानां सहक्रीडानुदर्शनम्।
यथासङ्कल्पसंसिद्धिः आज्ञाप्रतिहता गतिः॥७॥

त्रिकालज्ञत्वम् अद्वन्द्वं परचित्तादि अभिज्ञता।
अग्नि अर्क अम्बु विष आदीनां प्रतिष्टम्भः अपराजयः॥८॥

एताः च उद्देशतः प्रोक्ता योगधारणसिद्धयः।
यया धारणया या स्यात् यथा वा स्यात् निबोध मे॥९॥

भूतसूक्ष्म आत्मनि मयि तन्मात्रं धारयेत् मनः।
अणिमानम् अवाप्नोति तन्मात्र उपासकः मम॥१०॥

महति आत्मन् मयि परे यथासंस्थं मनः दधत्।
महिमानम् अवाप्नोति भूतानां च पृथक् पृथक्॥११॥

परमाणुमये चित्तं भूतानां मयि रञ्जयन्।
कालसूक्ष्मात्मतां योगी लघिमानम् अवाप्नुयात्॥१२॥

धारयन् मयि अहंतत्त्वे मनः वैकारिके अखिलम्।
सर्वेन्द्रियाणाम् आत्मत्वं प्राप्तिं प्राप्नोति मन्मनाः॥१३॥

महति आत्मनि यः सूत्रे धारयेत् मयि मानसम्।
प्राकाम्यं पारमेष्ठ्यं मे विन्दते अव्यक्तजन्मनः॥१४॥

विष्णौ त्र्यधि ईश्वरे चित्तं धारयेत् कालविग्रहे।
सः ईशित्वम् अवाप्नोति क्षेत्रक्षेत्रज्ञचोदनाम्॥१५॥

नारायणे तुरीयाख्ये भगवत् शब्दशब्दिते।
मनः मयि आदधत् योगी मत् धर्माः वहिताम् इयात्॥१६॥

निर्गुणे ब्रह्मणि मयि धारयन् विशदं मनः।
परमानन्दम् आप्नोति यत्र कामः अवसीयते॥१७॥

श्वेतदीपपतौ चित्तं शुद्धे धर्ममये मयि।
धारयन् श्वेततां याति षडूर्मिरहितः नरः॥१८॥

मयि आकाश आत्मनि प्राणे मनसा घोषम् उद्वहन्।
तत्र उपलब्धा भूतानां हंसः वाचः श्रुणोति असौ॥१९॥

चक्षुः त्वष्टरि संयोज्य त्वष्टारम् अपि चक्षुषि।
मां तत्र मनसा ध्यायन् विश्वं पश्यति सूक्ष्मदृक्॥२०॥

मनः मयि सुसंयोज्य देहं तदनु वायुना।
मद्धारण अनुभावेन तत्र आत्मा यत्र वै मनः॥२१॥

यदा मनः उपादाय यत् यत् रूपं बुभूषति।
तत् तत् भवेत् मनोरूपं मद्योगबलम् आश्रयः॥२२॥

परकायं विशन् सिद्धः आत्मानं तत्र भावयेत्।
पिण्डं हित्वा विशेत् प्राणः वायुभूतः षडङ्घ्रिवत्॥२३॥

पार्ष्ण्या आपीड्य गुदं प्राणं हृत् उरः कण्ठ मूर्धसु।
आरोप्य ब्रह्मरन्ध्रेण ब्रह्म नीत्वा उत्सृजेत् तनुम्॥२४॥

विहरिष्यन् सुराक्रीडे मत्स्थं सत्त्वं विभावयेत्।
विमानेन उपतिष्ठन्ति सत्त्ववृत्तीः सुरस्त्रियः॥२५॥

यथा सङ्कल्पयेत् बुद्ध्या यदा वा मत्परः पुमान्।
मयि सत्ये मनः युञ्जन् तथा तत् समुपाश्नुते॥२६॥

यः वै मद्भावम् आपन्नः ईशितुः वशितुः पुमान्।
कुतश्चित् न विहन्येत तस्य च आज्ञा यथा मम॥२७॥

मद्भक्त्या शुद्धसत्त्वस्य योगिनः धारणाविदः।
तस्य त्रैकालिकी बुद्धिः जन्म मृत्यु उपबृंहिता॥२८॥

अग्नि आदिभिः न हन्येत मुनेः योगम् अयं वपुः।
मद्योगश्रान्तचित्तस्य यादसाम् उदकं यथा॥२९॥

मद्विभूतिः अभिध्यायन् श्रीवत्स अस्त्रबिभूषिताः।
ध्वजातपत्रव्यजनैः सः भवेत् अपराजितः॥३०॥

उपासकस्य माम् एवं योगधारणया मुनेः।
सिद्धयः पूर्वकथिताः उपतिष्ठन्ति अशेषतः॥३१॥

जितेन्द्रियस्य दान्तस्य जितश्वास आत्मनः मुनेः।
मद्धारणां धारयतः का सा सिद्धिः सुदुर्लभा॥३२॥

अन्तरायान् वदन्ति एताः युञ्जतः योगम् उत्तमम्।
मया संपद्यमानस्य कालक्षेपणहेतवः॥३३॥

जन्म ओषधि तपो मन्त्रैः यावतीः इह सिद्धयः।
योगेन आप्नोति ताः सर्वाः न अन्यैः योगगतिं व्रजेत्॥३४॥

सर्वासाम् अपि सिद्धीनां हेतुः पतिः अहं प्रभुः।
अहं योगस्य साङ्ख्यस्य धर्मस्य ब्रह्मवादिनाम्॥३५॥

अहम् आत्मा अन्तरः बाह्यः अनावृतः सर्वदेहिनाम्।
यथा भूतानि भूतेषु बहिः अन्तः स्वयं तथा॥३६॥

इति श्रीमद्भागवते महापुराणे पारमहंस्यां
संहितायामेकादशस्कन्धे श्रीकृष्णोद्धवसंवादे
सिद्धनिरूपणयोगो नाम पञ्चदशोऽध्यायः॥१५॥

16 Lord's Wealth

English Rhyme

Uddhav spoke, his voice filled with awe,
"Lord, you are the Absolute, without flaw.

Beginningless, endless, the universal law,
Protector, life-giver, without a draw.

Though impious minds may fail to see,
You exist in all, in every tree.

But Brahmins, in truth, bow to thee,
In Vedic conclusion, they agree.

Tell me, Lord, of the sages' quest,
In devotion to you, how are they blessed?

Which forms of you, do they attest,
In their worship, in their zest?

Though you are the Parmatma, the soul,
You remain hidden, beyond control.

Living entities, in their role,
Cannot see you, though you patrol.

Supremely potent Lord, your power,
Manifests everywhere, every hour.

In earth, heaven, hell, in every flower,
I bow to you, in this hour."

The Lord replied, "Uddhav, listen well,
On Kuruksetra, a tale I'll tell.

Arjuna, desiring to quell,
His rivals, fell under a spell.

Thinking of killing his kin, he withdrew,
'I would be the killer,' he knew.

Thus, in mundane consciousness, he grew,
His duty, he could not pursue.

I enlightened Arjuna, with logic's light,
In the battle's front, in the fight.

He asked questions, in his plight,
Like you are now, in my sight.

I am the Parmatma, the soul within,
Naturally the well-wisher, kin.

Creator, maintainer, annihilator, in the din,
I am not different, from them, therein.

I am the goal, of those who seek,
I am time, for the meek.

I am the equilibrium, for the weak,
I am virtue, for the pious, unique.

Among qualities, I am nature's face,
Among great things, the cosmic space.

Among subtle, the Atma's trace,
Among the unconquerable, the mind's race.

Among the Vedas, I am Brahma, the seer,
Among mantras, the omkara, clear.

Among letters, 'a', near,
Among meters, the Gayatri, dear.

Among gods, I am Indra, the king,
Among Vasus, Agni's ring.

Among Aditi's sons, Visnu's wing,
Among Rudras, Shiv's spring.

Among Brahmins, Bhrigu, the sage,
Among kings, Manu, the page.

Among gods, Narada, the mage,
Among cows, Kamadhenu, the gauge.

Among beings, Kapila, the seer,
Among birds, Garuda, the flyer.

Among mankind, Daksa, the peer,
Among forefathers, Aryama, the deer."

Uddhav, among Diti's sons, I am Prahlada,
The saintly lord of asuras, the saga.

Among stars and herbs, I am Candra,
Among Yaksas and Raksasas, I am Kuvera.

Among elephants, I am Airavata, the lord,
Among aquatics, Varuna, in accord.

Among all that heat and illuminate, the sun,
Among humans, the king, second to none.

Among horses, Uccaihsrava, in the field,
Among metals, I am gold, the yield.

Among suppressors, I am Yamaraja,
Among serpents, Vasuki, the saga.

Among snakes, I am Anantadeva, the best,
Among horned beasts, the lion, the crest.

Among social orders, the fourth, the renounced,
Among occupations, the Brahmins, announced.

Among sacred flows, I am the Ganges, the holy,
Among waters, the ocean, the jolly.

Among weapons, the bow, in the fray,
Among wielders, Shiv, in the play.

Among residences, Mount Sumeru, the peak,
Among impervious, the Himalayas, unique.

Among trees, the holy fig, the sign,
Among plants, those that bear grains, the line.

Among priests, Vasistha Muni, the sage,
Among the cultured, Brihaspati, the page.

Among leaders, Kartikeya, the martial,
Among the advanced, Brahma, the partial.

Among sacrifices, study of the Veda, the rite,
Among vows, nonviolence, the light.

Among purifiers, wind, fire, sun, water, speech,
In all these forms, I each.

Among yoga states, samadhi, the end,
Among victors, prudent counsel, the friend.

Among discriminators, the science of the Atma,
Among philosophers, diversity of perception, the drama.

Among ladies, Satarupa, the dame,
Among males, her husband, Manu, the name.

Among sages, Narayana, the wise,
Among brahmacharis, Sanat-kumara, the prize.

Among principles, renunciation, the creed,
Among securities, Atma consciousness, the seed.

Of secrets, pleasant speech and silence,
Among pairs, Brahma, the essence.

Among cycles of time, the year, the span,
Among seasons, spring, the clan.

Among months, Margasirsa, the time,
Among lunar houses, Abhijit, the prime.

Among ages, Satya-yuga, the truth,
Among sages, Devala and Asita, the sleuth.

Among dividers of Vedas, Vedavyasa, the seer,
Among scholars, SukrAcharya, the peer.

Among the Bhagavans, I am Vasudeva,
And Uddhav, you represent me, the diva.

Among Kimpurusas, Hanuman, the servant,
Among Vidyadharas, Sudarsana, the observant.

Among jewels, the ruby, the gem,
Among beauties, the lotus cup, the stem.

Among grass, the sacred kusa, the strand,
Of oblations, ghee, the command.

Among the enterprising, I am fortune's hand,
Among the cheaters, gambling's sand.

I am forgiveness, in the tolerant's land,
And goodness's qualities, in its band.

Of the powerful, I am strength, body and mind,
In devotional activities, me, they find.

My devotees, in nine forms, bind,
Among which, Vasudeva, they're inclined.

Among Gandharvas, I am Visvavasu, the song,
Among Apsaras, Purvacitti, the throng.

I am the mountains' steadiness, strong,
And the earth's fragrant aroma, long.

I am water's sweet taste, the sip,
Among brilliant things, I am the sun's trip.

I am the effulgence, in every clip,
And the transcendental sound, the flip.

Among the cultured, I am Bali Maharaja, the son,
Among heroes, I am Arjuna, the one.

Indeed, I am creation, under the sun,
Maintenance and annihilation, all done.

I am the senses' functions, the feel,
The legs, speech, anus, hands, the real.

And the senses of knowledge, the deal,
Touch, sight, taste, hearing, smell, the wheel.

I am form, taste, aroma, touch, sound,
False ego, mahat-tattva, the ground.

Earth, water, fire, air, sky, the round,
The living entity, material nature, the bound.

As the Supreme Lord, I am the basis, the core,
Of the living entity, the modes, and more.

Thus, I am everything, the store,
Without me, nothing can explore.

Even if I count the universe's atoms, the speck,
My opulences, I could not check.

Within innumerable universes, on deck,
My manifestations, in every nook and neck.

Whatever power, beauty, fame, might be,
Humility, renunciation, pleasure, the spree,

Fortune, strength, tolerance, the key,
Or spiritual knowledge, is simply me.

I have described, in brief, my might,
My spiritual opulences, the light.

And the material features, in sight,
Perceived by the mind, in its flight.

Therefore, control your speaking, the word,
Subdue the mind, the bird.

Conquer the life air, the herd,
Regulate the senses, the third.

A transcendentalist, his words and mind, should steer,
By superior intelligence, clear.

Or his vows, austerities, charity, dear,
Flow away, like water, I fear.

Being surrendered to me, the goal,
Control the speech, mind, life air, the toll.

Through loving devotional intelligence, the role,
Fulfill the mission of life, the scroll.

Sanskrit Text 16

अथ षोडशोऽध्यायः।
उद्धवः उवाच।
त्वं ब्रह्म परमं साक्षात् अनादि अनन्तम् अपावृतम्।
सर्वेषाम् अपि भावानां त्राणस्थिति अप्यय उद्भवः॥१॥

उच्चावचेषु भूतेषु दुर्ज्ञेयम् अकृत आत्मभिः।
उपासते त्वां भगवन् याथातथ्येन ब्राह्मणाः॥२॥

येषु येषु च भावेषु भक्त्या त्वां परमर्षयः।
उपासीनाः प्रपद्यन्ते संसिद्धिं तत् वदस्व मे॥३॥

गूढः चरसि भूतात्मा भूतानां भूतभावन।
न त्वां पश्यन्ति भूतानि पश्यन्तं मोहितानि ते॥४॥

याः काः च भूमौ दिवि वै रसायाम् विभूतयः दिक्षु महाविभूते।
ताः मह्यम् आख्याहि अनुभाविताः ते नमामि ते तीर्थ पद
अङ्घ्रिपद्मम्॥५॥

श्रीभगवान् उवाच।
एवम् एतत् अहं पृष्टः प्रश्नं प्रश्नविदां वर।
युयुत्सुना विनशने सपत्नैः अर्जुनेन वै॥६॥

ज्ञात्वा ज्ञातिवधं गर्ह्यम् अधर्मं राज्यहेतुकम्।
ततः निवृत्तः हन्ता अहं हतः अयम् इति लौकिकः॥७॥

सः तदा पुरुषव्याघ्रः युक्त्या मे प्रतिबोधितः।
अभ्यभाषत माम् एवं यथा त्वं रणमूर्धनि॥८॥

अहम् आत्मा उद्धव आमीषां भूतानां सुहृत् ईश्वरः।
अहं सर्वाणि भूतानि तेषां स्थिति उद्भव अप्ययः॥९॥

अहं गतिः गतिमतां कालः कलयताम् अहम्।
गुणानां च अपि अहं साम्यं गुणिन्या उत्पत्तिकः गुणः॥१०॥

गुणिनाम् अपि अहं सूत्रं महतां च महान् अहम्।
सूक्ष्माणाम् अपि अहं जीवः दुर्जयानाम् अहं मनः॥११॥

हिरण्यगर्भः वेदानां मन्त्राणां प्रणवः त्रिवृत्।
अक्षराणाम् अकारः अस्मि पदानि छन्दसाम् अहम्॥१२॥

इन्द्रः अहं सर्वदेवानां वसूनामस्मि हव्यवाट्।
आदित्यानाम् अहं विष्णू रुद्राणां नीललोहितः॥१३॥

ब्रह्मर्षीणां भृगुः अहं राजर्षीणाम् अहं मनुः।
देवर्षिणां नारदः अहं हविर्धानि अस्मि धेनुषु॥१४॥

सिद्धेश्वराणां कपिलः सुपर्णः अहं पतत्रिणाम्।
प्रजापतीनां दक्षः अहं पितृइणाम् अहम् अर्यमा॥१५॥

मां विद्धि उद्धव दैत्यानां प्रह्लादम् असुरेश्वरम्।
सोमं नक्षत्र ओषधीनां धनेशं यक्षरक्षसाम्॥१६॥

ऐरावतं गजेन्द्राणां यादसां वरुणं प्रभुम्।
तपतां द्युमतां सूर्यं मनुष्याणां च भूपतिम्॥१७॥

उच्चैःश्रवाः तुरङ्गाणां धातूनाम् अस्मि काञ्चनम्।
यमः संयमतां च अहं सर्पाणाम् अस्मि वासुकिः॥१८॥

नागेन्द्राणा.म् अनन्तः अहं मृगेन्द्रः शृङ्गिदंष्ट्रिणाम्।
आश्रमाणाम् अहं तुर्यः वर्णानां प्रथमः अनघ॥१९॥

तीर्थानां स्रोतसां गङ्गा समुद्रः सरसाम् अहम्।
आयुधानां धनुः अहं त्रिपुरघ्नः धनुष्मताम्॥२०॥

धिष्ण्यानाम् अस्मि अहं मेरुः गहनानां हिमालयः।
वनस्पतीनाम् अश्वत्थः ओषधीनाम् अहं यवः॥२१॥

पुरोधसां वसिष्ठः अहं ब्रह्मिष्ठानां बृहस्पतिः।
स्कन्दः अहं सर्वसेनान्याम् अग्रण्यां भगवान् अजः॥२२॥

यज्ञानां ब्रह्मयज्ञः अहं व्रतानाम् अविहिंसनम्।
वायु अग्नि अर्क अम्बु वाक् आत्मा शुचीनाम् अपि अहं शुचिः॥२३॥

योगानाम् आत्मसंरोधः मन्त्रः अस्मि विजिगीषताम्।
आन्वीक्षिकी कौशलानां विकल्पः ख्यातिवादिनाम्॥२४॥

स्त्रीणां तु शतरूपा अहं पुंसां स्वायंभुवः मनुः।
नारायणः मुनीनां च कुमारः ब्रह्मचारिणाम्॥२५॥

धर्माणाम् अस्मि संन्यासः क्षेमाणाम् अबहिः मतिः।
गुह्यानां सूनृतं मौनं मिथुनानाम् अजः तु अहम्॥२६॥

संवत्सरः अस्मि अनिमिषाम् ऋतूनां मधुमाधवौ।
मासानां मार्गशीर्षः अहं नक्षत्राणां तथा अभिजित्॥२७॥

अहं युगानां च कृतं धीराणां देवलः असितः।
द्वैपायनः अस्मि व्यासानां कवीनां काव्यः आत्मवान्॥२८॥

वासुदेवः भगवतां त्वं भागवतेषु अहम्।
किंपुरुषाणां हनुमान् विद्याध्राणां सुदर्शनः॥२९॥

रत्नानां पद्मरागः अस्मि पद्मकोशः सुपेशसाम्।
कुशः अस्मि दर्भजातीनां गव्यम् आज्यं हविष्षु अहम्॥३०॥

व्यवसायिनाम् अहं लक्ष्मीः कितवानां छलग्रहः।
तितिक्षा अस्मि तितिक्षणां सत्त्वं सत्त्ववताम् अहम्॥३१॥

ओजः सहोबलवतां कर्म अहं विद्धि सात्त्वताम्।
सात्त्वतां नवमूर्तीनाम् आदिमूर्तिः अहं परा॥३२॥

विश्वावसुः पूर्वचित्तिः गन्धर्व अप्सरसाम् अहम्।
भूधराणाम् अहं स्थैर्यं गन्धमात्रम् अहं भुवः॥३३॥

अपां रसः च परमः तेजिष्ठानां विभावसुः।
प्रभा सूर्य इन्दु ताराणां शब्दः अहं नभसः परः॥३४॥

ब्रह्मण्यानां बलिः अहं विराणाम् अहम् अर्जुनः।
भूतानां स्थितिः उत्पत्तिः अहं वै प्रतिसङ्क्रमः॥३५॥

गति उक्ति उत्सर्ग उपादानम् आनन्द स्पर्श लक्षणम्।
आस्वाद श्रुति अवघ्राणम् अहं सर्वेन्द्रिय इन्द्रियम्॥३६॥

पृथिवी वायुः आकाशः आपः ज्योतिः अहं महान्।
विकारः पुरुषः अव्यक्तं रजः सत्त्वं तमः परम्।
अहम् एतत् प्रसङ्ख्यानं ज्ञानं सत्त्वविनिश्चयः॥३७॥

मया ईश्वरेण जीवेन गुणेन गुणिना विना।
सर्वात्मना अपि सर्वेण न भावः विद्यते क्वचित्॥३८॥

संख्यानं परमाणूनां कालेन क्रियते मया।
न तथा मे विभूतीनां सृजतः अण्डानि कोटिशः॥३९॥

तेजः श्रीः कीर्तिः ऐश्वर्यं ह्रीः त्यागः सौभगं भगः।
वीर्यं तितिक्षा विज्ञानं यत्र यत्र स मे अंशकः॥४०॥

एताः ते कीर्तिताः सर्वाः संक्षेपेण विभूतयः।
मनोविकाराः एव एते यथा वाचा अभिधीयते॥४१॥

वाचं यच्छ मनः यच्छ प्राणानि यच्छ इन्द्रियाणि च।
आत्मानम् आत्मना यच्छ न भूयः कल्पसे अध्वने॥४२॥

यः वै वाक् मनसि सम्यक् असंयच्छन् धिया यतिः।
तस्य व्रतं तपः दानं स्रवत्यामघटाम्बुवत्॥४३॥

तस्मात् मनः वचः प्राणान् नियच्छेत् मत् परायणः।
मत् भक्ति युक्तया बुद्ध्या ततः परिसमाप्यते॥४४॥

इति श्रीमद्भागवते महापुराणे पारमहंस्यां
संहितायामेकादशस्कन्धे श्रीकृष्णोद्धवसंवादे
विभूतियोगो नाम षोडशोऽध्यायः॥१६॥

17 Varnashram System

English Rhyme

Uddhav asked, his voice a soothing breeze,
"Lord, you outlined the path of devotees,

For Varnashram followers, and all species,
Now tell us, how can all achieve peace,

Strong-armed Lord, in Hamsa's form,
You enlightened Brahma, in the norm.

Those teachings, the world's adorn,
Will soon vanish, as time will transform.

Acyuta, there is none so deep,
On earth or in Brahma's keep.

When you depart, who'll sweep,
The lost wisdom, once in heap?

Therefore, my Lord, the seer of all,
Reveal the path, to prevent our fall.

How can beings, short and tall,
Serve you well, and heed your call?"

Sukadeva replied,
"Uddhav, the finest, of our fraternity,
Questioned the Lord, in all sincerity.

The Lord, delighted, answered
The Lord said, 'Uddhav, your query's glow,
Leads to perfection, pure as snow.

For all humans, and Varnashram's flight,
Learn from me, the religious rite.

In the beginning, in Satya-yuga's fold,
There's only one class, hamsa, bold.

All are devotees, young and old,
In Krta-yuga, as scholars told.

In Satya-yuga, the Veda's hum,
Is expressed by om, the sum.

I am the object, to which minds come,
As Hamsa, I am worshipped, by some.

In Treta-yuga, from my heart's seat,
Vedic knowledge, in three divisions, meet.

Rig, Sama, Yajur, in the heat,
From that knowledge, I greet.

In Treta-yuga, the social orders, four,
From my universal form, they pour.

Brahmins, ksatriyas, vaisyas, sudras, the core,
Each recognized, by duties they bore.

The married life, from my loins, did spring,
Celibate students, from my heart, sing.

Retired life, from my chest, bring,
Renounced life, in my head, cling.'"

In society's dawn, divisions take birth,
Ranked by nature's decree, of varied worth.

Brahmins guide with tranquility, restraint, and contentment,
Deeds marked by piety, compassion, honest commitment.

Ksatriyas radiate with might, vigor, and liberality,
Governance and devotion to Brahmins, a natural ability.

Vaisyas, loyal to Vedic culture, treasure prosperity,
Their service to Brahmins, a testament to their sincerity.

Sudras assist with simplicity, their earnings a pleasure,
Service to Brahmins, cows, gods, their virtuous measure.

Those beyond Varnashram, in deceit they flounder,
Temperament marked by wrath, desire, a bitter encounter.

Ahimsa, satya, honesty, the universal appeal,
Wishing for others' wellbeing, a responsibility real.

The twice-born, through rituals, attains a new birth,
In the guru's ashram, they discover their worth.

The brahmachari, in straw and deerskin, is attired,
Sacred thread, aksa beads, a staff, their spiritual desired.

Shunning luxury, they carry pristine kusa grass,
Teeth unadorned, their garments un-dyed, they surpass.

Silent during bathing, eating, sacrifices, and japa,
They do not cut nails and hair, following the map.

Observing celibacy, they control their breath,
Chanting the Gayatri hymn, they ward off death.

In purity, they worship the fire-god, sun, and guru,
Acharya, cows, Brahmins, their devotion ever true.

Seeing the Acharya as Myself, respect they direct,
For he embodies all gods, a truth they protect.

In the morning and evening, they collect and offer food,
Accepting for oneself, in self-controlled mood.

In the service of the spiritual master, humility is our coat,
Walking behind, as he strides, we follow in his float.

When he rests his eyes, nearby we also lay,
Awake or asleep, in his service, we always stay.

Massaging his lotus feet, rendering services due,
Standing with folded hands, awaiting orders to pursue.

In this manner, the spiritual master, we always revere,
A humble servant in his ashram, we appear.

The student of Vedic wisdom, in the ashram resides,
Free of material desires, in celibacy he abides.

If Maharloka or Brahmaloka, he aspires to see,
To the spiritual master, surrender completely he must be.

Enlightened in Vedic knowledge, by the guru's grace,
Freed from sins, duality, Parmatma's presence he can trace.

In fire, in self, in all living entities, He resides,
Worship the Parmatma, the scripture guides.

Men of celibacy - sannyasis, vanaprasthas, brahmacharis,
Not mingle with women, nor indulge in such narratives.

Purity, devotion, and japa, should be their daily ritual,
Recalling Parmatma's presence, keeping Him in visual.

The Brahmin, with celibacy's vow, becomes brilliant like fire,
Burning material desires, reaching higher and higher.

Once Vedic education is complete, household life he yearns,
To the spiritual master, proper remuneration he returns.

With the guru's permission, to his home he may go,
Or if material desires persist, a family life he may sow.

A householder seeking purity, may enter the forest wide,
While a purified Brahmin, in renounced life may abide.

To establish a family, marry a wife of your class,
Younger and without reproach, for a life that will last.

All twice-born men – Brahmins, Kshatriyas, and Vaisyas,
Must do sacrifice, study Vedas, give alms in their areas.

A Brahmin, fearing charity may tarnish his fame,
Teach Vedic knowledge, perform sacrifice in God's name.

If these too compromise his position, he believes,
He should live off grains, in independence, he achieves.

The body of a Brahmin, not for sense gratification,
Accepting austerities, for post-death jubilation.

A Brahmin householder, in mind satisfied,
Gleans rejected grains, his needs supplied.

Free of personal desire, in me absorbed,
Practices magnanimous principles, by me adored.

Just as a ship rescues those at sea,
I rescue those who uplift devotees in poverty.

Like the chief bull elephant, strong and grand,
A fearless king protects his land.

An earthly king, removing sins from his reign,
Will with Indra, in sun-bright planes, remain.

A Brahmin, suffering, unable to maintain,
May become a merchant, his livelihood regain.

If poverty persists, a ksatriya he may become,
But never a dog, under an ordinary master, succumb.

A king, unable to maintain, may change his role,
But never a sudra's profession, should he enroll.

A vaisya, unable to sustain, may a sudra be,
Making baskets and mats, in duress surely.

But when difficulties pass, he must reassess,
And give up the substitute occupation, no less.

One in the grihasta order, should daily pray,
Worship the sages, the forefathers, in their own way.

Offer shares of meals, to all living entities,
Perform these five sacrifices, with sincerities.

A householder should maintain his dependents well,
With money that comes on its own, or by honest sell.

Perform sacrifices, religious ceremonies, as means allow,
Care for many, but material attachment disavow.

The association of kin, like travelers meeting brief,
With each change of body, comes separation and grief.

A liberated Atma, at home, should live like a guest,
Unbound, unentangled, in domestic affairs, at rest.

A householder devotee, in family duties immersed,
May stay at home, or take sannyasa, if so versed.

Worshiping me, in holy place, or at home,
In execution of duties, wherever he may roam.

A householder, his mind attached to his abode,
Disturbed by desires, in illusion's road.

Lusty after women, with a miser's sight,
Thinks, "All is mine, in day and night."

"My elderly parents, my wife and child so small,
My young children, on me they all fall.

Without me, they have no protector, no guide,
How will they live, in life's tide?"

Thus, with foolish mentality, he is never content,
His heart overwhelmed, on relatives his time spent.

Constantly meditating, in family's embrace,
He enters the darkness, losing life's race.

Sanskrit Text 17

अथ सप्तदशोऽध्यायः।
उद्धवः उवाच।
यः त्वया अभितः पूर्वं धर्मः त्वत् भक्तिलक्षणः।
वर्णाश्रम आचारवतां सर्वेषां द्विपदाम् अपि॥१॥

यथा अनुष्ठीयमानेन त्वयि भक्तिः नृणां भवेत्।
स्वधर्मेण अरविन्दाक्ष तत् समाख्यातुम् अर्हसि॥२॥

पुरा किल महाबाहो धर्मं परमकं प्रभो।
यत् तेन हंसरूपेण ब्रह्मणे अभ्यात्थ माधव॥३॥

सः इदानीं सुमहता कालेन अमित्रकर्शन।
न प्रायः भविता मर्त्यलोके प्राक् अनुशासितः॥४॥

वक्ता कर्ता अविता न अन्यः धर्मस्य अच्युत ते भुवि।
सभायाम् अपि वैरिञ्च्यां यत्र मूर्तिधराः कलाः॥५॥

कर्त्रा अवित्रा प्रवक्त्रा च भवता मधुसूदन।
त्यक्ते महीतले देव विनष्टं कः प्रवक्ष्यति॥६॥

तत्त्वं नः सर्वधर्मज्ञ धर्मः त्वत् भक्तिलक्षणः।
यथा यस्य विधीयेत तथा वर्णय मे प्रभो॥७॥

श्रीशुकः उवाच।
इत्थं स्वभृत्यमुख्येन पृष्टः सः भगवान् हरिः।
प्रीतः क्षेमाय मर्त्यानां धर्मान् आह सनातनान्॥८॥

श्रीभगवान् उवाच।
धर्म्यः एष तव प्रश्नः नैःश्रेयसकरः नृणाम्।
वर्णाश्रम आचारवतां तम् उद्धव निबोध मे॥९॥

आदौ कृतयुगे वर्णः नृणां हंसः इति स्मृतः।
कृतकृत्याः प्रजाः जात्याः तस्मात् कृतयुगं विदुः॥१०॥

वेदः प्रणवः एव अग्रे धर्मः अहं वृषरूपधृक्।
उपासते तपोनिष्ठां हंसं मां मुक्तकिल्बिषाः॥११॥

त्रेतामुखे महाभाग प्राणात् मे हृदयात् त्रयी।
विद्या प्रादुः अभूत् तस्याः अहम् आसं त्रिवृन्मखः॥१२॥

विप्र क्षत्रिय विट् शूद्राः मुख बाहु उरु पादजाः।
वैराजात् पुरुषात् जाताः यः आत्माचारलक्षणाः॥१३॥

गृहाश्रमः जघनतः ब्रह्मचर्यं हृदः मम।
वक्षःस्थानात् वने वासः न्यासः शीर्षणि संस्थितः॥१४॥

वर्णानाम् आश्रमाणां च जन्मभूमि अनुसारिणीः।
आसन् प्रकृतयः नृणां नीचैः नीच उत्तम उत्तमाः॥१५॥

शमः दमः तपः शौचं सन्तोषः क्षान्तिः आर्जवम्।
मद्भक्तिः च दया सत्यं ब्रह्मप्रकृतयः तु इमाः॥१६॥

तेजः बलं धृतिः शौर्यं तितिक्षा औदार्यम् उद्यमः।
स्थैर्यं ब्रह्मणि अत ऐश्वर्यं क्षत्रप्रकृतयः तु इमाः॥१७॥

आस्तिक्यं दाननिष्ठा च अदम्भः ब्रह्मसेवनम्।
अतुष्टिः अर्थ उपचयैः वैश्यप्रकृतयः तु इमाः॥१८॥

शुश्रूषणं द्विजगवां देवानां च अपि अमायया।
तत्र लब्धेन सन्तोषः शूद्रप्रकृतयः तु इमाः॥१९॥

अशौचम् अनृतं स्तेयं नास्तिक्यं शुष्कविग्रहः।
कामः क्रोधः च तर्षः च स्वभावः अन्तेवसायिनाम्॥२०॥

अहिंसा सत्यम् अस्तेयम् अकामक्रोधलोभता।
भूतप्रियहितेहा च धर्मः अयं सार्ववर्णिकः॥२१॥

द्वितीयं प्राप्य अनुपूर्व्यात् जन्म उपनयनं द्विजः।
वसन् गुरुकुले दान्तः ब्रह्म अधीयीत च आहुतः॥२२॥

मेखला अजिन दण्ड अक्ष ब्रह्मसूत्र कमण्डलून्।
जटिलः अधौतदद्वासः अरक्तपीठः कुशान् दधत्॥२३॥

स्नान भोजन होमेषु जप उच्चारे च वाग्यतः।
न च्छिन्द्यात् नख रोमाणि कक्ष उपस्थगतानि अपि॥२४॥

रेतः न अवकिरेत् जातु ब्रह्मव्रतधरः स्वयम्।
अवकीर्णे अवगाह्य अप्सु यतासुः त्रिपदीं जपेत्॥२५॥

अग्नि अर्क आचार्य गो विप्र गुरु वृद्ध सुरान् शुचिः।
समाहितः उपासीत सन्ध्ये च यतवाक् जपन्॥२६॥

आचार्यं मां विजानीयात् न अवमन्येत कर्हिचित्।
न मर्त्यबुद्धि आसूयेत सर्वदेवमयः गुरुः॥२७॥

सायं प्रातः उपानीय भैक्ष्यं तस्मै निवेदयेत्।
यत् च अन्यत् अपि अनुज्ञातम् उपयुञ्जीत संयतः॥२८॥

शुश्रूषमाणः आचार्यं सदा उपासीत नीचवत्।
यान शय्या आसन स्थानैः न अतिदूरे कृताञ्जलिः॥२९॥

एवंवृत्तः गुरुकुले वसेत् भोगविवर्जितः।
विद्या समाप्यते यावत् बिभ्रत् व्रतम् अखण्डितम्॥३०॥

यदि असौ छन्दसां लोकम् आरोक्ष्यन् ब्रह्मविष्टपम्।
गुरवे विन्यसेत् देहं स्वाध्यायार्थं वृहत् व्रतः॥३१॥

अग्नौ गुरौ आत्मनि च सर्वभूतेषु मां परम्।
अपृथक् धीः उपासीत ब्रह्मवर्चस्वी अकल्मषः॥३२॥

स्त्रीणां निरीक्षण स्पर्श संलाप क्ष्वेलन आदिकम्।
प्राणिनः मिथुनीभूतान् अगृहस्थः अग्रतः त्यजेत्॥३३॥

शौचम् आचमनं स्नानं सन्ध्या उपासनम् आर्जवम्।
तीर्थसेवा जपः अस्पृश्य अभक्ष्य असंभाष्य वर्जनम्॥३४॥

सर्व आश्रम प्रयुक्तः अयं नियमः कुलनन्दन.
मद्भावः सर्बभूतेषु मनोवाक्काय संयमः॥३५॥

एवं बृहत् व्रतधरः ब्राह्मणः अग्निः इव ज्वलन्।
मद्भक्तः तीव्रतपसा दग्धकर्म आशयः अमलः॥३६॥

अथ अनन्तरम् आवेक्ष्यन् यथा जिज्ञासित आगमः।
गुरवे दक्षिणां दत्त्वा स्नायत् गुरु अनुमोदितः॥३७॥

गृहं वनं वा उपविशेत् प्रव्रजेत् वा द्विज उत्तमः।
आश्रमात् आश्रमं गच्छेत् न अन्यथा मत्परः चरेत्॥३८॥

गृहार्थी सदृशीं भार्याम् उद्वहेत् अजुगुप्सिताम्।
यवीयसीं तु वयसा यां सवर्णाम् अनुक्रमात्॥३९॥

इज्य अध्ययन दानानि सर्वेषां च द्विजन्मनाम्।
प्रतिग्रहः अध्यापनं च ब्राह्मणस्य एव याजनम्॥४०॥

प्रतिग्रहं मन्यमानः तपः तेजोयशोनुदम्।
अन्याभ्याम् एव जीवेत शिलैः वा दोषदृक् तयोः॥४१॥

ब्राह्मणस्य हि देहः अयं क्षुद्रकामाय न इष्यते।
कृच्छ्राय तपसे च इह प्रेत्य अनन्तसुखाय च॥४२॥

शिलोञ्छवृत्त्या परितुष्टचित्तः धर्मं महान्तं विरजं जुषाणः।
मयि अर्पितात्मा गृहः एव तिष्ठन् न अतिप्रसक्तः समुपैति
शान्तिम्॥४३॥

समुद्धरन्ति ये विप्रं सीदन्तं मत्परायणम्।
तान् उद्धरिष्ये न चिरात् आपद्भ्यः नौः इव अर्णवात्॥४४॥

सर्वाः समुद्धरेत् राजा पिता इव व्यसनात् प्रजाः।
आत्मानम् आत्मना धीरः यथा गजपतिः गजान्॥४५॥

एवंविधः नरपतिः विमानेन अर्कवर्चसा।
विधूय इह अशुभं कृत्स्नम् इन्द्रेण सह मोदते॥४६॥

सीदन् विप्रः वणिक् वृत्त्या पण्यैः एव आपदं तरेत्।
खड्गेन वा आपदाक्रान्तः न श्ववृत्त्या कथंचन॥४७॥

वैश्यवृत्त्या तु राजन् यः जीवेत् मृगयया आपदि।
चरेत् वा विप्ररूपेण न श्ववृत्त्या कथंचन॥४८॥

शूद्रवृत्तिं भजेत् वैश्यः शूद्रः कारुकटप्रियाम्।
कृच्छ्रात् मुक्तः न गर्ह्येण वृत्तिं लिप्सेत कर्मणा॥४९॥

वेद अध्याय स्वधा स्वाहा बलि अन्न आद्यैः यथा उदयम्।
देवर्षि पितृभूतानि मद्रूपाणि अन्वहं यजेत्॥५०॥

यदृच्छया उपपन्नेन शुक्लेन उपार्जितेन वा।
धनेन अपीडयन् भृत्यान् न्यायेन एव आहरेत् क्रतून्॥५१॥

कुटुंबेषु न सज्जेत न प्रमाद्येत् कुटुंबि अपि।
विपश्चित् नश्वरं पश्येत् अदृष्टम् अपि दृष्टवत्॥५२॥

पुत्र दारा आप्त बन्धूनां सङ्गमः पान्थसङ्गमः।
अनुदेहं वियन्ति एते स्वप्नः निद्रानुगः यथा॥५३॥

इत्थं परिमृशन् मुक्तः गृहेषु अतिथिवत् वसन्।
न गृहैः अनुबध्येत निर्ममः निरहङ्कृतः॥५४॥

कर्मभिः गृहम् एधीयैः इष्ट्वा माम् एव भक्तिमान्।
तिष्ठेत् वनं वा उपविशेत् प्रजावान् वा परिव्रजेत्॥५५॥

यः तु आसक्तम् अतिः गेहे पुत्र वित्तैषण आतुरः।
स्त्रैणः कृपणधीः मूढः मम अहम् इति बध्यते॥५६॥

अहो मे पितरौ वृद्धौ भार्या बालात्मजा आत्मजाः।
अनाथाः माम् ऋते दीनाः कथं जीवन्ति दुःखिताः॥५७॥

एवं गृह आशय आक्षिप्त हृदयः मूढधीः अयम्।
अतृप्तः तान् अनुध्यायन् मृतः अन्धं विशते तमः॥५८॥

इति श्रीमद्भागवते महापुराणे पारमहंस्यां
संहितायामेकादशस्कन्धे श्रीकृष्णोद्धवसंवादे
ब्रह्मचर्यगृहस्थकर्मधर्मनिरूपणे सप्तदशोऽध्यायः॥१७॥

18 Varnashram Dharma

English Rhyme

The Lord said, with wisdom divine,
"Enter the forest, let peace be thine.

Leave your wife with mature sons, or take her along,
In the third order of life, vanaprastha, be strong.

Dress in tree bark, grass, leaves, or skins,
Eat bulbs, roots, fruits, cleanse your sins.

Groom not your hair, nails, nor seek dental shine,
Bathe thrice daily, on the ground recline.

Subject yourself to summer's fiery blaze,
To winter's icy waters, and rain's cold daze.

Eat grains prepared with fire, or fruits ripe with time,
Grind your food with mortar, stone, or teeth in line.

Collect what you need, considering time, place, capacity,
Never hoard for the future, embrace simplicity.

Perform seasonal sacrifices, offer oblations of caru,
But never offer animal sacrifices, even those known to you.

Perform the agnihotra, darsa, paurnamasa, as before,
And the vows and sacrifices of caturmasya, explore.

Emaciated, skin and bones, through penances severe,
Worship me, reach Maharloka, have no fear.

Long attempts at painful penance, for liberation ultimate,
Yet seeking sense gratification, is a fool's unfortunate fate.

Overtaken by old age, trembling, unable to execute,
Place the sacrificial fire within, let your body be mute.

Comprehend the sorrow of Brahmaloka, let go of fruitive ties,
Embrace the sannyasa life, calm the inner cries.

In worship, to the priest your possessions gift,
Enter sannyasa, let your spirit lift.

'This man taking sannyasa, will surpass us, indeed,
Will go back home, back to Godhead,' the gods concede.

They create stumbling blocks, in attractive forms appear,
But the sannyasi pays no heed, his path is clear."

If the sannyasi desires more than a kaupina's fold,
He may use another cloth, if he be so bold.

But in no emergency, should he accept,
Anything besides his danda and waterpot, he must respect.

A saintly person steps with care,
Ensuring no creature suffers despair.

Drinks water filtered through cloth, pure and neat,
Speaks only truth, performs actions discreet.

Without internal disciplines three,
A sannyasi, one can never be.

Avoiding useless speech, activities, controlling life air,
Carrying bamboo rods, does not a sannyasi declare.

Rejecting houses polluted, untouchable, in sight,
Approach seven houses, with no prior plight.

Beg and be satisfied, with what is obtained,
Approach each occupational order, as needed, unstrained.

Food gathered through begging, take in hand,
Leave populated areas, seek a secluded land.

Distribute portions of food, without a word,
Eat everything on the plate, like a free bird.

Without material attachment, senses controlled,
Remain enthusiastic, in the Supreme Lord consoled.

Travel about the earth alone, with equal vision,
Steady on the spiritual platform, make that decision.

Dwell in a safe and solitary place, mind pure,
Concentrate on the Atma, in me, secure.

Ascertain the nature of the Atma's bondage and liberation,
Control of senses constitutes liberation's foundation.

Travel in sanctified places, by rivers flowing,
In solitude of mountains and forests, knowledge growing.

Approach ordinary working men, beg bare sustenance,
Practice taking charity, achieve spiritual abundance.

Never see as ultimate reality, material things that perish,
Retire from all activities, material progress relinquish.

Consider the universe, within the Lord, to be,
Products of illusory energy, in the self, see.

Grasp Brahmaloka's pain, from fruitive outcomes, free,
Choose the sannyasa path, let your turmoil be.

In devotion, to the priest, your wealth bestow,
Embrace sannyasa, let your spirit glow.

The paramahamsa, wise and grand,
Lives like a child, in life's vast land.

Oblivious to honour, dishonour, no constraint,
Behaves like a stunted, incompetent saint.

Speaks like an insane, though most learned,
In Vedic regulations, unrestricted, he's turned.

A devotee, in fruitive rituals, never engaged,
Nor atheistic, nor in useless arguments, enraged.

A saintly person, calm and serene,
Never frightens, never mean.

Tolerates insults, never belittles,
For the material body, no hostility kindles.

The Supreme Lord, in all, does reside,
Like the moon's reflection, far and wide.

In joy or sorrow, be not swayed,
Understand both situations, by God, are made.

Strive for sufficient food, maintain health,
Contemplate spiritual truth, achieve stealth.

Accept food, clothing, bedding, as they come,
Of excellent or inferior quality, welcome.

Just as the Supreme Lord, free will exercises,
One with realized knowledge, cleanliness prioritizes.

Purifies hands with water, takes a bath,
Executes regulative duties, follows the path.

A realized Atma, sees no separation,
From me, destroys illusory perception.

At death, achieves opulences divine,
Equal to mine, in glory, they shine.

Detached from sense gratification, desiring perfection,
Approach a learned spiritual master, seek direction.

Render service to the guru, with faith and respect,
Until spiritual knowledge, you introspect.

Uncontrolled illusions, attachment to material things,
Denies gods, self, Supreme Lord, contamination clings.

Ruins religious principles, adopts sannyasa for living,
Is deviated, lost, in this life and the coming.

Sannyasi's duties, equanimity, nonviolence,
Vanaprastha's austerity, Atma's science.

Householder gives shelter, performs sacrifices,
Brahmachari serves the guru, fulfills his services.

A householder, in time prescribed, may seek his wife,
For begetting children, in their shared life.

Practice celibacy, austerity, cleanliness of mind and body,
Find satisfaction in natural position, friendship embody.

Worship of me, by all, should be practiced,
Regardless of social or occupational tactics.

One who worships me, with no other aim,
Achieves unflinching devotional service, in my name.

Dear Uddhav, I the Supreme Being, all realms in my sway,
I birth and annihilate this cosmos, the ultimate source, I say.

I am the Ultimate Reality, to me, the devotee turns,
With firm devotional service, spiritual rhythm churns.

One who sanctifies his existence, performs duties right,
Comprehends my supreme stature, in scriptural insight,

Blessed with enlightened knowledge, reaches me,
In the Varnashram system, discovers the key.

Embracing spiritual values, in sanctioned tradition's sight,
Devote Varnashram duties to me, in loving service, ignite.

They bestow the supreme culmination of life, a gem,
In me, find the ultimate stem.

Dear virtuous Uddhav, to you I narrate,
The means for my devotee, in set duty, to participate,

To return to me, the Lord, in devotion's wave,
In perfect commitment, let this be your brave.

Sanskrit Text 18

अथ अष्टादशोऽध्यायः।
श्रीभगवान् उवाच।
वनं विविक्षुः पुत्रेषु भार्यां न्यस्य सह एव वा।
वनः एव वसेत् शान्तः तृतीयं भागम् आयुषः॥१॥

कन्दमूलफलैः वन्यैः मेध्यैः वृत्तिं प्रकल्पयेत्।
वसीत वल्कलं वासः तृणपर्ण अजिनानि च॥२॥

केशरोमनखश्मश्रुमलानि बिभृयात् अतः।
न धावेत् अप्सु मज्जेत त्रिकालं स्थण्डिलेशयः॥३॥

ग्रीष्मे तप्येत पञ्चाग्नीन् वर्षास्वासारषाड् जले।
आकण्ठमग्नः शिशिरः एवंवृत्तः तपश्चरेत्॥४॥

अग्निपक्वं समश्नीयात् कालपक्वम् अथ अपि वा।
उलूखल अश्मकुट्टः वा दन्त उलूखलः एव वा॥५॥

स्वयं संचिनुयात् सर्वम् आत्मनः वृत्तिकारणम्।
देशकालबल अभिज्ञः न आददीत अन्यदा आहृतम्॥६॥

वन्यैः चरुपुरोडाशैः निर्वपेत् कालचोदितान्।
न तु श्रौतेन पशुना मां यजेत वनाश्रमी॥७॥

अग्निहोत्रं च दर्शः च पूर्णमासः च पूर्ववत्।
चातुर्मास्यानि च मुनेः आम्नातानि च नैगमैः॥८॥

एवं चीर्णेन तपसा मुनिः धमनिसन्ततः।
मां तपोमयम् आराध्य ऋषिलोकात् उपैति माम्॥९॥

यः तु एतत् कृच्छ्रतः चीर्णं तपः निःश्रेयसं महत्।
कामाय अल्पीयसे युञ्ज्यात् वालिशः कः अपरः ततः॥१०॥

यदा असौ नियमे अकल्पः जरया जातवेपथुः।
आत्मनि अग्नीन् समारोप्य मच्चित्तः अग्निं समाविशेत्॥११॥

यदा कर्मविपाकेषु लोकेषु निरय आत्मसु।
विरागः जायते सम्यक् न्यस्त अग्निः प्रव्रजेत् ततः॥१२॥

इष्ट्वा यथा उपदेशं मां दत्त्वा सर्वस्वम् ऋत्विजे।
अग्नीन् स्वप्राणः आवेश्य निरपेक्षः परिव्रजेत्॥१३॥

विप्रस्य वै संन्यसतः देवाः दारादिरूपिणः।
विघ्नान् कुर्वन्ति अयं हि अस्मान् आक्रम्य समियात् परम्॥१४॥

बिभृयात् चेत् मुनिः वासः कौपीन आच्छादनं परम्।
त्यक्तं न दण्डपात्राभ्याम् अन्यत् किंचित् अनापदि॥१५॥

दृष्टिपूतं न्यसेत् पादं वस्त्रपूतं पिबेत् जलम्।
सत्यपूतां वदेत् वाचं मनःपूतं समाचरेत्॥१६॥

मौन अनीहा अनिल आयामाः दण्डाः वाक् देह चेतसाम्।
नहि एते यस्य सन्ति अङ्गः वेणुभिः न भवेत् यतिः॥१७॥

भिक्षां चतुषु वर्णेषु विगर्ह्यान् वर्जयन् चरेत्।
सप्तागारान् असंक्लृप्तान् तुष्येत् लब्धेन तावता॥१८॥

बहिः जलाशयं गत्वा तत्र उपस्पृश्य वाग्यतः।
विभज्य पावितं शेषं भुञ्जीत अशेषम् आहृतम्॥१९॥

एकः चरेत् महीम् एतां निःसङ्गः संयतेन्द्रियः।
आत्मक्रीडः आत्मरतः आत्मवान् समदर्शनः॥२०॥

विविक्तक्षेमशरणः मद्भावविमलाशयः।
आत्मानं चिन्तयेत् एकम् अभेदेन मया मुनिः॥२१॥

अन्वीक्षेत आत्मनः बन्धं मोक्षं च ज्ञाननिष्ठया।
बन्धः इन्द्रियविक्षेपः मोक्षः एषां च संयमः॥२२॥

तस्मात् नियम्य षड्वर्गं मद्भावेन चरेत् मुनिः।
विरक्तः क्षुल्लकामेभ्यः लब्ध्वा आत्मनि सुखं महत्॥२३॥

पुरग्रामव्रजान् सार्थान् भिक्षार्थं प्रविशन् चरेत्।
पुण्यदेशसरित् शैलवन आश्रमवतीं महीम्॥२४॥

वानप्रस्थ आश्रम पदेषु अभीक्ष्णं भैक्ष्यम् आचरेत्।
संसिध्यत्याश्वसंमोहः शुद्धसत्त्वः शिलान्धसा॥२५॥

न एतत् वस्तुतया पश्येत् दृश्यमानं विनश्यति।
असक्तचित्तः विरमेत् इह अमुत्र चिकीर्षितात्॥२६॥

यत् एतत् आत्मनि जगत् मनोवाक्प्राणसंहतम्।
सर्वं माया इति तर्केण स्वस्थः त्यक्त्वा न तत् स्मरेत्॥२७॥

ज्ञाननिष्ठः विरक्तः वा मद्भक्तः वा अनपेक्षकः।
सलिङ्गान् आश्रमां त्यक्त्वा चरेत् अविधिगोचरः॥२८॥

बुधः बालकवत् क्रीडेत् कुशलः जडवत् चरेत्।
वदेत् उन्मत्तवत् विद्वान् गोचर्यां नैगमः चरेत्॥२९॥

वेदवादरतः न स्यात् न पाखण्डी न हैतुकः।
शुष्कवादविवादे न कंचित् पक्षं समाश्रयेत्॥३०॥

न उद्विजेत जनात् धीरः जनं च उद्वेजयेत् न तु।
अतिवादान् तितिक्षेत न अवमन्येत कंचन।
देहम् उद्दिश्य पशुवत् वैरं कुर्यात् न केनचित्॥३१॥

एकः एव परः हि आत्मा भूतेषु आत्मनि अवस्थितः।
यथा इन्दुः उदपात्रेषु भूतानि एकात्मकानि च॥३२॥

अलब्ध्वा न विषीदेत काले काले अशनं क्वचित्।
लब्ध्वा न हृष्येत् धृतिम् आनुभयं दैवतन्त्रितम्॥३३॥

आहारार्थं समीहेत युक्तं तत् प्राणधारणम्।
तत्त्वं विमृश्यते तेन तत् विज्ञाय विमुच्यते॥३४॥

यत् ऋच्छया उपपन्नात् अन्नम् अद्यात् श्रेष्ठम् उत अपरम्।
तथा वासः तथा शय्यां प्राप्तं प्राप्तं भजेत् मुनिः॥३५॥

शौचम् आचमनं स्नानं न तु चोदनया चरेत्।
अन्यान् च नियमान् ज्ञानी यथा अहं लीलया ईश्वरः॥३६॥

नहि तस्य विकल्पाख्या या च मद्वीक्षया हता।
आदेहान्तात् क्वचित् ख्यातिः ततः संपद्यते मया॥३७॥

दुःख उदर्केषु कामेषु जातनिर्वेदः आत्मवान्।
अजिज्ञासित मद्धर्मः गुरुं मुनिम् उपाव्रजेत्॥३८॥

तावत् परिचरेत् भक्तः श्रद्धावान् अनसूयकः।
यावत् ब्रह्म विजानीयात् माम् एव गुरुम् आदृतः॥३९॥

यः तु असंयत षड्वर्गः प्रचण्ड इन्द्रिय सारथिः।
ज्ञान वैराग्य रहितः त्रिदण्डम् उपजीवति॥४०॥

सुरान् आत्मानम् आत्मस्थं निह्नुते मां च धर्महा।
अविपक्व कषायः अस्मात् उष्मात् च विहीयते॥४१॥

भिक्षोः धर्मः शमः अहिंसा तपः ईक्षा वनौकसः।
गृहिणः भूतरक्ष इज्याः द्विजस्य आचार्यसेवनम्॥४२॥

ब्रह्मचर्यं तपः शौचं सन्तोषः भूतसौहृदम्।
गृहस्थस्य अपि ऋतौ गन्तुः सर्वेषां मदुपासनम्॥४३॥

इति मां यः स्वधर्मेण भजन् नित्यम् अनन्यभाक्।
सर्वभूतेषु मद्भावः मद्भक्तिं विन्दते अचिरात्॥४४॥

भक्त्या उद्धव अनपायिन्या सर्वलोकमहेश्वरम्।
सर्व उत्पत्ति अपि अयं ब्रह्म कारणं मा उपयाति सः॥४५॥

इति स्वधर्म निर्णिक्त सत्त्वः निर्ज्ञात् मद्गतिः।
ज्ञान विज्ञान संपन्नः न चिरात् समुपैति माम्॥४६॥

वर्णाश्रमवतां धर्मः एषः आचारलक्षणः।
सः एव मद्भक्तियुतः निःश्रेयसकरः परः॥४७॥

एतत् ते अभिहितं साधो भवान् पृच्छति यत् च माम्।
यथा स्वधर्मसंयुक्तः भक्तः मां समियात् परम्॥४८॥

इति श्रीमद्भागवते महापुराणे पारमहंस्यां
संहितायामेकादशस्कन्धे श्रीकृष्णोद्धवसंवादे
वानप्रस्थसंन्यासधर्मनिरूपणं नामाष्टादशोऽध्यायः॥१८॥

19 Spiritual Knowledge Perfection

English Rhyme

The Lord said, with wisdom profound,
"Scriptural knowledge, in enlightenment found,
Understanding the universe as illusion, let it be,
Surrender unto me, both knowledge and the means to see.

For philosophers, self-realized, learned and wise,
I am the only object of worship, the desired prize.

The goal of life, the means to achieve,
The conclusion of all knowledge, in me, they believe.

Those who've achieved perfection, complete and whole,
Recognize my lotus feet as the supreme goal.

The learned transcendentalist, dear to me,
Maintains me in happiness, through knowledge, free.

Perfection, by a fraction of spiritual knowledge, gained,
Cannot be duplicated, though austerities are strained.

Visiting holy places, chanting silent prayers,
Giving in charity, engaging in pious affairs.

Therefore, dear Uddhav, through knowledge, understand,
Your actual self, in Vedic knowledge, stand.

Worship me, in the mood of loving devotion,
Advance by clear realization, in steady motion.

Formerly, great sages, in sacrifice of knowledge, Vedic,
Worshiped me within, the Supreme Lord, majestic.

Knowing me as the Parmatma, in every heart,
Achieved supreme perfection, made a fresh start.

Dear Uddhav, the material body and mind, in illusion, dwell,
Attach themselves to you, a story they tell.

But they exist only at present, with no ultimate existence,
How can they relate to your eternal self, in this instance?

Uddhav said, with a plea in his voice,
'Lord of the universe, I have no choice.

On the terrible path of birth and death, I tread,
Overwhelmed by threefold miseries, in dread.

Almighty Lord, be merciful, uplift this living entity,
Fallen into the dark hole of material reality.

Despite detestable conditions, for material pleasure, rife,
Save me, my Lord, awaken me to spiritual life.

The Lord said, with a gentle nod,
'Dear Uddhav, just as you inquire of God,

So did King Yudhisthira, with no enemy in sight,
Inquire from Bhisma, in religious principles, bright.

After the great Battle of Kuruksetra, overwhelmed by death,
He inquired about path of liberation, with his last breath."

The Lord said, with wisdom profound,
"Religious principles of Vedic knowledge, in Bhisma, found.

Detachment, self-realization, faith, devotional service, pure,
Heard directly from his mouth, of this be sure.

I approve of that knowledge, unique and great,
Seeing the combination of elements, in a state.

Nine, eleven, five and three, in all living entities,
Ultimately one element, within those twenty-eight mysteries.

When one not sees the separated elements, twenty-eight,
But sees the cause itself, the Lord, contemplate.

At that time, one's direct experience, so fine,
Is called viGyan, or self-realization divine.

Start, termination, maintenance, stages of causation,
With all material phases, from creation to annihilation.

That which remains, when all material phases are gone,
Is the one eternal, shining like the dawn.

From four types of signal, Vedic knowledge, practice, direct,
Traditional wisdom, logical induction, perfect.

Realize the temporary, insubstantial situation, material world,
Become detached from the duality, let the truth be unfurled.

An intelligent person sees, any material activity,
Subject to constant transformation, a proclivity.

Even on Brahma's planet, there is simply unhappiness,
All within the universe, have a beginning, an end, express.

Sinless Uddhav, because you love me, so true,
I explained the process of devotional service, to you.

Now I will again explain, the supreme process, so divine,
For achieving loving service unto me, a sacred line.

Firm faith in the blissful narration of my pastimes, hold,
Constant chanting of my glories, be bold.

Unwavering attachment to ceremonial worship of me,
Praising me through beautiful hymns, let your heart be free.

In my service, offer obeisance, respect great and whole,
Worship my devotees, let this be your role.

See me in all living entities, consciousness be,
In my devotional service, let your activities free.

Use words to describe my qualities, to me, your mind offer,
From wealth, all material desires, do buffer.

Renounce sense gratification, happiness material,
Let your devotion show, in activities ethereal.

When consciousness, in goodness, finds peace, strength,
Fixed on the Lord, extends its length.

Attains religiosity, wisdom, detachment, and wealth,
Rewarded for steadfast devotion, in spiritual health.

When consciousness is fixed on body, home, alike,
Chasing material objects, life's hike.

Affected by passion, consciousness, dedicated,
To impermanent things, life's path, dictated.

True faith guides to my service, devotion's call,
Real wisdom unveils my presence, in all.

Detachment is dispassion for worldly pleasure,
Opulence is mystic perfection, a spiritual treasure.

Uddhav said, with a plea in his voice,
"Dear Krishna, tell me the choice,

Of disciplinary regulations, daily duties, how many,
Mental equilibrium, self-control, tell me if any.

What is tolerance, steadfastness, charity, austerity,
Heroism, reality, truth, in their entirety?

What is renunciation, wealth, what is desirable,
What is sacrifice, religious remuneration, reliable?

How to understand strength, opulence, profit,
What is the best education, humility, benefit?

What is real beauty, happiness, unhappiness,
Who is learned, who is a fool, in this mess?

What are the true and false paths, heaven and hell,
Who is a true friend, one's real home, do tell.

Who is a rich man, a poor man, who is wretched,
Who is an actual controller, these matters, sketched."

The Lord said, with wisdom profound,
"Nonviolence, truthfulness, not coveting, abound,

Detachment, humility, freedom from possessiveness,
Trust in religion, celibacy, silence, expressiveness.

Firmness, mercy, fearlessness, primary principles, twelve,
Internal cleanliness, external cleanliness, within delve.

Chanting holy names, austerity, sacrifice, faith,
Hospitality, worship of me, visiting holy places, saith.

Acting for supreme interest, satisfaction, servicing master,
Regular prescribed duties, twelve, a spiritual plaster.

These twenty-four elements, all desired blessings bestow,
On those who devotedly cultivate them, in life's flow.

Absorbing intelligence in me, mental equilibrium,
Complete discipline of senses, self-control, minimum.

Tolerance, patiently enduring unhappiness, steadfastness,
Conquering the tongue and genitals, in impressiveness.

Greatest charity, giving up all aggression,
Renunciation of lust, real austerity, confession.

Real heroism, conquering tendency to enjoy material life,
Reality, seeing the Lord everywhere, in strife.

Truthfulness, speaking the truth in a pleasing way,
Cleanliness, detachment in fruitive activities, sway.

Renunciation, the sannyasa order of life,
True desirable wealth, religiousness, without strife.

I, the Lord, am sacrifice, religious remuneration,
Devotion to the Acharya, acquiring spiritual instruction.

Greatest strength, the pranayama system, breath control,
These are the answers, Uddhav, to your soul."

Actual opulence, my nature as the Lord,
Exhibiting six unlimited opulences, in accord.

Supreme gain in life, devotional service to me,
Actual education, nullifying Atma's duality.

Real modesty, disgusted with improper acts,
Beauty is detachment, a matter of facts.

Real happiness, transcending material bounds,
Real misery, in sex pleasure, it confounds.

A wise man knows freedom from bondage, the way,
A fool identifies with body and mind, in dismay.

The real path in life, that which leads to me,
The wrong path, sense gratification, a spree.

Actual heaven, the mode of goodness, predominant,
Hell is ignorance, its presence constant.

I am everyone's true friend, the universe's spiritual master,
One's home is the human body, life's plaster.

Dear friend Uddhav, enriched with good qualities, truly rich,
Unsatisfied in life, truly poor, life's glitch.

A wretched person, cannot control his senses,
Not attached to sense gratification, real control commences.

One who attaches to sense gratification, a slave,
Uddhav, I have elucidated, matters you crave.

No need for more description, good and bad qualities,
To constantly see good and bad, itself a bad quality.

The best quality, to transcend material good and evil,
A path to spiritual liberation, in life's upheaval.

Sanskrit Text 19

अथ एकोनविंशः अध्यायः।
श्रीभगवान् उवाच।
यः विद्याश्रुतसंपन्नः आत्मवान् न अनुमानिकः।
मायामात्रम् इदं ज्ञात्वा ज्ञानं च मयि संन्यसेत्॥१॥

ज्ञानिनः तु अहम् एव इष्टः स्वार्थः हेतुः च संमतः।
स्वर्गः च एव अपवर्गः च न अन्यः अर्थः मद्दते प्रियः॥२॥

ज्ञानविज्ञानसंसिद्धाः पदं श्रेष्ठं विदुः मम।
ज्ञानी प्रियतमः अतः मे ज्ञानेन असौ बिभर्ति माम्॥३॥

तपः तीर्थं जपः दानं पवित्राणि इतराणि च।
न अलं कुर्वन्ति तां सिद्धिं या ज्ञानकलया कृता॥४॥

तस्मात् ज्ञानेन सहितं ज्ञात्वा स्वात्मानम् उद्धव।
ज्ञानविज्ञानसंपन्नः भज मां भक्तिभावतः॥५॥

ज्ञानविज्ञानयज्ञेन माम् इष्ट्वा आत्मानम् आत्मनि।
सर्वयज्ञपतिं मां वै संसिद्धिं मुनयः अगमन्॥६॥

त्वयि उद्धव आश्रयति यः त्रिविधः विकारः मायान्तरा आपतति न आदि अपवर्गयोः यत्।
जन्मादयः अस्य यत् अमी तव तस्य किं स्युः आदि अन्तयोः यत् असतः अस्ति तत् एव मध्ये॥७॥

उद्धवः उवाच।
ज्ञानं विशुद्धं विपुलं यथा एतत् वैराग्यविज्ञानयुतं पुराणम्।
आख्याहि विश्वेश्वर विश्वमूर्ते त्वत् भक्तियोगं च महत् विमृग्यम्॥८॥

तापत्रयेण अभिहतस्य घोरे सन्तप्यमानस्य भवाध्वनीश।
पश्यामि न अन्यत् शरणं तवाङ्घ्रि द्वन्द्व आतपत्रात् अमृत

अभिवर्षात्॥९॥

दष्टं जनं संपतितं बिले अस्मिन् कालाहिना क्षुद्रसुखोः उतर्षम्।
समुद्धर एनं कृपया अपवर्ग्यैः वचोभिः आसिञ्च महानुभाव॥१०॥

श्रीभगवान् उवाच।
इत्थम् एतत् पुरा राजा भीष्मं धर्मभृतां वरम्।
अजातशत्रुः पप्रच्छ सर्वेषां नः अनुश्रुण्वताम्॥११॥

निवृत्ते भारते युद्धे सुहृत् निधनविह्वलः।
श्रुत्वा धर्मान् बहून् पश्चात् मोक्षधर्मान् अपृच्छत॥१२॥

तान् अहं ते अभिधास्यामि देवव्रतमुखात् श्रुतान्।
ज्ञानवैराग्यविज्ञानश्रद्धाभक्ति उपबृंहितान्॥१३॥

नव एकादश पञ्च त्रीन् भावान् भूतेषु येन वै।
ईक्षेत अथ एकम् अपि एषु तत् ज्ञानं मम निश्चितम्॥१४॥

एतत् एव हि विज्ञानं न तथा एकेन येन यत्।
स्थिति उत्पत्ति अपि अयान् पश्येत् भावानां त्रिगुण आत्मनाम्॥१५॥

आदौ अन्ते च मध्ये च सृज्यात् सृज्यं यत् अन्वियात्।
पुनः तत् प्रतिसंक्रामे यत् शिष्येत तत् एव सत्॥१६॥

श्रुतिः प्रत्यक्षम् ऐतिह्यम् अनुमानं चतुष्टयम्।
प्रमाणेषु अनवस्थानात् विकल्पात् सः विरज्यते॥१७॥

कर्मणां परिणामित्वात् आविरिञ्चात् अमङ्गलम्।
विपश्चित् नश्वरं पश्येत् अदृष्टम् अपि दृष्टवत्॥१८॥

भक्तियोगः पुरा एव उक्तः प्रीयमाणाय ते अनघ।
पुनः च कथयिष्यामि मद्भक्तेः कारणं परम्॥१९॥

श्रद्धा अमृतकथायां मे शश्वत् मत् अनुकीर्तनम्।
परिनिष्ठा च पूजायां स्तुतिभिः स्तवनं मम॥२०॥

आदरः परिचर्यायां सर्वाङ्गैः अभिवन्दनम्।
मद्भक्तपूजाभ्यधिका सर्वभूतेषु मन्मतिः॥२१॥

मदर्थेषु अङ्गचेष्टा च वचसा मद्गुणेरणम्।
मय्यर्पणं च मनसः सर्वकामविवर्जनम्॥२२॥

मदर्थे अर्थ परित्यागः भोगस्य च सुखस्य च।
इष्टं दत्तं हुतं जप्तं मदर्थं यत् व्रतं तपः॥२३॥

एवं धर्मैः मनुष्याणाम् उद्धव आत्मनिवेदिनाम्।
मयि संजायते भक्तिः कः अन्यः अर्थः अस्य अवशिष्यते॥२४॥

यदा आत्मनि अर्पितं चित्तं शान्तं सत्त्व उपबृंहितम्।
धर्मं ज्ञानं सवैराग्यम् ऐश्वर्यं च अभिपद्यते॥२५॥

यत् अर्पितं तत् विकल्पे इन्द्रियैः परिधावति।
रजस्वलं च आसन् निष्ठं चित्तं विद्धि विपर्ययम्॥२६॥

धर्मः मद्भक्तिकृत् प्रोक्तः ज्ञानं च एकात्म्यदर्शनम्।
गुणेषु असङ्गः वैराग्यम् ऐश्वर्यं च अणिम् आदयः॥२७॥

उद्धवः उवाच।
यमः कतिविधः प्रोक्तः नियमः वा अरिकर्शन।
कः शमः कः दमः कृष्ण का तितिक्षा धृतिः प्रभो॥२८॥

किं दानं किं तपः शौर्यं किं सत्यम् ऋतम् उच्यते।
कः त्यागः किं धनं चेष्टं कः यज्ञः का च दक्षिणा॥२९॥

पुंसः किंस्वित् बलं श्रीमन् भगः लाभः च केशव।
का विद्या ह्रीः परा का श्रीः किं सुखं दुःखम् एव च॥३०॥

कः पण्डितः कः च मूर्खः कः पन्थाः उत्पथः च कः।
कः स्वर्गः नरकः कः स्वित् कः बन्धुः उत किं गृहम्॥३१॥

कः आढ्यः कः दरिद्रः वा कृपणः कः ईश्वरः।
एतान् प्रश्नान् मम ब्रूहि विपरीतान् च सत्पते॥३२॥

श्रीभगवान् उवाच।
अहिंसा सत्यम् अस्तेयम् असङ्गः ह्रीः असंचयः।
आस्तिक्यं ब्रह्मचर्यं च मौनं स्थैर्यं क्षमा अभयम्॥३३॥

शौचं जपः तपः होमः श्रद्धा आतिथ्यं मत् अर्चनम्।
तीर्थाटनं परार्थेहा तुष्टिः आचार्यसेवनम्॥३४॥

एते यमाः सनियमाः उभयोः द्वादश स्मृताः।
पुंसाम् उपासिताः तात यथाकामं दुहन्ति हि॥३५॥

शमः मत् निष्ठता बुद्धेः दमः इन्द्रियसंयमः।
तितिक्षा दुःखसंमर्षः जिह्वा उपस्थजयः धृतिः॥३६॥

दण्डन्यासः परं दानं कामत्यागः तपः स्मृतम्।
स्वभावविजयः शौर्यं सत्यं च समदर्शनम्॥३७॥

ऋतं च सूनृता वाणी कविभिः परिकीर्तिता।
कर्मस्वसङ्गमः शौचं त्यागः संन्यासः उच्यते॥३८॥

धर्मः इष्टं धनं नृणां यज्ञः अहं भगवत्तमः।
दक्षिणा ज्ञानसन्देशः प्राणायामः परं बलम्॥३९॥

भगः मे ऐश्वरः भावः लाभः मद्भक्तिः उत्तमः।
विद्या आत्मनि भिद अबाधः जुगुप्सा ह्रीः अकर्मसु॥४०॥

श्रीः गुणाः नैरपेक्ष्य आद्याः सुखं दुःखसुख अत्ययः।
दुःखं कामसुख अपेक्षा पण्डितः बन्धमोक्षवित्॥४१॥

मूर्खः देह आदि अहं बुद्धिः पन्थाः मत् निगमः स्मृतः।
उत्पथः चित्तविक्षेपः स्वर्गः सत्त्वगुण उअदयः॥४२॥

नरकः तमः उन्नहः बन्धुः गुरुः अहं सखे।
गृहं शरीरं मानुष्यं गुणाढ्यः हि आढ्यः उच्यते॥४३॥

दरिद्रः यः तु असन्तुष्टः कृपणः यः अजितेन्द्रियः।
गुणेषु असक्तधीः ईशः गुणसङ्गः विपर्ययः॥४४॥

एतः उद्धव ते प्रश्नाः सर्वे साधु निरूपिताः।
किं वर्णितेन बहुना लक्षणं गुणदोषयोः।
गुणदोष दृशिः दोषः गुणः तु उभयवर्जितः॥४५॥

इति श्रीमद्भागवते महापुराणे पारमहंस्यां
संहितायामेकादशस्कन्धे भगवदुधवसंवादे
एकोनविंशोऽध्यायः॥१९॥

20 Devotion, Knowledge, Detachment

English Rhyme

In the realm of the lotus-eyed Krishna, divine,
Where Vedic literatures intertwine.

Positive, negative injunctions, they state,
On work's qualities, they deliberate.

Varnashram's variety, the Vedic literature's narration,
Born of pious, sinful modes of family foundation.

Piety, sin, the constant frame,
In heaven, hell, they stake their claim.

Without seeing sin and piety's separation,
How to comprehend your Vedic revelation?

Without such scriptures, liberation's key,
How can humans reach life's apogee?

To understand beyond our sensory perception,
Forefathers, gods, humans seek your direction.

In Vedic literatures, your laws, they delve,
The highest evidence, revelation itself.

The distinction between sin and piety's creation,
Comes from your own Vedic foundation.

If the same scripture nullifies this distinction,
It will certainly lead to confusion.

Dear Uddhav, for human perfection's motivation,
I present three paths for their elevation.

Knowledge, work, devotion, the trinity,
Beyond these, no other path to divinity.

Gyan-yoga, for those weary of material life's tale,
Karma-yoga, for those with desires on a grand scale.

By fortune's grace, if one finds faith in my narration,
They should strive for perfection through loving devotion.

Until desire for worldly gains does not cease,
And the allure of devotion is yet to release,

One must persistently tread with ease,
The path outlined by Vedic decrees.

A person in his duty, with Vedic worship's dedication,
Not desiring the fruitive result of such action,

Will not ascend to heavenly stations,
Nor descend to hellish locations.

In one's duty firmly situated,
From sin's taint, we're liberated.

In this life, we find education,
Transcendental, or devotion's initiation.

Heavenly, hellish beings yearn for human birth,
For it lays the path to divine love's worth.

Neither heavenly nor hellish forms,
Offer such a chance, in their realms.

A wise soul should never yearn,
For heavenly rise or hellish turn.

Nor covet an earthly stay,
It leads to folly, self-interest astray.

A wise person, in life's grand theatre,
Knows the body's death, yet its feature,

Can award life's perfection, a treasure,
Neglect not this opportunity, a measure.

A bird, without attachment's chain,
Leaves the tree, bearing pain,

When cruel men, like death's reign,
Cut it down, yet finds joy again.

Knowing life, a fleeting game,
Cut down by days and nights' claim,

One should fear, in life's frame,
Give up desire, peace to reclaim.

The human body, a rare feat,
By nature's laws, a seat,

A boat perfect, a retreat,
Unused, one's soul, they cheat.

A transcendentalist, in despair,
Finds no joy in worldly affair,

Controls the senses, takes care,
Fixes the mind, in spiritual layer.

The mind, a wild horse in motion,
Deviation its notion,

Control it with devotion,
By prescribed means, the potion.

Never lose sight, the goal,
Conquer senses, pay the toll,

With goodness, play the role,
Bring the mind, under control.

An expert horseman, in his art,
Tames the horse, plays his part,

So does yoga, impart,
Control of mind, a start.

Study the world, in reflection,
Its temporary nature, a dissection,

Observe creation, and its direction,
And annihilation, the correction.

Disgusted with the world, a mirage,
Guided by the master, a sage,

Gives up false matter, a cage,
In the mind, a new page.

Through yoga, a purification,
Or logic, an education,

Engage the mind, in adoration,
Remember the Lord, the foundation.

A yogi, in his mission,
May err, in a session,

Burns the sin, in submission,
By yoga, without any concession.

Transcendentalists, in their station,
Adherence, a real piety's indication,

Sin, a neglect of duty's violation,
Gives up sense gratification, a liberation.

Awakened faith, in glories told,
Disgusted by the material fold.

Knowing well, the misery's root,
Yet, renouncing not, the sensory loot.

My devotee, in joy, should dwell,
In faith and conviction, none can quell.

Engaged sometimes, in sense's play,
He knows the misery that lies in sway.

An intelligent soul, in worship deep,
In loving service, a vigil he keeps.

His heart in me, firmly cast,
Material desires, from his heart, are past.

The knot in the heart, is pierced in sight,
Misgivings cut, in the Lord's light.

Fruitive actions, find their end,
When I, the Lord, am seen as a friend.

For a devotee, in service true,
Knowledge and renunciation, are but a few.

The highest perfection, he does see,
In loving service, unto me.

All that's achieved, by penance and deed,
By knowledge, detachment, in every creed,

Is easily won, in service divine,
If my devotee, does in love, align.

My devotees, of behaviour saintly,
Dedicate themselves, to me, quite quaintly.

Desiring not, but me alone,
Even liberation, they have disowned.

Detachment complete, is freedom's peak,
No personal desire, does the devotee seek.

In loving service, unto me,
He finds himself, in joy, free.

Material piety, and sin's sway,
In my devotees, find no way.

Free from hankering, they remain,
In steady consciousness, they attain.

Those who follow, these methods true,
Attain freedom, from illusion's hue.

Reaching my abode, they see,
The Absolute Truth, in its glory.

Sanskrit Text 20

अथ विंशः अध्यायः।
उद्धवः उवाच।
विधिः च प्रतिषेधः च निगमः हि ईश्वरस्य ते।
अवेक्षते अरविन्दाक्ष गुणं दोषं च कर्मणाम्॥१॥

वर्णाश्रम विकल्पं च प्रतिलोम अनुलोमजम्।
द्रव्य देश वयः कालान् स्वर्गं नरकम् एव च॥२॥

गुण दोष भिदा दृष्टिम् अन्तरेण वचः तव।
निःश्रेयसं कथं नृणां निषेध विधि लक्षणम्॥३॥

पितृदेवमनुष्याणां वेदः चक्षुः तव ईश्वर।
श्रेयः तु अनुपलब्धे अर्थे साध्यसाधनयोः अपि॥४॥

गुणदोषभिदादृष्टिः निगमात् ते न हि स्वतः।
निगमेन अपवादः च भिदायाः इति हि भ्रमः॥५॥

श्रीभगवान् उवाच।
योगाः त्रयः मया प्रोक्ता नृणां श्रेयोविधित्सया।
ज्ञानं कर्म च भक्तिः च न उपायः अन्यः अस्ति कुत्रचित्॥६॥

निर्विण्णानां ज्ञानयोगः न्यासिनाम् इह कर्मसु।
तेषु अनिर्विण्णचित्तानां कर्मयोगः ति कामिनाम्॥७॥

यदृच्छया मत् कथा आदौ जातश्रद्धः तु यः पुमान्।
न निर्विण्णः न अतिसक्तः भक्तियोगः अस्य सिद्धिदः॥८॥

तावत् कर्माणि कुर्वीत न निर्विद्येत यावता।
मत् कथाश्रवण आदौ वा श्रद्धा यावत् न जायते॥९॥

स्वधर्मस्थः यजन्यज्ञैः अनाशीः कामः उद्धव।
न याति स्वर्गनरकौ यदि अन्यत्र समाचरेत्॥१०॥

अस्मिन् लोके वर्तमानः स्वधर्मस्थः अनघः शुचिः।
ज्ञानं विशुद्धम् आप्नोति मद्भक्तिं वा यदृच्छया॥११॥

स्वर्गिणः अपि एतम् इच्छन्ति लोकं निरयिणः तथा।
साधकं ज्ञानभक्तिभ्याम् उभयं तत् असाधकम्॥१२॥

न नरः स्वर्गतिं कांक्षेत् नारकीं वा विचक्षणः।
न इमं लोकं च कांक्षेत देह आवेशात् प्रमाद्यति॥१३॥

एतत् विद्वान् पुरा मृत्योः अभवाय घटेत सः।
अप्रमत्तः इदं ज्ञात्वा मर्त्यम् अपि अर्थसिद्धिदम्॥१४॥

छिद्यमानं यमैः एतैः कृतनीडं वनस्पतिम्।
खगः स्वकेतम् उत्सृज्य क्षेमं याति हि अलम्पटः॥१५॥

अहोरात्रैः छिद्यमानं बुद्ध्वायुः भयवेपथुः।
मुक्तसङ्गः परं बुद्ध्वा निरीह उपशाम्यति॥१६॥

नृदेहम् आद्यं सुलभं सुदुर्लभम् प्लवं सुकल्पं गुरुकर्णधारम्।
मया अनुकूलेन नभस्वतेरितम् पुमान् भवाब्धिं न तरेत् सः
आत्महा॥१७॥

यदा आरम्भेषु निर्विण्णः विरक्तः संयतेन्द्रियः।
अभ्यासेन आत्मनः योगी धारयेत् अचलं मनः॥१८॥

धार्यमाणं मनः यः हि भ्राम्यदाशु अनवस्थितम्।
अतन्द्रितः अनुरोधेन मार्गेण आत्मवशं नयेत्॥१९॥

मनोगतिं न विसृजेत् जितप्राणः जितेन्द्रियः।
सत्त्वसंपन्नया बुद्ध्या मनः आत्मवशं नयेत्॥२०॥

एषः वै परमः योगः मनसः संग्रहः स्मृतः।
हृदयज्ञत्वम् अन्विच्छन् दम्यस्य एव अर्वतः मुहुः॥२१॥

सांख्येन सर्वभावानां प्रतिलोम अनुलोमतः।
भव अपि अयौ अनुध्ययेत् मनः यावत् प्रसीदति॥२२॥

निर्विण्णस्य विरक्तस्य पुरुषस्य उक्तवेदिनः।
मनः त्यजति दौरात्म्यं चिन्तितस्य अनुचिन्तया॥२३॥

यम आदिभिः योगपथैः आन्वीक्षिक्या च विद्यया।
मम अर्चोपासनाभिः वा न अन्यैः योग्यं स्मरेत् मनः॥२४॥

यदि कुर्यात् प्रमादेन योगी कर्म विगर्हितम्।
योगेन एव दहेत् अंहः न अन्यत् तत्र कदाचन॥२५॥

स्वे स्वे अधिकारे या निष्ठा सः गुणः परिकीर्तितः।
कर्मणां जाति अशुद्धानाम् अनेन नियमः कृतः।
गुणदोषविधानेन सङ्गानां त्याजनेच्छया॥२६॥

जातश्रद्धः मत्कथासु निर्विण्णः सर्वकर्मसु।
वेद दुःखात्मकान् कामान् परित्यागे अपि अनीश्वरः॥२७॥

ततः भजेत मां प्रीतः श्रद्धालुः दृढनिश्चयः।
जुषमाणः च तान् कामान् दुःख उदर्कान् च गर्हयन्॥२८॥

प्रोक्तेन भक्तियोगेन भजतः मा असकृत् मुनेः।
कामाः हृदय्याः नश्यन्ति सर्वे मयि हृदि स्थिते॥२९॥

भिद्यते हृदयग्रन्थिः छिद्यन्ते सर्वसंशयाः।
क्षीयन्ते च अस्य कर्माणि मयि दृष्टे अखिल आत्मनि॥३०॥

तस्मात् मद्भक्तियुक्तस्य योगिनः वै मत् आत्मनः।
न ज्ञानं न च वैराग्यं प्रायः श्रेयः भवेत् इह॥३१॥

यत् कर्मभिः यत् तपसा ज्ञानवैराग्यतः च यत्।
योगेन दानधर्मेण श्रेयोभिः इतरैः अपि॥३२॥

सर्वं मद्भक्तियोगेन मद्भक्तः लभते अञ्जसा।
स्वर्ग अपवर्गं मत् धाम कथंचित् यदि वाञ्छति॥३३॥

न किंचित् साधवः धीराः भक्ताः हि एकान्तिनः मम।
वाञ्छति अपि मया दत्तं कैवल्यम् अपुनर्भवम्॥३४॥

नैरपेक्ष्यं परं प्राहुः निःश्रेयसम् अनल्पकम्।
तस्मात् निराशिषः भक्तिः निरपेक्षस्य मे भवेत्॥३५॥

न मयि एकान्तभक्तानां गुणदोष उद्भवाः गुणाः।
साधूनां समचित्तानां बुद्धेः परम् उपेयुषाम्॥३६॥

एवम् एतत् मया आदिष्टान् अनुतिष्ठन्ति मे पथः।
क्षेमं विन्दन्ति मत् स्थानं यत् ब्रह्म परमं विदुः॥३७॥

इति श्रीमद्भागवते महापुराणे पारमहंस्यां
संहितायामेकादशस्कन्धे भगवदुद्धवसंवादे
वेदत्रयीविभागयोगो नाम विंशोऽध्यायः॥२०॥

21 Vedic Gita

English Rhyme

The Lord spoke with a voice so clear,
"Give up the senses, hold me dear.

Devotion, philosophy, duties regulated,
Else, in material existence, you'll be fated.

Steadiness in position, the true piety,
Deviation from it, the real impiety.

Evaluate objects in their category,
To understand life's true story.

For those burdened by mundane rites,
I reveal the path to spiritual heights.

Earth, water, fire, air, and ether,
From me, they emanate together.

All bodies of the same elements made,
Yet, in Vedic texts, different grades.

To restrict materialistic strides,
I set what's proper on all sides.

Places bereft of the spotted antelope,
Or devoid of Brahmin's hope,

Where cleanliness is neglected,
Are as contaminated, reflected.

Time is pure when it's right,
For duty's performance, in its light.

Purity or impurity, in an object's name,
Is established in many a game.

Impure things may or may not bind,
Depending on one's strength of mind.

Grains, utensils, things of bone,
By time, wind, fire, are known.

The self is cleansed by charity, age,
By remembrance of me, the sage.

A mantra chanted with knowledge true,
And work offered to me, makes you anew.

Sometimes piety becomes a sin,
And sin becomes piety, from within.

Such are the rules, so unique,
In the path of truth, that we seek."

The same acts that degrade the high,
Cause no further fall for those who lie,

Already fallen, on the ground, they sigh,
Material association, by nature's tie, they comply.

Refraining from sin, from materialistic spree,
Frees one from bondage, sets the spirit free.

Such renunciation, a basis it be,
For religious life, from suffering, illusion, fear, we flee.

Material objects, when seen as desirable,
Lead to attachment, unbreakable, undeniable.

From such attachment, lust takes birth,
Creating quarrels on this earth.

From quarrel arises anger, hard to bear,
Followed by ignorance, a blinding glare.

This ignorance overtakes intelligence wide,
In its darkness, wisdom cannot abide.

Saintly Uddhav, a person devoid of true sense,
Is considered to have lost everything hence.

Deviated from life's purpose, in ignorance, they dwell,
Like a dead person, in life's well.

Absorbed in sense gratification, in pleasure's tree,
One fails to recognize oneself, fails to see.

Living in ignorance, like a tree, they stand,
Breathing like a bellows, on life's sand.

Scriptures promise rewards, a fruitive spree,
Not prescribing the ultimate good, the highest glee.

Like candy promised to a child, to take medicine,
They entice one towards religious discipline.

By material birth, humans get attached,
To sense gratification, to life protracted.

Their minds absorbed in what defeats their interest,
In strength, potency, family and friends, they invest.

Those ignorant of their real self-interest, wander,
On the path of material existence, they ponder.

Heading toward darkness, they heed Vedic injunctions,
Why would the Vedas encourage their sense functions?

Persons with perverted intelligence, in confusion,
Misunderstand the purpose of Vedic conclusion.

They propagate flowery Vedic promises as truth,
Those in actual knowledge, never speak in that booth.

Full of lust, avarice, and greed, they mistake,
Mere flowers to be life's fruit, a false uptake.

Bewildered by fire's glare, suffocated by smoke,
They fail to recognize their true identity, under life's yoke.

Dear Uddhav, those dedicated to sense gratification,
Cannot understand my universal situation.

Like persons whose eyes are covered by fog,
They fail to see me, in every heart's cog.

Sworn to sense gratification, they fail to comprehend,
The confidential conclusion of Vedic knowledge, my friend.

Taking pleasure in violence, they slaughter the innocent,
Such passion for violence, in Vedic sacrifice, isn't meant.

Just as a foolish businessman, in speculation lost,
Gives up real wealth, paying a heavy cost.

Foolish persons, in life's grand scheme,
Pursue material heaven, an unreal dream.

Established in passion, goodness, ignorance, they stand,
Worship gods and deities, across the land.

Failing to worship me, in their earthly spree,
Lost in modes of nature, they fail to see.

Worshipers of gods, in their pride and greed,
Think, "By sacrifices, to heaven, we'll proceed.

And when that enjoyment ends, we'll return,
As great householders, for worldly concern."

The Vedas, in three divisions, ultimately reveal,
The living entity as spirit, the truth they seal.

Yet, they deal in esoteric terms, so deep,
And I am pleased by such secrets they keep.

The Vedic sound, difficult to comprehend,
On different levels, it does descend.

Unlimited, deep, like the ocean's call,
It's perceived subtly, like a lotus stalk, tall.

Just as a spider spins its web, so grand,
I manifest as the primeval vital strand.

From the ethereal sky of my heart, I create,
The great Vedic sound, in a state so sedate.

The Vedic sound branches out, in thousands of ways,
Adorned with letters, in the syllable 'om' it plays.

Elaborated by verbal varieties, in different meters,
Ultimately, I withdraw this sound, the universe's greeter.

In the entire world, none but me,
Understands the Vedic knowledge, the secret key.

People do not know, what the Vedas prescribe,
In karma-kanda, upasana-kanda, they ascribe.

I am the sacrifice, the worshipable Deity,
Presented as hypotheses, refuted by reality.

The Vedic sound establishes me, in every way,
Negating all duality, achieving its own sway.

Sanskrit Text 21

अथ एकविंशः अध्यायः।
श्रीभगवान् उवाच।
यः एतान् मत्पथः हित्वा भक्तिज्ञानक्रियात्मकान्।
क्षुद्रान् कामान् चलैः प्राणैः जुषन्तः संसरन्ति ते॥१॥

स्वे स्वे अधिकारे या निष्ठा सः गुणः परिकीर्तितः।
विपर्ययः तु दोषः स्यात् उभयोः एषः निश्चयः॥२॥

शुद्धि अशुद्धी विधीयेते समानेषु अपि वस्तुषु।
द्रव्यस्य विचिकित्सार्थं गुणदोषौ शुभ अशुभौ॥३॥

धर्मार्थं व्यवहारार्थं यात्रार्थम् इति च अनघ।
दर्शितः अयं मया आचारः धर्मम् उद्वहतां धुरम्॥४॥

भूमि अम्बु अग्नि अनिल आकाशाः भूतानां पञ्च धातवः।
आब्रह्म स्थावर आदीनां शरीराः आत्मसंयुताः॥५॥

वेदेन नामरूपाणि विषमाणि समेषु अपि।
धातुषु उद्धव कल्प्यन्तः एतेषां स्वार्थसिद्धये॥६॥

देश काल आदि भावानां वस्तूनां मम सत्तम।
गुणदोषौ विधीयेते नियमार्थं हि कर्मणाम्॥७॥

अकृष्णसारः देशानाम् अब्रह्मण्यः अशुचिः भवेत्।
कृष्णसारः अपि असौवीर कीकट असंस्कृतेरिणम्॥८॥

कर्मण्यः गुणवान् कालः द्रव्यतः स्वतः एव वा।
यतः निवर्तते कर्म सः दोषः अकर्मकः स्मृतः॥९॥

द्रव्यस्य शुद्धि अशुद्धी च द्रव्येण वचनेन च।
संस्कारेण अथ कालेन महत्त्व अल्पतया अथवा॥१०॥

शक्त्या अशक्त्या अथवा बुद्ध्या समृद्ध्या च यत् आत्मने।
अघं कुर्वन्ति हि यथा देश अवस्था अनुसारतः॥११॥

धान्य दारु अस्थि तन्तूनां रस तैजस चर्मणाम्।
काल वायु अग्नि मृत्तोयैः पार्थिवानां युत अयुतैः॥१२॥

अमेध्यलिप्तं यत् येन गन्धं लेपं व्यपोहति।
भजते प्रकृतिं तस्य तत् शौचं तावत् इष्यते॥१३॥

स्नान दान तपः अवस्था वीर्य संस्कार कर्मभिः।
मत् स्मृत्या च आत्मनः शौचं शुद्धः कर्म आचरेत् द्विजः॥१४॥

मन्त्रस्य च परिज्ञानं कर्मशुद्धिः मदर्पणम्।
धर्मः संपद्यते षड्भिः अधर्मः तु विपर्ययः॥१५॥

क्वचित् गुणः अपि दोषः स्यात् दोषः अपि विधिना गुणः।
गुणदोषार्थनियमः तत् भिदाम् एव बाधते॥१६॥

समानकर्म आचरणं पतितानां न पातकम्।
औत्पत्तिकः गुणः सङ्गः न शयानः पतति अधः॥१७॥

यतः यतः निवर्तेत विमुच्येत ततः ततः।
एषः धर्मः नृणां क्षेमः शोकमोहभय अपहः॥१८॥

विषयेषु गुणाध्यासात् पुंसः सङ्गः ततः भवेत्।
सङ्गात् तत्र भवेत् कामः कामात् एव कलिः नृणाम्॥१९॥

कलेः दुर्विषहः क्रोधः तमः तम् अनुवर्तते।
तमसा ग्रस्यते पुंसः चेतना व्यापिनी द्रुतम्॥२०॥

तया विरहितः साधो जन्तुः शून्याय कल्पते।
ततः अस्य स्वार्थविभ्रंशः मूर्च्छितस्य मृतस्य च॥२१॥

विषयाभिनिवेशेन न आत्मानं वेद न अपरम्।
वृक्षजीविकया जीवन् व्यर्थं भस्त्र इव यः श्वसन्॥२२॥

फलश्रुतिः इयं नृणां न श्रेयः रोचनं परम्।
श्रेयोविवक्षया प्रोक्तं यथा भैषज्यरोचनम्॥२३॥

उत्पत्ति एव हि कामेषु प्राणेषु स्वजनेषु च।
आसक्तमनसः मर्त्या आत्मनः अनर्थहेतुषु॥२४॥

न तान् अविदुषः स्वार्थं भ्राम्यतः वृजिनाध्वनि।
कथं युञ्ज्यात् पुनः तेषु तान् तमः विशतः बुधः॥२५॥

एवं व्यवसितं केचित् अविज्ञाय कुबुद्धयः।
फलश्रुतिं कुसुमितां न वेदज्ञाः वदन्ति हि॥२६॥

कामिनः कृपणाः लुब्धाः पुष्पेषु फलबुद्धयः।
अग्निमुग्धा धुमतान्ताः स्वं लोकं न विन्दन्ति ते॥२७॥

न ते माम् अङ्गः जानन्ति हृदिस्थं यः इदं यतः।
उक्थशस्त्राः हि असुतृपः यथा नीहारचक्षुषः॥२८॥

ते मे मतम् अविज्ञाय परोक्षं विषयात्मकाः।
हिंसायां यदि रागः स्यात् यज्ञः एव न चोदना॥२९॥

हिंसाविहाराः हि अलब्धैः पशुभिः स्वसुखएच्छया।
यजन्ते देवताः यज्ञैः पितृभूतपतीन् खलाः॥३०॥

स्वप्न् उपमम् अमुं लोकम् असन्तं श्रवणप्रियम्।
आशिषः हृदि सङ्कल्प्य त्यजन्ति अर्थान् यथा वणिक्॥३१॥

रजःसत्त्वतमोनिष्ठाः रजःसत्त्वतमोजुषः।
उपासतः इन्द्रमुख्यान् देवादीन् न तथा एव माम्॥३२॥

इष्ट्वा इह देवताः यज्ञैः गत्वा रंस्यामहे दिवि।
तस्य अन्तः इह भूयास्मः महाशाला महाकुलाः॥३३॥

एवं पुष्पितया वाचा व्याक्षिप्तमनसां नृणाम्।
मानिनान् च अतिस्तब्धानां मद्वार्ता अपि न रोचते॥३४॥

वेदाः ब्रह्मात्मविषयाः त्रिकाण्डविषयाः इमे।
परोक्षवादाः ऋषयः परोक्षं मम च प्रियम्॥३५॥

शब्दब्रह्म सुदुर्बोधं प्राण इन्द्रिय मनोमयम्।
अनन्तपारं गम्भीरं दुर्विगाह्यं समुद्रवत्॥३६॥

मया उपबृंहितं भूम्ना ब्रह्मणा अनन्तशक्तिना।
भूतेषु घोषरूपेण बिसेषु ऊर्ण इव लक्ष्यते॥३७॥

यथा ऊर्णनाभिः हृदयात् ऊर्णाम् उद्वमते मुखात्।
आकाशात् घोषवान् प्राणः मनसा स्पर्शरूपिणा॥३८॥

छन्दोमयः अमृतमयः सहस्रपदवीं प्रभुः।
ओङ्कारात् व्यञ्जित स्पर्श स्वर उष्म अन्तस्थ भूषिताम्॥३९॥

विचित्रभाषाविततां छन्दोभिः चतुर उत्तरैः।
अनन्तपारां बृहतीं सृजति आक्षिपते स्वयम्॥४०॥

गायत्री उष्णिक् अनुष्टुप् च बृहती पङ्क्तिः एव च।
त्रिष्टुप् जगती अतिच्छन्दः हि अत्यष्टि अतिजगत् विराट्॥४१॥

किं विधत्ते किम् आचष्टे किम् अनूद्य विकल्पयेत्।
इति अस्याः हृदयं लोके न अन्यः मत् वेद कश्चन॥४२॥

मां विधत्ते अभिधत्ते मां विकल्प्य अपोह्यते तु अहम्।
एतावान् सर्ववेदार्थः शब्दः आस्थाय मां भिदाम्।
मायामात्रम् अनूद्य अन्ते प्रतिषिध्य प्रसीदति॥४३॥

इति श्रीमद्भागवते महापुराणे पारमहंस्यां
संहितायामेकादशस्कन्धे भगवदुद्धवसंवादे
वेदत्रयविभागनिरूपणं नाम एकविंशोऽध्यायः॥२१॥

22 Material Creation Elements

English Rhyme

Uddhav inquired, with a mind so keen,
"Dear Lord, how many elements have been seen?

Twenty-eight, twenty-six, or twenty-five,
Seven, nine, six, four, or five?

Eleven, seventeen, sixteen, or thirteen,
What did these sages mean?

Supreme eternal, kindly explain,
The creative elements, make it plain."

Krishna replied, with a voice so clear,
"All material elements, far and near,

Are present everywhere, it's true,
Analyzed differently, from each sage's view.

When philosophers argue, 'I don't choose,
To analyze this case, as you do use,'

It's my own energies, that motivate,
Their analytic disagreements, that they state.

By interaction of my energies, arise,
Different opinions, under the skies.

But for those who fix their intelligence on me,
Differences disappear, they are set free.

Best among men, subtle and gross elements blend,
Philosophers calculate, on their personal trend.

All subtle elements, in their gross effects reside,
All gross elements, in their subtle causes hide.

No matter which thinker is speaking,
Whether they include elements, in their seeking,

Within their previous subtle causes, or manifest products,
I accept their conclusions, in all their constructs.

As a person, covered by ignorance, cannot see,
The Absolute Truth, there must be,

Another personality, who can impart,
This knowledge to him, from the heart.

According to knowledge, in the mode of goodness,
No difference, between living entity and supreme witness.

The imagination of difference, is speculation, baseless,
Nature exists, in three material modes, faceless.

Goodness, passion, ignorance, they are,
The effective causes, near and far,

Of creation, maintenance, and destruction,
Of this universe, in its construction.

In this world, goodness is knowledge, passion is work,
Darkness is ignorance, where dangers lurk.

Time is perceived, as the agitated interaction,
Of the material modes, in their action.

I have described, the nine basic elements,
As the enjoying Atma, nature, and its developments.

Ether, air, fire, water, and earth,
And the five senses, of knowledge and worth."

Sound, touch, taste, smell, and form,
Objects of senses, in their norm.

Movement, speech, excretion, and craft,
Functions of working senses, fore and aft.

In creation's beginning, nature assumes,
Forms of subtle causes, in myriad rooms.

The Lord does not enter, but merely glances,
On nature's dance, as it advances.

Material elements, by the Supreme Lord's glance,
Receive their potencies, in a divine dance.

Amalgamated by nature's power, they create,
The universal egg, in a state so great.

Some philosophers propose, with elements seven,
Earth, water, fire, air, and heaven.

Along with the conscious spirit, and the Supreme,
From these seven elements, all phenomena gleam.

Others state, there are elements six,
The five physical elements, in the mix.

And the sixth element, the Lord so divine,
Creates the universe, in a design so fine.

Some propose, elements four,
Three emanate from the Self, forevermore.

Once existing, these elements give birth,
To the cosmic manifestation, on this earth.

Some calculate, elements seventeen,
Five gross elements, in the scene.

Five objects of perception, senses five,
The mind, and the Atma, make seventeen thrive.

According to the calculation, of elements sixteen,
The Atma is identified with the mind, it's seen.

If we think in terms of five elements, senses, and mind,
The individual Atma and the Supreme, thirteen we find.

Counting eleven, there are the Atma, elements, and senses,
Eight elements plus the Supreme, suspense lessens.

Thus great philosophers, in many ways,
Have analyzed the elements, in their essays.

Uddhav inquired, with a mind so keen,
"Nature and the living entity, what does it mean?

They appear to be within each other,
The Atma in nature, and nature in the other."

Lotus-eyed Krishna, omniscient Lord, so bright,
Cut this doubt out of my heart, with your light.

From you alone, knowledge arises,
And by your potency, that knowledge disguises.

The Lord said, with a voice so clear,
"Best among men, let me steer,

Material nature and its enjoyer, are distinct,
This creation transforms, in nature's instinct.

Dear Uddhav, my material energy, in modes three,
Manifests creation's variety.

The result of transformation, in aspects three,
Adhyatmic, adhidaivic, adhibhautic, you see.

Sight, form, and the sun's reflected beam,
Work together, in a unified theme.

But the original sun, in the sky, self-manifested,
Like the Supreme Atma, separately rested.

The sense organs, and the subtle body's function,
Can be analyzed, in a threefold junction.

Sense, object of perception, and presiding deity,
Form the basis of this reality.

When nature's modes are agitated, they create,
False ego, in phases three, they generate.

This false ego, from the mahat-tattva, takes birth,
Becomes the cause of all illusion on earth.

The argument of philosophers, in their quest,
'This world is real,' 'No, it's not,' they jest.

Based on incomplete knowledge, of the Supreme Atma,
They're unable to give up, this enigma.

Uddhav said, with a heart so pure,
'Supreme master, please ensure,

Explain how persons, by their deeds,
Accept bodies, and then such bodies, cedes.

Krishna said, 'The material mind of men,
Is shaped by fruitive work, again and again.

Along with the senses, it travels wide,
From one body to another, in life's tide.

The mind, bound to reactions, of fruitive work,
On the objects of senses, it does lurk.

Thus, the mind appears to come into being,
And to suffer annihilation, in its seeing.

When the living entity, from the present body, departs,
To the next body, which his own karma imparts,

He becomes absorbed, in sensations new,
And forgets the experience, of the body he outgrew.

What is called birth, is identification,
With a new body, a total fixation.

One accepts the new body, as reality,
Just as one accepts, a dream's duality.

Just as a person, in a dream or daydream,
Does not remember, the previous dream's theme,

A person, in his present body, thinks anew,
That he has only recently, come into view.'"

The mind, the senses' resting place,
Creates identification with a new face.

High, middle, low, the material variety,
Appears within the Atma's reality.

Material bodies, in constant flux,
By time's force, that no one ducks.

Like a candle's flame, a river's flow,
Or a tree's fruits, that grow.

The lamp's illumination, in constant change,
Yet, a person with illusory range,

Says, "This is the light of the lamp," in sight,
Falsely stating, "This is the river's might."

A person does not take birth, from past deeds,
Nor dies, despite life's creeds.

By illusion, appears to be born and to die,
Like fire with firewood, under the sky.

Impregnation, gestation, birth, and more,
Infancy, childhood, youth, lore,

Middle age, old age, and death,
Are the body's nine ages, in breath.

Although the body is different from the self,
One falsely identifies, in material wealth.

Sometimes, a fortunate one can give up,
Such mental concoction, in life's cup.

By the death of one's father, one can see,
One's own death, in life's decree.

By the birth of one's son, one can understand,
The condition of one's own birth, in this land.

One who observes a tree's birth and death,
Remains a distinct observer, in breath.

Similarly, the witness of the body's rise and fall,
Remains separate from it, through it all.

An unintelligent man, in confusion,
Thinks nature to be real, in illusion.

By contact with it, he becomes bewildered,
Enters the cycle of material existence, considered.

Made to wander, because of his work,
The conditioned Atma, does lurk.

By contact with the modes, takes birth,
Among sages, gods, or on earth.

Just as one may imitate, those dancing and singing,
The Atma, captivated by material intelligence, is bringing,

Its qualities to imitate, in life's spree,
Although never the doer of material activities, is he.

The Atma's material life, his sense gratification,
Is actually false, a mere imitation.

Like trees' quivering, reflected in water,
Or the earth's spinning, in life's quarter.

For one meditating on sense gratification,
Material life, lacking factual foundation,

Does not go away, just as a dream,
Does not, despite its unreal theme.

Therefore, Uddhav, seek not to enjoy,
Sense gratification, a mere ploy.

See how illusion, based on dualities,
Prevents one from realizing the self's realities.

Even though neglected, insulted, or envied,
Or agitated, beaten, tied up, and derided,

One who desires the highest goal,
Should use his intelligence, to play this role.

Keep safe on the spiritual platform, stand tall,
Despite all difficulties, do not fall.

Uddhav asked, with a heart so pure,
"Best of speakers, make me secure.

How may I understand, this grand design?
Atma of the universe, make it mine."

The conditioning in material life, is strong,
Tolerating offenses, is hard and long.

Only your devotees, in your loving service,
Achieve peace, at your lotus feet, they surface.

Able to tolerate offenses, they rise,
In your loving service, they find their prize.

Sanskrit Text 22

अथ द्वाविंशः अध्यायः।
उद्धवः उवाच।
कति तत्त्वानि विश्वेश संख्यातानि ऋषिभिः प्रभो।
नव एकादश पञ्च त्रीणि आत्थ त्वम् इह शुश्रुम॥१॥

केचित् षड्विंशतिं प्राहुः अपरे पञ्चविंशतिम्।
सप्त एके नव षट् केचित् चत्वारि एकादश अपरे।
केचित् सप्तदश प्राहुः षोडश एके त्रयोदश॥२॥

एतावत् त्वम् हि संख्यानाम् ऋषयः यत् विवक्षया।
गायन्ति पृथक् आयुष्मन् इदं नः वक्तुम् अर्हसि॥३॥

श्रीभगवान् उवाच।
युक्तं च सन्ति सर्वत्र भाषन्ते ब्राह्मणाः यथा।
मायां मदीयाम् उद्गृह्य वदतां किं नु दुर्घटम्॥४॥

न एतत् एवं यथा आत्थ त्वं यत् अहं वच्मि तत् तथा।
एवं विवदतां हेतुं शक्तयः मे दुरत्ययाः॥५॥

यासां व्यतिकरात् आसीत् विकल्पः वदतां पदम्।
प्राप्ते शमदमे अपि एति वादस्तमनु शाम्यति॥६॥

परस्परान् अनुप्रवेशात् तत्त्वानां पुरुषर्षभ।
पौर्व अपर्य प्रसंख्यानं यथा वक्तुः विवक्षितम्॥७॥

एकस्मिन् अपि दृश्यन्ते प्रविष्टानि इतराणि च।
पूर्वस्मिन् वा परस्मिन् वा तत्त्वे तत्त्वानि सर्वशः॥८॥

पौर्व अपर्यम् अतः अमीषां प्रसंख्यानम् अभीप्सताम्।
यथा विविक्तं यत् वक्त्रं गृह्णीमः युक्तिसंभवात्॥९॥

अनादि अविद्यायुक्तस्य पुरुषस्य आत्मवेदनम्।
स्वतः न संभवात् अन्यः तत्त्वज्ञः ज्ञानदः भवेत्॥१०॥

पुरुष ईश्वरयोः अत्र न वैलक्षण्यम् अणु अपि।
तत् अन्यकल्पनापार्था ज्ञानं च प्रकृतेः गुणः॥११॥

प्रकृतिः गुणसाम्यं वै प्रकृतेः न आत्मनः गुणाः।
सत्त्वं रजः तमः इति स्थिति उत्पत्ति अन्तहेतवः॥१२॥

सत्त्वं ज्ञानं रजः कर्म तमः अज्ञानम् इह उच्यते।
गुणव्यतिकरः कालः स्वभावः सूत्रम् एव च॥१३॥

पुरुषः प्रकृतिः व्यक्तम् अहंकारः नभः अनिलः।
ज्योतिः आपः क्षितिः इति तत्त्वानि उक्तानि मे नव॥१४॥

श्रोत्रं त्वक् दर्शनं घ्राणः जिह्वा इति ज्ञानशक्तयः।
वाक् पाणि उपस्थ पायु अंघ्रिः कर्माण्यङ्ग उभयं मनः॥१५॥

शब्दः स्पर्शः रसः गन्धः रूपं च इति अर्थजातयः।
गति उक्ति उत्सर्ग शिल्पानि कर्म आयतन सिद्धयः॥१६॥

सर्ग आदौ प्रकृतिः हि अस्य कार्य कारण रूपिणी।
सत्त्व आदिभिः गुणैः धत्ते पुरुषः अव्यक्तः ईक्षते॥१७॥

व्यक्त आदयः विकुर्वाणाः धातवः पुरुष ईक्षया।
लब्धवीर्याः सृजन्ति अण्डं संहताः प्रकृतेः बलात्॥१८॥

सप्त एव धातवः इति तत्र अर्थाः पञ्च खादयः।
ज्ञानम् आत्मा उभय आधारः ततः देह इन्द्रिय आसवः॥१९॥

षड् इति अत्र अपि भूतानि पञ्च षष्ठः परः पुमान्।
तैः युक्तः आत्मसंभूतैः सृष्ट्वा इदं समुपाविशत्॥२०॥

चत्वारि एव इति तत्र अपि तेजः आपः अन्नम् आत्मनः।
जातानि तैः इदं जातं जन्म अवयविनः खलु॥२१॥

संख्याने सप्तदशके भूतमात्र इन्द्रियाणि च।
पञ्चपञ्च एक मनसा आत्मा सप्तदशः स्मृतः॥२२॥

तद्वत् षोडशसंख्याने आत्मा एव मनः उच्यते।
भूतेन्द्रियाणि पञ्च एव मनः आत्मा त्रयोदशः॥२३॥

एकादशत्वः आत्मा असौ महाभूतेन्द्रियाणि च।
अष्टौ प्रकृतयः च एव पुरुषः च नव इति अथ॥२४॥

इति नाना प्रसंख्यानं तत्त्वानाम् ऋषिभिः कृतम्।
सर्वं न्याय्यं युक्तिमत्वात् विदुषां किम् अशोभनम्॥२५॥

उद्धवः उवाच।
प्रकृतिः पुरुषः च उभौ यदि अपि आत्मविलक्षणौ।
अन्योन्य अपाश्रयात् कृष्ण दृश्यते न भिदा तयोः।
प्रकृतौ लक्ष्यते हि आत्मा प्रकृतिः च तथा आत्मनि॥२६॥

एवं मे पुण्डरीकाक्ष महान्तं संशयं हृदि।
छेत्तुम् अर्हसि सर्वज्ञ वचोभिः नयनैपुणैः॥२७॥

त्वत्तः ज्ञानं हि जीवानां प्रमोषः ते अत्र शक्तितः।
त्वम् एव हि आत्म मायाया गतिं वेत्थ न च अपरः॥२८॥

श्रीभगवान् उवाच।
प्रकृतिः पुरुषः च इति विकल्पः पुरुषर्षभ।
एषः वैकारिकः सर्गः गुणव्यतिकरात्मकः॥२९॥

मम अङ्ग माया गुणमयी अनेकधा विकल्पबुद्धीः च गुणैः विधत्ते।
वैकारिकः त्रिविधः अध्यात्मम् एकम् अथ अधिदैवम् अधिभूतम्
अन्यत्॥३०॥

दृक् रूपम् आर्कं वपुः अत्र रन्ध्रे परस्परं सिध्यति यः स्वतः खे।
आत्मा यत् एषम् अपरः यः आद्यः स्वया अनुभूत्य अखिलसिद्धसिद्धिः।
एवं त्वक् आदि श्रवणादि चक्षुः जिह्व आदि नास आदि च
चित्तयुक्तम्॥३१॥

यः असौ गुणक्षोभकृतौ विकारः प्रधानमूलात् महतः प्रसूतः।
अहं त्रिवृत् मोहविकल्पहेतुः वैकारिकः तामसः ऐन्द्रियः च॥३२॥

आत्मापरिज्ञानमयः विवादः हि अस्ति इति न अस्ति इति भिदार्थनिष्ठः।
व्यर्थः अपि न एव उपरमेत पुंसां मत्तः परावृत्तधियां स्वलोकात्॥३३॥

उद्धवः उवाच।
त्वत्तः परावृत्तधियः स्वकृतैः कर्मभिः प्रभो।
उच्च अवचान् यथा देहान् गृह्णन्ति विसृजन्ति च॥३४॥

तत् मम आख्याहि गोविन्द दुर्विभाव्यम् अनात्मभिः।
न हि एतत् प्रायशः लोके विद्वांसः सन्ति वञ्चिताः॥३५॥

श्रीभगवान् उवाच।
मनः कर्ममयं नृणाम् इन्द्रियैः पञ्चभिः युतम्।
लोकात् लोकं प्रयाति अन्यः आत्मा तत् अनुवर्तते॥३६॥

ध्यायन् मनः अनुविषयान् दृष्टान् वा अनुश्रुतान् अथ।
उद्यत् सीदत् कर्मतन्त्रं स्मृतिः तत् अनुशाम्यति॥३७॥

विषय अभिनिवेशेन न आत्मानं यत् स्मरेत् पुनः।
जन्तोः वै कस्यचित् हेतोः मृत्युः अत्यन्तविस्मृतिः॥३८॥

जन्म तु आत्मतया पुंसः सर्वभावेन भूरिद।
विषय स्वीकृतिं प्राहुः यथा स्वप्नमनोरथः॥३९॥

स्वप्नं मनोरथं च इत्थं प्राक्तनं न स्मरति असौ।
तत्र पूर्वम् इव आत्मानम् अपूर्वं च अनुपश्यति॥४०॥

इन्द्रिय आयन सृष्ट्या इदं त्रैविध्यं भाति वस्तुनि।
बहिः अन्तः भिदाहेतुः जनः असत् जनकृत् यथा॥४१॥

नित्यदा हि अङ्गः भूतानि भवन्ति न भवन्ति च।
कालेन अलक्ष्यवेगेन सूक्ष्मत्वात् तत् न दृश्यते॥४२॥

यथा अर्चिषां स्रोतसां च फलानां वा वनस्पतेः।
तथा एव सर्वभूतानां वयः अवस्था आदयः कृताः॥४३॥

सः अयं दीपः अर्चिषां यद्वत् स्रोतसां तत् इदं जलम्।
सः अयं पुमान् इति नृणां मृषाः गीः धीः मृषा आयुषाम्॥४४॥

मा स्वस्य कर्मबीजेन जायते सः अपि अयं पुमान्।
म्रियते वामरः भ्रान्त्या यथा अग्निः दारु संयुतः॥४५॥

निषेकगर्भजन्मानि बाल्यकौमारयौवनम्।
वयोमध्यं जरा मृत्युः इति अवस्थाः तनोः नव॥४६॥

एताः मनोरथमयीः हि अन्यस्य उच्चावचाः तनूः।
गुणसङ्गात् उपादत्ते क्वचित् कश्चित् जहाति च॥४७॥

आत्मनः पितृपुत्राभ्याम् अनुमेयौ भवाप्ययौ।
न भवाप्ययवस्तूनाम् अभिज्ञः द्वयलक्षणः॥४८॥

तरोः बीजविपाकाभ्यां यः विद्वात् जन्मसंयमौ।
तरोः विलक्षणः द्रष्टा एवं द्रष्टा तनोः पृथक्॥४९॥

प्रकृतेः एवम् आत्मानम् अविविच्य अबुधः पुमान्।
तत्त्वेन स्पर्शसंमूढः संसारं प्रतिपद्यते॥५०॥

सत्त्वसङ्गात् ऋषीन् देवान् रजसा असुरमानुषान्।
तमसा भूततिर्यक्त्वं भ्रामितः याति कर्मभिः॥५१॥

नृत्यतः गायतः पश्यन् यथा एव अनुकरोति तान्।
एवं बुद्धिगुणान् पश्यन् अनीहः अपि अनुकार्यते॥७२॥

यथा अम्भसा प्रचलता तरवः अपि चलाः इव।
चक्षुषा भ्राम्यमाणेन दृश्यते भ्रमति इव भूः॥७३॥

यथा मनोरथधियः विषयानुभवः मृषा।
स्वप्नदृष्टाः च दाशार्ह तथा संसारः आत्मनः॥७४॥

अर्थे हि अविद्यमाने अपि संसृतिः न निवर्तते।
ध्यायतः विषयान् अस्य स्वप्ने अनर्थ आगमः यथा॥७५॥

तस्मात् उद्धव मा भुङ्क्ष्व विषयान् असत् इन्द्रियैः।
आत्मा अग्रहणनिर्भातं पश्य वैकल्पिकं भ्रमम्॥७६॥

क्षिप्तः अवमानितः असद्भिः प्रलब्धः असूयितः अथवा।
ताडितः संनिबद्धः वा वृत्त्या वा परिहापितः॥७७॥

निष्ठितः मूत्रितः बहुधा एवं प्रकम्पितः।
श्रेयस्कामः कृच्छ्रगतः आत्मना आत्मानम् उद्धरेत्॥७८॥

उद्धवः उवाच।
यथा एवम् अनुबुद्ध्येयं वद नः वदतां वर।
सुदुःसहम् इमं मन्यः आत्मनि असत् अतिक्रमम्॥७९॥

विदुषम् अपि विश्वात्मन् प्रकृतिः हि बलीयसी।
ऋते त्वत् धर्मनिरतान् शान्ताः ते चरणालयान्॥८०॥

इति श्रीमद्भागवते महापुराणे पारमहंस्यां
संहितायामेकादशस्कन्धे भगवदुद्धवसंवादे
द्वाविंशोऽध्यायः॥२२॥

23 Avanti Brahman Gita

English Rhyme

Sukadeva said, with a voice so clear,
"Mukunda, the chief of the Dasarhas, hear,

Uddhav, the best of devotees, did request,
And the Lord, with glorious exploits, began his quest.

Krishna said, 'Disciple of Brihaspati, in this land,
No saintly man can understand,

How to resettle his own mind,
After insults by uncivilized men, unkind.

Sharp arrows, which pierce one's heart,
Do not cause as much hurt,

As harsh, insulting words, that start,
When spoken by uncivilized men, they assert.

Dear Uddhav, a pious story is told,
Please listen, with attention bold.

Once a sannyasi, insulted in many ways,
Remembered he was suffering, his own karma's plays.

In Avanti, lived a Brahmin, rich and grand,
Engaged in commerce, wealth at hand.

But he was miserly, lusty, greedy, and prone to anger,
In his home, no respect, even with words, did he offer.

His sons, in-laws, wife, daughters, and servants,
Began to feel inimical, in their observants.

Disgusted, they never treated him with affection,
Thus, he felt the deities' rejection.

By his neglect of the gods, he paid the price,
Lost his piety, and all things nice.

His wealth was taken, by kin, thieves, and fate,
By time's swift passage, by men who hate.

Finally, when his wealth was no more,
He who shunned faith and pleasure, felt the sore.

Ignored by his kin, anxiety was his guest,
Having lost all his wealth, he felt unrest.

The Brahmin spoke, 'What great misfortune, I see,
I have tormented myself, uselessly.

The wealth of misers, never allows happiness,
In this life, it causes self-torment, in excess.

Whatever pure fame the renowned do hold,
Is tarnished by greed, uncontrolled.

In pursuit, attainment, growth, safeguarding treasure,
In spending, loss, and in wealth's pleasure,

All men endure toil, in measures untold,
Fear grips their heart, anxiety takes hold.

In the stealth of life, under wealth's spell,
They tread a path, known too well.

Theft, violence, lies, and duplicity,
Lust, anger, perplexity, and complicity,

Pride, quarreling, enmity, faithlessness, and envy,
Dangers of women, gambling, intoxication, a spree.

Fifteen undesirable qualities, that contaminate men,
Because of greed for wealth, again and again.

Although these qualities are undesirable, it's true,
Men falsely ascribe value, in their view.

One desiring to achieve life's real benefit,
Should remain aloof from wealth, counterfeit.

Even a man's brothers, wife, parents, and friends,
Will break off their affection, when love ends.

Over a single coin, they become enemies,
For even a small amount of money, brings miseries.

Their anger is inflamed, they become rivals,
They give up all sentiments of goodwill, for survival.

Those who obtain human life, a gift so grand,
Prayed for even by the gods, in every land.

If they disregard this opportunity, so fortunate,
They kill their own self-interest, an unfortunate fate.

What mortal man, having achieved this life,
Would willingly become attached to strife?

Material property, an abode of worthlessness,
One who fails to distribute his wealth, is a mess.

To the gods, sages, forefathers, and all,
To his relatives, in-laws, and self, he should call.

Discriminating persons, with money, youth, and strength,
Can achieve perfection, at any length.

But I have squandered these, in a useless attempt,
For further wealth, with contempt.

Now that I am old, what can I achieve?
Why must an intelligent man, in vain, believe?

For one in the grips of death, what is the use,
Of wealth, sense gratification, or any excuse?

The Supreme Personality of Godhead, Hari, so divine,
Must be satisfied with me, in this suffering line.

He has brought me to this condition, so severe,
Forced me to experience detachment, clear.

If there is any time remaining, in my life,
I will perform austerities, and end this strife.

I shall pursue that which constitutes my self-interest,
And remain satisfied within the self, in this quest.

Thus may the presiding gods, show their mercy on me,
Like Maharaja Khatvanga, in a single moment, free.

His mind thus determined, the Avanti Brahmin,
Untied the knots of desire, within.

He assumed the role of a peaceful sannyasi,
A silent mendicant, in life's journey.

He wandered about the earth, with control so fine,
Over his intelligence, senses, and life's line.

To beg charity, he traveled alone, far and wide,
His advanced spiritual position, he did not confide.

Kind Uddhav saw him, an old, dirty beggar,
Rowdy persons dishonored him, with insults they'd trigger.

They took away his sannyasi rod, his waterpot, his seat,
His chanting beads, his ragged clothing, in deceit.

Sitting on the river bank, about to partake,
Of the food from his begging, a break,

Sinful rascals would come, pass urine on it,
Dare to spit on his head, in a fit.

Although he had taken a vow of silence, they'd insist,
Make him speak, beat him with fists.

Others would chastise him, "This man is a thief,"
Bind him up with rope, beyond belief.

They'd criticize and insult him, "A hypocrite, a cheat,"
"Lost all his wealth, his family gave him the beat."

Some ridicule him, "A sage, steadfast as the mountains,"
"By silence, he strives, like a duck," they'd maintain.

The Brahmin understood, all his suffering,
From beings, nature, and his own buffering,

Was unavoidable, allotted by providence, in this life,
Even while insulted, he remained steady, in strife.

The Brahmin said, "These people are not the cause,
Of my happiness and distress, or any applause.

Neither are the gods, my body, the planets, or time,
It's the mind alone, that causes the chime.

The powerful mind actuates, the material modes,
From which evolve, the different roads.

Of material activities, in goodness, ignorance, and passion,
From these activities, develop the corresponding fashion.

Although present with the struggling mind, in the body,
The Parmatma is not attempting, already embodying,

Transcendental enlightenment, acting as my friend,
Witnessing from a transcendental position, without end.

I, the infinitesimal spirit Atma, have embraced this mind,
Reflecting the image of the material world, entwined.

Thus I have become engaged, in enjoying desire,
And am entangled, due to nature's fire.

Charity, duties, principles, hearing from scripture,
Pious works, purifying vows, form the picture.

All aim at subduing the mind, indeed,
Mind's concentration on the Supreme, the highest creed.

If one's mind is perfectly fixed, pacified, then tell,
What need to perform rituals, to dwell?

And if one's mind remains uncontrolled, lost in ignorance,
Then of what use are these engagements, in this dance?"

All the senses, under the mind's control,
Since time immemorial, playing their role.

The mind, stronger than the strongest, and fearsome,
Master it, and become the senses' sum.

Failing to conquer this enemy, the mind,
Many are bewildered, in a bind.

Creating quarrels, useless and vain,
Seeing others as friends, enemies, or plain.

Persons who identify with this body, so blind,
Are lost in "I" and "mine," they find.

In their illusion, they wander in darkness, endless,
In the maze of material bodies, senseless.

If you say, these people cause my joy and pain,
Then where does the Atma, in such a concept, remain?

This joy and pain, to the Atma, do not pertain,
But to the interactions of material bodies, again.

If you say, the gods cause suffering,
Still, how can such suffering, to the spirit Atma, bring?

This acting and being acted on, merely interactions,
Of the changeable senses, and their factions.

If the Atma were the cause of joy and distress,
Then we could not blame others, no less.

Since happiness and distress would be the Atma's nature,
Why become angry at oneself, or any creature?

And if we say, the planets cause suffering and bliss,
Then where is the Atma's place, in this?

The effect of the planets, applies only to birth,
So, against whom should he vent his anger, on this earth?

If we assume, fruitive work is the cause,
We still are not dealing with the Atma's laws.

Idea of material work, arises when there's a spiritual actor,
And a material body, undergoing transformation, a factor.

If we accept time as the cause of joy and pain,
That experience still cannot, to the spirit Atma, pertain.

Since time is a manifestation, of Lord's spiritual potency,
At whom should one become angry, in this density?

The false ego shapes the illusory existence,
Experiences material happiness and resistance.

But the spirit Atma, transcendental and pure,
Is never affected, of this be sure.

A person who understands this, has no fear,
From the material creation, far or near.

"I shall cross over the ocean of nescience," he said,
"By being firmly fixed in Krishna's service, as led.

This was approved by the previous Acharyas, so wise,
Fixed in firm devotion to the Lord, their prize.

Thus, becoming detached on the loss of his property,
This sage gave up his moroseness, in austerity.

He left home, taking sannyasa, began to roam,
Even when insulted, he chanted a song, his tome.

No other force, besides his own mental confusion,
Makes the Atma experience happiness and illusion.

His perception of friends, enemies, neutral parties,
And the material life he builds, are simply arties.

Dear Uddhav, fix your intelligence on me,
Control the mind, this is the essence of the decree.

Anyone who listens to this song of the sannyasi,
Of scientific knowledge of the Absolute, so classy,

And meditates on it with full attention,
Will never be overwhelmed by dualities' tension."

Sanskrit Text 23

अथ त्रयोविंशः अध्यायः।
बादरायणिः उवाच।
सः एवम् आशंसितः उद्धवेन भागवतमुख्येन दाशार्हमुख्यः।
सभाजयन् बृत्यवचः मुकुन्दः तम् आबभाषे श्रवणीयवीर्यः॥१॥

श्रीभगवान् उवाच।
बर्हस्पत्य सः वै न अत्र साधुः वै दुर्जन् ईरितैः।
दुरुक्तैः भिन्नम् आत्मानं यः समाधातुम् ईश्वरः॥२॥

न तथा तप्यते विद्धः पुमान् बाणैः सुमर्मगैः।
यथा तुदन्ति मर्मस्थाः हि असतां परुषेषवः॥३॥

कथयन्ति महत्पुण्यम् इतिहासम् इह उद्धव।
तम् अहं वर्णयिष्यामि निबोध सुसमाहितः॥४॥

केनचित् भिक्षुणा गीतं परिभूतेन दुर्जनैः।
स्मरताः धृतियुक्तेन विपाकं निजकर्मणाम्॥५॥

अवनिषु द्विजः कश्चित् आसीत् आढ्यतमः श्रिया।
वार्तावृत्तिः कदर्यः तु कामी लुब्धः अतिकोपनः॥६॥

ज्ञातयः अतिथयः तस्य वाङ्मात्रेण अपि न अर्चिताः।
शून्य अवसथः आत्मा अपि काले कामैः अनर्चितः॥७॥

दुःशीलस्य कदर्यस्य द्रुह्यन्ते पुत्रबान्धवाः।
दारा दुहितरः भृत्याः विषण्णाः न आचरन् प्रियम्॥८॥

तस्य एवं यक्षवित्तस्य च्युतस्य उभयलोकतः।
धर्मकामविहीनस्य चुक्रुधुः पञ्चभागिनः॥९॥

तत् अवध्यान विस्रस्त पुण्य स्कन्धस्य भूरिद।
अर्थः अपि अगच्छन् निधनं बहु आयास परिश्रमः॥१०॥

ज्ञातयः जगृहुः किंचित् किंचित् अस्यवः उद्धव।
दैवतः कालतः किंचित् ब्रह्मबन्धोः नृपार्थिवात्॥११॥

सः एवं द्रविणे नष्टे धर्मकामविवर्जितः।
उपेक्षितः च स्वजनैः चिन्ताम् आप दुरत्ययाम्॥१२॥

तस्य एवं ध्यायतः दीर्घं नष्टरायः तपस्विनः।
खिद्यतः बाष्पकण्ठस्य निर्वेदः सुमहान् अभूत्॥१३॥

सः च आह इदम् अहो कष्टं वृथा आत्मा मे अनुतापितः।
न धर्माय न कामाय यस्य अर्थ आयासः ईदृशः॥१४॥

प्रायेण अर्थाः कदर्याणां न सुखाय कदाचन।
इह च आत्मोपतापाय मृतस्य नरकाय च॥१५॥

यशः यशस्विनां शुद्धं श्लाघ्याः ये गुणिनां गुणाः।
लोभः स्वल्पः अपि तान् हन्ति श्वित्रः रूपम् इव इप्सितम्॥१६॥

अर्थस्य साधने सिद्धः उत्कर्षे रक्षणे व्यये।
नाश उपभोगः आयासः त्रासः चिन्ता भ्रमः नृणाम्॥१७॥

स्तेयं हिंसा अनृतं दम्भः कामः क्रोधः स्मयः मदः।
भेदः वैरम् अविश्वासः संस्पर्धा व्यसनानि च॥१८॥

एते पञ्चदशान् अर्थाः हि अर्थमूलाः मताः नृणाम्।
तस्मात् अनर्थम् अर्थाख्यं श्रेयः अर्थी दूरतः त्यजेत्॥१९॥

भिद्यन्ते भ्रातरः दाराः पितरः सुहृदः तथा।
एकास्निग्धाः काकिणिना सद्यः सर्वे अरयः कृताः॥२०॥

अर्थेन अल्पीयसा हि एते संरब्धा दीप्तम् अन्यवः।
त्यजन्ति आशु स्पृधः घ्नन्ति सहसा उत्सृज्य सौहृदम्॥२१॥

लब्ध्वा जन्म अमरप्रार्थ्यं मानुष्यं तत् द्विज अग्र्यताम्।
तत् अनादृत्य ये स्वार्थं घ्नन्ति यान्ति अशुभां गतिम्॥२२॥

स्वर्ग अपवर्गयोः द्वारं प्राप्य लोकम् इमं पुमान्।
द्रविणे कः अनूषज्जेत मर्त्यः अनर्थस्य धामनि॥२३॥

देवर्षि पितृ भूतानि ज्ञातीन् बन्धून् च भागिनः।
असंविभज्य च आत्मानं यक्षवित्तः पतति अधः॥२४॥

व्यर्थया अर्थेहया वित्तं प्रमत्तस्य वयः बलम्।
कुशलाः येन सिध्यन्ति जरठः किं नु साधये॥२५॥

कस्मात् संक्लिश्यते विद्वान् व्यर्थया अर्थेहया असकृत्।
कस्यचित् मायया नूनं लोकः अयं सुविमोहितः॥२६॥

किं धनैः धनदैः वा किं कामैः वा कामदैः उत।
मृत्युना ग्रस्यमानस्य कर्मभिः वा उत जन्मदैः॥२७॥

नूनं मे भगवान् तुष्टः सर्वदेवमयः हरिः।
येन नीतः दशाम् एतां निर्वेदः च आत्मनः प्लवः॥२८॥

सः अहं कलौ अशेषेण शोषयिहह्ये अङ्गम् आत्मनः।
अप्रमत्तः अखिलस्वार्थे यदि स्यात् सिद्धः आत्मनि॥२९॥

तत्र माम् अनुमोदेरन् देवाः त्रिभुवनेश्वराः।
मुहूर्तेन ब्रह्मलोकं खट्वाङ्गः समसाधयत्॥३०॥

श्रीभगवान् उवाच।
इति अभिप्रेत्य मनसा हि आवन्त्यः द्विजसत्तमः।
उन्मुच्य हृदयग्रन्थीन् शान्तः भिक्षुः अभूत् मुनिः॥३१॥

सः चचार महीम् एतां संयत आत्मेन्द्रिय अनिलः।
भिक्षार्थं नगर ग्रामान् असङ्गः अलक्षितः अविशत्॥३२॥

तं वै प्रवयसं भिक्षुम् अवधूतम् असज्जनाः।
दृष्ट्वा पर्यभवन् भद्रः बह्वीभिः परिभूतिभिः॥३३॥

केचित् त्रिवेणुं जगृहुः एके पात्रं कमण्डलुम्।
पीठं च एके अक्षसूत्रं च कन्थां चीराणि केचन॥३४॥

प्रदाय च पुनः तानि दर्शितानि आददुः मुनेः।
अन्नं च भैक्ष्यसम्पन्नं भुञ्जानस्य सरित् तटे॥३५॥

मूत्रयन्ति च पापिष्ठाः ष्ठीवन्ति अस्य च मूर्धनि।
यतवाचं वाचयन्ति ताडयन्ति न वक्ति चेत्॥३६॥

तर्जयन्ति अपरे वाग्भिः स्तेनः अयम् इति वादिनः।
बध्नन्ति रज्ज्वा तं केचित् बध्यतां बध्यताम् इति॥३७॥

क्षिपन्ति एके अवजानन्तः एषः धर्मध्वजः शठः।
क्षीणवित्तः इमां वृत्तिम् अग्रहीत् स्वजन उज्झितः॥३८॥

अहो एषः महासारः धृतिमान् गिरिः आडिव।
मौनेन साधयति अर्थं बकवत् दृढनिश्चयः॥३९॥

इति एके विहसन्ति एनम् एके दुर्वातयन्ति च।
तं बबन्धुः निरुरुधुः यथा क्रीडनकं द्विजम्॥४०॥

एवं सः भौतिकं दुःखं दैविकं दैहिकं च यत्।
भोक्तव्यम् आत्मनः दिष्टं प्राप्तं प्राप्तम् अबुध्यत॥४१॥

परिभूतः इमां गाथाम् अगायत नराधमैः।
पातयद्भिः स्वधर्मस्थः धृतिम् आस्थाय सात्विकीम्॥४२॥

द्विजः उवाच।
न अयं जनः मे सुखदुःखहेतुः न देवतात्मा ग्रहकर्मकालाः।
मनः परं कारणम् आमनन्ति संसारचक्रं परिवर्तयेत् यत्॥४३॥

मनः गुणान् वै सृजते बलीयः ततः च कर्माणि विलक्षणानि।
शुक्लानि कृष्णानि अथ लोहितानि तेभ्यः सवर्णाः सृतयः भवन्ति॥४४॥

अनीहः आत्मा मनसा समीहता हिरण्मयः मत्सखः उद्विचष्टे।
मनः स्वलिङ्गं परिगृह्य कामान् जुषन् निबद्धः गुणसङ्गतः
असौ॥४५॥

दानं स्वधर्मः नियमः यमः च श्रुतं च कर्माणि च सद्व्रतानि।
सर्वे मनोनिग्रहलक्षणान्ताः परः हि योगः मनसः समाधि॥४६॥

समाहितं यस्य मनः प्रशान्तम् दानादिभिः किं वद तस्य कृत्यम्।
असंयतं यस्य मनः विनश्यत् दानादिभिः चेत् अपरं किमेभिः॥४७॥

मनोवशे अन्ये हि अभवन् स्म देवाः मनः च न अन्यस्य वशं समेति।
भीष्मः हि देवः सहसः सहीयान् युञ्ज्यात् वशे तं सः हि देवदेवः॥४८॥

तं दुर्जयं शत्रुम् असह्यवेगं मरुन्तुदं तत् न विजित्य केचित्।
कुर्वन्ति असत् विग्रहम् अत्र मर्त्यैः मित्राणि उदासीन रिपून्
विमूढाः॥४९॥

देहं मनोमात्रम् इमं गृहीत्वा मम अहम् इति अन्ध धियः मनुष्याः।
एषः अहम् अन्यः अयम् इति भ्रमेण दुरन्तपारे तमसि भ्रमन्ति॥५०॥

जनः तु हेतुः सुखदुःखयोः चेत् किम् आत्मनः च अत्र ह भौमयोः तत्।
जिह्वां क्वचित् सन्दशति स्वदद्भिः तत् वेदनायां कतमाय कुप्येत्॥५१॥

दुःखस्य हेतुः यदि देवताः तु किम् आत्मनः तत्र विकारयोः तत्।
यत् अङ्गम् अङ्गेन निहन्यते क्वचित् क्रुध्येत कस्मै पुरुषः
स्वदेहे॥५२॥

आत्मा यदि स्यात् सुखदुःखहेतुः किम् अन्यतः तत्र निजस्वभावः।
न हि आत्मनः अन्यत् यदि तत् मृषा स्यात् क्रुध्येत कस्मात् न सुखं न दुःखम्॥५३॥

ग्रहाः निमित्तं सुखदुःखयोः चेत् किम् आत्मनः अजस्य जनस्य ते वै।
ग्रहैः ग्रहस्य एव वदन्ति पीडाम् क्रुध्येत कस्मै पुरुषः ततः अन्यः॥५४॥

कर्माः तु हेतुः सुखदुःखयोः चेत् किम् आत्मनः तत् हि जडाजडत्वे।
देहः तु अचित्पुरुषः अयं सुपर्णः क्रुध्येत कस्मै न हि कर्ममूलम्॥५५॥

कालः तु हेतुः सुखदुःखयोः चेत् किम् आत्मनः तत्र तत् आत्मकः असौ।
न अग्नेः हि तापः न हिमस्य तत् स्यात् क्रुध्येत कस्मै न परस्य द्वन्द्वम्॥५६॥

न केनचित् क्व अपि कथंचन अस्य द्वन्द्व उपरागः परतः परस्य।
यथाहमः संसृतिरूपिणः स्यात् एवं प्रबुद्धः न बिभेति भूतैः॥५७॥

एतां सः आस्थाय परात्मनिष्ठाम् अध्यासितां पूर्वतमैः महर्षिभिः।
अहं तरिष्यामि दुरन्तपारम् तमः मुकुन्द अङ्घ्रिनिषेवया एव॥५८॥

श्रीभगवान् उवाच।
निर्विद्य नष्टद्रविणः गतक्लमः प्रव्रज्य गां पर्यटमानः इत्थम्।
निराकृतः असद्भिः अपि स्वधर्मात् अकम्पितः अमुं मुनिः आह गाथाम्॥५९॥

सुखदुःखप्रदः न अन्यः पुरुषस्य आत्मविभ्रमः।
मित्र उदासीनरिपवः संसारः तमसः कृतः॥६०॥

तस्मात् सर्वात्मना तात निगृहाण मनो धिया।
मयि आवेशितया युक्तः एतावान् योगसंग्रहः॥६१॥

यः एतां भिक्षुणा गीतां ब्रह्मनिष्ठां समाहितः।
धारयन् श्रावयन् श्रुण्वन् द्वन्द्वैः न एव अभिभूयते॥६२॥

इति श्रीमद्भागवते महापुराणे पारमहंस्यां
संहितायामेकादशस्कन्धे भगवदुद्धवसंवादे
बिक्षुगीतनिरूपणं नाम त्रयोविंशोऽध्यायः॥२३॥

24 Sankhya Philosophy

English Rhyme

Krishna said:
I shall describe to you Sankhya philosophy,
Which established by ancient authorities be,

By its understanding a person can instantly,
Shed all the illusions of the material duality.

During the Krita-yuga the men originally,
Were experts in spiritual discrimination truly,

During the period of annihilation previously,
Seer alone, nondifferent from seen object be.

That one Absolute Truth, but remaining free,
From material dualities; speech, mind cut be,

Divided Self in material nature, living entities,
Trying to enjoy manifestations of nature truly.

One the material nature, which but embodies,
Subtle causes, manifesting matter products be,

The other is the very conscious living entity,
Which designated as the enjoyer does be.

When material nature agitated by my look be,
Goodness, passion, ignorance: materials three,

Modes manifested to fulfill pending desires truly,
Just of the conditioned Atmas unquestionably.

From these then arose primeval sutra clearly,
Along with the mahat-tattva but undisputedly,

Mahat-tattva transformation created ego falsely,
The cause of the living bewilderment entities'.

False ego, cause of physical sensation be,
The senses, and mind, encompasses clearly,

Both spirit, matter - showing in these varieties:
Of goodness, passion, ignorance: modes three.

False ego in ignorance physical insights be,
From it gross elements but generated be,

False ego in passion came the senses truly,
From it goodness mode arose eleven deities.

All these elements joint, impelled by Me,
Just to function in a fashion very orderly,

Together gave birth to universal egg truly,
Which My excellent place of residence be.

I Myself appeared within that egg clearly,
Which but floating on the causal water be,

From my navel arose universal lotus truly,
The birthplace of self-born Brahma surely.

Brahma, Atma of the universe, endowed be,
With mode of passion, doing great austerities,

And thus created planetary divisions three,
Bhur, Bhuvar Svar, with their presiding deities.

Heaven established as residence of gods be,
The Bhuvarloka as that for the spirits ghostly,

Earth for humans and mortal creatures worldly,
Mystics striving for liberation beyond them be.

Below earth for demons and Naga snakes be,
Thus destinations arranged for the worlds three,

As corresponding reactions for different work be,
As performed within the modes of nature three.

By mystic yoga, great austerities but attained be,
Renounced order of life, pure destinations surely,

Of Maharlok, Janolok, Tapolok, Satyalok truly,
But by devotional yoga, my abode attained be.

All results of fruitive work set in world by Me,
Supreme Creator acting as force of time clearly,

At times these modes of nature are seen surely,
Rising up or submerging in this river mighty,

Whatever features exist within the world visibly,
Be they small or great, thin or stout physically,

They contain both the material nature certainly,
And its actual enjoyer, the spirit, the Atma be.

Gold and earth existing as ingredients initially,
From gold one may fashion golden jewelry,

From earth clay pots, saucers fashion be,
Ingredients exist before, even if smashed be.

Material object made of crucial ingredient be,
Creates another object by alteration clearly,

A created object basis of another object be,
Having nature of its origin, destination finally.

Material universe may considered real be,
Having its novel ingredient in all stages truly,

In basic form, on creation of objects plainly,
Or even if those creations but destroyed be,

Maha-Vishnu the resting place of nature be,
Which is manifest by the power of time surely.

Thus nature, the Lord Vishnu, the Almighty,
And time are truly never different from Me,

As long as the Lord glancing on nature be,
The material world continues to exist clearly,

Manifesting through procreation perpetually,
Great, rainbow flow of universal creation be.

I universal form basis, with endless variety,
With creation, maintenance, destruction be,

Within all planets in dormant state originally,
Merging five elements forming infinite varieties.

At annihilation, the mortal body just food be,
Food merges as grains, grain back in earth be,

Earth fuses in subtle sensation, fragrance truly,
Fragrance into water, water into its taste quality.

Taste merges in fire, which merges into form be,
Form fuses in touch, touch merging in ether be,

Ether merges into the sensation of sound finally,
And senses merge into their origin subsequently.

Back to presiding gods, who fuse certainly,
Into mind, which as false ego in goodness be.

Sound into false ego in ignorance mode be,
First of physical elements, into nature totally.

The total material nature, primary repository,
Of three basic modes, merging into modes be,

Nature modes fusing into unmanifest nature be,
That unmanifest form merges into time clearly.

Time in Supreme, omniscient Maha-purush be,
Original activator of all, all life merges into Me,

Unborn Supreme Atma, alone, within self be,
From Him creation, annihilation manifested be.

As rising sun removes darkness of sky totally,
Cosmic scientific knowledge annihilation rids fully,

All illusory duality from the mind of a devotee,
Even if it enters heart, it cannot remain surely.

Thus I, perfect seer of material, spiritual fully,
Have stated this knowledge of Sankhya clearly,

Which destroys all the illusion of doubt totally,
By scientific creation analysis, annihilation truly.

Sanskrit Text 24

अथ चतुर्विंशोऽध्यायः।
श्रीभगवान् उवाच।
अथ ते संप्रवक्ष्यामि सांख्यं पूर्वैः विनिश्चितम्।
यत् विज्ञाय पुमान् सद्यः जह्यात् वैकल्पिकं भ्रमम्॥१॥

आसीत् ज्ञानम् अथः हि अर्थः एकम् एव अविकल्पितम्।
यदा विवेकनिपुणाः आदौ कृतयुगे अयुगे॥२॥

तत् मायाफलरूपेण केवलं निर्विकल्पितम्।
वाङ्मनः अगोचरं सत्यं द्विधा समभवत् बृहत्॥३॥

तयोः एकतरः हि अर्थः प्रकृतिः सोभयात्मिका।
ज्ञानं तु अन्यतरः भावः पुरुषः सः अभिधीयते॥४॥

तमः रजः सत्त्वम् इति प्रकृतेः अभवन् गुणाः।
मया प्रक्षोभ्यमाणायाः पुरुष अनुमतेन च॥५॥

तेभ्यः समभवत् सूत्रं महान् सूत्रेण संयुतः।
ततः विकुर्वतः जातः यः अहंकारः विमोहनः॥६॥

वैकारिकः तैजसः च तामसः च इति अहं त्रिवृत्।
तन्मात्र इन्द्रिय मनसां कारणं चित् अचित् मयः॥७॥

अर्थः तन्मात्रिकात् जज्ञे तामसात् इन्द्रियाणि च।
तैजसात् देवताः आसन् एकादश च वैकृतात्॥८॥

मया संचोदिताः भावाः सर्वे संहति अकारिणः।
अण्डम् उत्पादयामासुः मम आयतनम् उत्तमम्॥९॥

तस्मिन् अहं समभवम् अण्डे सलिलसंस्थितौ।
मम नाभ्याम् अभूत् पद्मं विश्वाख्यं तत्र च आत्मभूः॥१०॥

सः असृजत् तपसा युक्तः रजसा मत् अनुग्रहात्।
लोकान् सपालान् विश्वात्मा भूः भुवः स्वः इति त्रिधा॥११॥

देवानाम् ओकः आसीत् स्वः भूतानां च भुवः पदम्।
मर्त्य आदीनां च भूः लोकः सिद्धानां त्रितयात् परम्॥१२॥

अधः असुराणां नागानां भूमेः ओकः असृजत् प्रभुः।
त्रिलोक्यां गतयः सर्वाः कर्मणां त्रिगुण आत्मनाम्॥१३॥

योगस्य तपसः च एव न्यासस्य गतयः अमलाः।
महः जनः तपः सत्यं भक्तियोगस्य मद्गतिः॥१४॥

मया कालात्मना धात्रा कर्मयुक्तम् इदं जगत्।
गुणप्रवाहः एतस्मिन् उन्मज्जति निमज्जति॥१५॥

अणुः बृहत् कृशः स्थूलः यः यः भावः प्रसिध्यति।
सर्वः अपि उभयसंयुक्तः प्रकृत्या पुरुषेण च॥१६॥

यः तु यस्य आदिः अन्तः च सः वै मध्यं च तस्य सन्।
विकारः व्यवहारार्थः यथा तैजस पार्थिवाः॥१७॥

यत् उपादाय पूर्वः तु भावः विकुरुते अपरम्।
आदिः अन्तः यदा यस्य तत् सत्यम् अभिधीयते॥१८॥

प्रकृतिः हि अस्य उपादानम् आधारः पुरुषः परः।
सतः अभिव्यञ्जकः कालः ब्रह्म तत् त्रितयं तु अहम्॥१९॥

सर्गः प्रवर्तते तावत् पौर्व अपर्येण नित्यशः।
महान् गुणविसर्ग अर्थः स्थिति अन्तः यावत् ईक्षणम्॥२०॥

विराट् मया आसाद्यमानः लोककल्पविकल्पकः।
पञ्चत्वाय विशेषाय कल्पते भुवनैः सह॥२१॥

अन्ने प्रलीयते मर्त्यम् अन्नं धानासु लीयते।
धानाः भूमौ प्रलीयन्ते भूमिः गन्धे प्रलीयते॥२२॥

अप्सु प्रलीयन्ते गन्धः आपः च स्वगुणे रसे।
लीयते ज्योतिषि रसः ज्योती रूपे प्रलीयते॥२३॥

रूपं वायौ सः च स्पर्शे लीयते सः अपि च अम्बरे।
अम्बरं शब्दतन्मात्रः इन्द्रियाणि स्वयोनिषु॥२४॥

योनिः वैकारिके सौम्य लीयते मनसि ईश्वरे।
शब्दः भूतादिम् अपि एति भूतादिः महति प्रभुः॥२५॥

सः लीयते महान् स्वेषु गुणेषु गुणवत्तमः।
ते अव्यक्ते संप्रलीयन्ते तत्कले लीयते अव्यये॥२६॥

कालः मायामये जीवे जीवः आत्मनि मयि अजे।
आत्मा केवलः आत्मस्थः विकल्प अपाय लक्षणः॥२७॥

एवम् अन्वीक्षमाणस्य कथं वैकल्पिकः भ्रमः।
मनसः हृदि तिष्ठेत व्योम्नि इव अर्क उदये तमः॥२८॥

एषः सांख्यविधिः प्रोक्तः संशयग्रन्थिभेदनः।
प्रतिलोम अनुलोमाभ्यां परावरदृशा मया॥२९॥

इति श्रीमद्भागवते महापुराणे पारमहंस्यां
संहितायामेकादशस्कन्धे श्रीकृष्णोद्धवसंवादे
प्रकृतिपुरुषसाङ्ख्ययोगो नाम चतुर्विंशोऽध्यायः॥२४॥

25 Three Nature Modes & Beyond

English Rhyme

The Lord said, "Best among men, lend your ear,
Understand how entities, by modes, their nature wear.

Mind control, tolerance, truthfulness, and more,
Are qualities of goodness, opening wisdom's door.

Material desire, audacity, false pride, and gain,
Are qualities of passion, leading to struggle and pain.

Anger, stinginess, delusion, and fear,
Are qualities of ignorance, making the path unclear.

Dear Uddhav, the three modes combine,
In the mentality of 'I' and 'mine'.

The transactions of this world, in modes, they bask,
In religiosity, wealth, and sensual tasks.

A man desiring sense gratification, attached to family life,
Finds in religious and occupational duties, the modes rife.

Goodness is self-control, passion is lust,
Ignorance is anger, in these modes, we trust.

Any soul, be it man or woman, who worships divine,
Without worldly attachment, in goodness, they shine.

But one who worships for worldly gain,
In passion's domain, seeks violence, in ignorance's chain.

Three modes of nature, goodness, passion, and ignorance,
Influence the living entity, but not the divine stance.

They bind the living entity, to material forms they bind,
In the mode of goodness, joy and wisdom, they find.

When passion takes over, it leads to fame and wealth,
But also to anxiety and struggle, disrupting health.

When ignorance prevails, it obscures one's sight,
Leading to sorrow, illusion, and fright.

When consciousness is lucid, and senses from matter, free,
Fearlessness within the body, one can see.

This is the mode of goodness, pure and bright,
Where one has the opportunity, to realize the divine light.

The mode of passion, by symptoms, discern,
Too much activity, the senses, from objects, can't turn.

The mind is perplexed, the organs in strife,
Such is the passion-filled life.

When higher awareness fails, and can't concentrate,
The mind is ruined, ignorance does it demonstrate.

With the rise of ignorance, the wicked grow strong,
In this mode, many go wrong.

Alertness from goodness, dreaming sleep from passion,
Deep sleep from ignorance, in a fashion.

But the fourth state of consciousness, so grand,
Is transcendental, beyond these modes, it stands.

Those in goodness, to higher positions, elevate,
While ignorance forces one, to a lower state.

Those in passion, through human bodies, migrate,
But those free from all modes, to me, they relate.

Work offered to me, without desire for the fruit,
Is in the mode of goodness, absolute.

Work done for enjoyment, is in passion,
And work done in violence, shows ignorance in action.

Knowledge is in goodness, if it's absolute,
In passion, if it's dual, in ignorance, if it's brute.

But knowledge based on me, is transcendental,
Beyond the modes, it's fundamental.

Abode in forest, shows goodness, in town, shows passion,
In a gambling house, ignorance is in fashion.

But residence where I reside, is transcendental,
Beyond the modes, it's fundamental.

A worker free of attachment, is in goodness, so pure,
Blinded by desire, in passion, for sure.

Forgetting right from wrong, in ignorance, they fall,
But those who take shelter in me, transcend them all.

Faith in spiritual life, is in goodness, so bright,
Work fruit, it's in passion, in irreligious activities, it's not right.

But faith in my service, is purely transcendental,
Beyond the modes, it's fundamental.

Food that's wholesome, is in goodness, so pure,
That which pleases senses, in passion, for sure.

Unclean food, in ignorance, does distress,
But happiness found in me, is transcendental, no less.

Material substance, place, and time,
Work, faith, and life's climb,

All are based on the three modes of nature,
In every death, and in every creature.

Best of humans, understand this truth,
All states of being, in youth and in ruth,

Are related to the Atma and nature's interaction,
In all that is seen, heard, or only a fraction.

Gentle Uddhav, all phases of life,
Arise from work, in peace and in strife.

One who conquers these modes, so rife,
Can dedicate self to me, cutting ignorance with a knife.

Having achieved this human form, so rare,
Which allows one to knowledge, compare,

The intelligent should free themselves from every snare,
Engage in loving service to me, laying their hearts bare.

A wise sage, free from all material tie,
Should subdue his senses, to ignorance say goodbye.

Engaging in goodness, letting passion, ignorance lie,
He can then reach me, in the spiritual sky.

Freed from the mind's subtle condition,
And from the modes of material rendition,

The living entity finds complete satisfaction,
In experiencing my transcendental position.

Sanskrit Text 25

अथ पञ्चविंशोऽध्यायः।
श्रीभगवानुवाच।
गुणानाम् असमिश्राणां पुमान्येन यथा भवेत्।
तन्मे पुरुषवर्य इअदम् उपधारय शंसतः॥१॥

समः दमः तितिक्षा ईक्षा तपः सत्यं दया स्मृतिः।
तुष्टिः त्यागः अस्पृहा श्रद्धा ह्रीः दया आदिः स्वनिर्वृतिः॥२॥

कामः ईहा मदः तृष्णा स्तम्भः आशीः भिदा सुखम्।
मद उत्साहः यशः प्रीतिः हास्यं वीर्यं बल उद्यमः॥३॥

क्रोधः लोभः अनृतं हिंसा याञ्चा दम्भः क्लमः कलिः।
शोकमोहौ विषादार्ती निद्रा आशा भीः अनुद्यमः॥४॥

सत्त्वस्य रजसः च एताः तमसः च अनुमूर्वशः।
वृत्तयः वर्णितप्रायाः संनिपातम् अथः श्रुणु॥५॥

संनिपातः तु अहम् इति मम इति उद्धव या मतिः।
व्यवहारः संनिपातः मनोमात्र इन्द्रियासुभिः॥६॥

धर्मे च अर्थे च कामे च यदा असौ परिनिष्ठितः।
गुणानां संनिकर्षः अयं श्रद्धाः अतिधनावहः॥७॥

प्रवृत्तिलक्षणे निष्ठा पुमान् यः हि गृहाश्रमे।
स्वधर्मे च अनुतिष्ठेत गुणानां समितिः हि सा॥८॥

पुरुषं सत्त्वसंयुक्तम् अनुमीयात् शम आदिभिः।
कामादिभी रजोयुक्तं क्रोधाद्यैः तमसा युतम्॥९॥

यदा भजति मां भक्त्या निरपेक्षः स्वकर्मभिः।
तं सत्त्वप्रकृतिं विद्यात् पुरुषं स्त्रियम् एव वा॥१०॥

यदा आशिषः आशास्य मां भजेत स्वकर्मभिः।
तं रजःप्रकृतिं विद्यात् हिंसाम् आशास्य तामसम्॥११॥

सत्त्वं रजः तमः इति गुणाः जीवस्य न एव मे।
चित्तजा यैः तु भूतानां सज्जमानः निबध्यते॥१२॥

यदेतरौ जयेत् सत्त्वं भास्वरं विशदं शिवम्।
तदा सुखेन युज्येत धर्मज्ञान आदिभिः पुमान्॥१३॥

यदा जयेत् तमः सत्त्वं रजः सङ्गं भिदा चलम्।
तदा दुःखेन युज्येत कर्मणा यशसा श्रिया॥१४॥

यदा जयेत् रजः सत्त्वं तमः मूढः लयं जडम्।
युज्येत शोकमोहाभ्यां निद्रया हिंसया आशया॥१५॥

यदा चित्तं प्रसीदेत इन्द्रियाणां च निर्वृतिः।
देहे अभयं मनोसङ्गं तत् सत्त्वं विद्धि मत्पदम्॥१६॥

विकुर्वन् क्रियया च अधीर निर्वृतिः च चेतसाम्।
गात्रास्वास्थ्यं मनः भ्रान्तं रजः एतैः निशामय॥१७॥

सीदत् चित्तं विलीयेत चेतसः ग्रहणे अक्षमम्।
मनः नष्टं तमः ग्लानिः तमः तत् उपधारय॥१८॥

एधमाने गुणे सत्त्वे देवानां बलम् एधते।
असुराणां च रजसि तमसि उद्धव रक्षसाम्॥१९॥

सत्त्वात् जगरणं विद्यात् रजसा स्वप्नम् आदिशेत्।
प्रस्वापं तमसा जन्तोः तुरीयं त्रिषु सन्ततम्॥२०॥

उपर्युपरि गच्छन्ति सत्त्वेन आब्रह्मणः जनाः।
तमसा अधः अधः आमुख्यात् रजसा अन्तरचारिणः॥२१॥

सत्त्वे प्रलीनाः स्वः यान्ति नरलोकं रजोलयाः।
तमोलयाः तु निरयं यान्ति माम् एव निर्गुणाः॥२२॥

मदर्पणं निष्फलं वा सात्विकं निजकर्म तत्।
राजसं फलसङ्कल्पं हिंसाप्रायादि तामसम्॥२३॥

कैवल्यं सात्विकं ज्ञानं रजः वैकल्पिकं च यत्।
प्राकृतं तामसं ज्ञानं मन्निष्ठं निर्गुणं स्मृतम्॥२४॥

वनं तु सात्विकः वासः ग्रामः राजसः उच्यते।
तामसं द्यूतसदनं मन्निकेतनं तु निर्गुणम्॥२५॥

सात्विकः कारकः असङ्गी रागान्धः राजसः स्मृतः।
तामसः स्मृतिविभ्रष्टः निर्गुणः मदपाश्रयः॥२६॥

सात्त्विकी आध्यात्मिकी श्रद्धा कर्मश्रद्धा तु राजसी।
तामस्यधर्मे या श्रद्धा मत्सेवायां तु निर्गुणा॥२७॥

पथ्यं पूतम् अनायः तम् आहार्यं सात्त्विकं स्मृतम्।
राजसं च इन्द्रियप्रेष्ठं तामसं च आर्तिद अशुचि॥२८॥

सात्त्विकं सुखम् आत्मोत्थं विषयोत्थं तु राजसम्।
तामसं मोहदैनोत्थं निर्गुणं मदपाश्रयम्॥२९॥

द्रव्यं देशः फलं कालः ज्ञानं कर्म च कारकाः।
श्रद्धा अवस्था आकृतिः निष्ठा त्रैगुण्यः सर्वः एव हि॥३०॥

सर्वे गुणमयाः भावाः पुरुष अव्यक्त धिष्ठिताः।
एताः संसृतयः पुंसः गुणकर्मनिबन्धनाः॥३१॥

येन इमे निर्जिताः सौम्य गुणाः जीवेन चित्तजाः।
भक्तियोगेन मन्निष्ठः मद्भावाय प्रपद्यते॥३२॥

तस्मात् अहम् इमं लब्ध्वा ज्ञानविज्ञानसंभवम्।
गुणसङ्गं विनिर्धूय मां भजन्तु विचक्षणाः॥३३॥

निःसङ्गः मां भजेत् विद्वान् अप्रमत्तः जितेन्द्रियः।
रजः तमः च अभिजयेत् सत्त्वसंसेवया मुनिः॥३४॥

सत्त्वं च अभिजयेत् युक्तः नैरपेक्ष्येण शान्तधीः।
संपद्यते गुणैः मुक्तः जीवः जीवं विहाय माम्॥३५॥

जीवः जीवविनिर्मुक्तः गुणैः च आशयसंभवैः।
मया एव ब्रह्मणा पूर्णः न बहिः न अन्तरः चरेत्॥३६॥

इति श्रीमद्भागवते महापुराणे पारमहंस्यां
संहितायामेकादशस्कन्धे श्रीकृष्णोद्धवसंवादे
गुणनिर्गुणनिरूपणं नाम पञ्चविंशोऽध्यायः॥२५॥

26 Aila Gita

English Rhyme

The Lord once said with divine decree,
"Human life, a chance to realize me.

In my service, find your role,
Reach for me, the pleasure's sole.

I am the Supreme Atma, can't you see?
Residing in hearts, in you and me."

A person of knowledge, transcendent and pure,
Sees the illusion, of nature's allure.

Unreal are its products, its modes but a game,
In this constant change, he remains the same.

Beware of the materialists, in pleasure they drown,
Chasing their desires, they wear a fool's crown.

Like a blind man following another,
Into darkness, they pull each other.

A song was sung by Emperor Pururava,
Of his wife Urvasi, he was in awe.

But when she left, he felt the sting,
In his nakedness, he felt the king.

"My wife, my wife!" he cried in vain,
His heart aflame, consumed by pain.

Years of pleasure, yet unsatisfied,
In the arms of night, his senses lied.

King Aila lamented his pitiful state,
In the grip of lust, he met his fate.

"Alas!" he cried, "See my delusion!
In the arms of a goddess, I found confusion."

Days turned to years, in a blink,
Under her spell, he didn't think.

A mighty emperor, reduced to a toy,
In the hands of women, he found no joy.

Naked and shamed, he followed her still,
A blade of grass against her will.

His power, his influence, all for naught,
In the face of desire, he was caught.

What use is knowledge, austerity, and grace,
When one's mind is lost in a woman's embrace?

To hell with me! I am a fool,
In the game of love, there is no rule.

Even the nectar of Urvasi's lips,
Couldn't quench his heart's eclipse.

Like a fire that burns, never to cease,
In the arms of desire, he found no peace.

Only the Lord, beyond our sight,
Can save a soul from such a plight.

For I am ignorant of my spiritual part,
A snake in the grass, close to my heart.

What is this body, polluted and vile,
Full of odors, devoid of style?

Attracted was I, by a woman's grace,
But what are these features, but illusion's face?

Who owns this body, can one ever tell?
Parents, wife, or employer who yell?

Is it the fire's, or the jackal's feast,
Or the Atma within, to say the least?

Yet, when a man at a woman stares,
He thinks, "What beauty, none compares!"

But what difference is there, let's discuss,
Between us and worms, in this body of pus?

Even one who knows the body's lore,
Should avoid the company that makes the mind sore.

For the senses, when with their objects they meet,
Inevitably cause the mind's defeat.

The mind is calm, when it doesn't hear or see,
Thus, restricting senses sets it free.

So, never let your senses roam,
In the company of those, who call illusion home.

The Lord then said, with a voice so sweet,
"Maharaja Pururava, accept defeat.

Give up your position, let go of the vice,
Understand me as the Supreme, and achieve paradise.

An intelligent person should choose to be,
In the company of devotees, who set the mind free.

My devotees, with minds fixed on me,
Are peaceful, equal, from ego, they flee.

Greatly fortunate Uddhav, in such company,
There is constant discussion of me, in harmony.

Those who partake, in this divine feast,
Are purified of sins, to say the least.

Whoever hears, chants, and takes to heart,
These topics about me, they become a part,

Of my devotional service, they achieve the divine,
What more is left, for the devotee so fine?

Just as cold, fear, and darkness take flight,
For one who approaches the sacrificial light,

So dullness, fear, and ignorance cease,
For one engaged in serving the devotees in peace.

The devotees of the Lord, in knowledge, they bask,
Are the ultimate shelter, for those who ask.

They are like a strong boat, in the ocean of strife,
Rescuing those, who are drowning in life."

Just as food gives life to all creatures,
And I am the shelter when distress features,

Just as religion is the wealth of those,
Who from this world, choose to repose,

So are my devotees, the only refuge,
For those fearful of misery, on the verge.

My devotees bestow divine sight,
Unlike the sun, that gives light only in daylight.

They are the real deities, worthy of praise,
They are the real family, that one should raise.

They are one's own self, this is no lie,
Ultimately, they are nondifferent from I.

Thus, Maharaja Pururava, let go of his desire,
To be on the same planet as Urvasi, the celestial choir.

He began to wander the earth, free of all ties,
Completely satisfied within the self, he cut all ties.

Sanskrit Text 26

अथ षड्विंशोऽध्यायः।
श्रीभगवान् उवाच।
मत् लक्षणम् इमं कायं लब्ध्वा मद्धर्मः आस्थितः।
आनन्दं परमात्मानम् आत्मस्थं समुपैति माम्॥१॥

गुणमय्याः जीवयोन्याः विमुक्तः ज्ञाननिष्ठया।
गुणेषु मायामात्रेषु दृश्यमानेषु अवस्तुतः।
वर्तमानः अपि न पुमान् युज्यते अवस्तुभिः गुणैः॥२॥

सङ्गं न कुर्यात् असतां शिश्न उदर तृपां क्वचित्।
तस्य अनुगतः तमसि अन्धे पतति अन्ध अनुगान्धवत्॥३॥

ऐलः सम्राट् इमां गाथाम् अगायत बृहच्छ्रवाः।
उर्वशी विरहात् मुह्यन् निर्विण्णः शोकसंयमे॥४॥

त्यक्त्वा आत्मानं व्रजन्तीं तां नग्नः उन्मत्तवत् नृपः।
विलपन् अन्वगात् जाये घोरे तिष्ठ इति विक्लवः॥५॥

कामान् अतृप्तः अनुजुषन् क्षुल्लकान् वर्षयामिनीः।
न वेद यान्तीः न अयान्तीः उर्वशी आकृष्टचेअतनः॥६॥

ऐलः उवाच।
अहो मे मोहविस्तारः कामकष्मलचेतसः।
देव्याः गृहीतकण्ठस्य न आयुःखण्डाः इमे स्मृताः॥७॥

न अहं वेद अभिनिर्मुक्तः सूर्यः वा अभ्युदितः अमुया।
मुषितः वर्षपूगानां बत अहानि गतानि उत॥८॥

अहो मे आत्मसंमोहः येन आत्मा योषितां कृतः।
क्रीडामृगः चक्रवर्ती नरदेवशिखामणिः॥९॥

सपरिच्छदम् आत्मानं हित्वा तृणम् इव ईश्वरम्।
यान्तीं स्त्रियं च अन्वगमं नग्नः उन्मत्तवत् रुदन्॥१०॥

कुतः तस्य अनुभावः स्यात् तेजः ईशत्वम् एव वा।
यः अन्वगच्छं स्त्रियं यान्तीं खरवत् पादताडितः॥११॥

किं विद्यया किं तपसा किं त्यागेन श्रुतेन वा।
किं विविक्तेन मौनेन स्त्रीभिः यस्य मनः हृतम्॥१२॥

स्वार्थस्य अकोविदं धिङ् मां मूर्खं पण्डित मानिनम्।
यः अहम् ईश्वरतां प्राप्य स्त्रीभिः गो खरवत् जितः॥१३॥

सेवतः वर्षपूगात् मे उर्वश्यः अधरासवम्।
न तृप्यति आत्मभूः कामः वह्निः आहुतिभिः यथा॥१४॥

पुंश्चल्या अपहृतं चित्तं कोन्वन्यः मोचितुं प्रभुः।
आत्मारामेश्वरम् ऋते भगवन्तम् अधोक्षजम्॥१५॥

बोधितस्य अपि देव्या मे सूक्तवाक्येन दुर्मतेः।
मनोगतः महामोहः न अपयाति अजितात्मनः॥१६॥

किम् एतया नः अपकृतं रज्ज्वा वा सर्पचेतसः।
रज्जुस्वरूप अविदुषः यः अहं यत् अजितेन्द्रियः॥१७॥

क्व अयं मलोमसः कायः दौर्गन्धि आदि आत्मकः अशुचिः।
क्व गुणाः सौमनस्य आद्याः हि अध्यासः अविद्यया कृतः॥१८॥

पित्रोः किं स्वं नु भार्यायाः स्वामिनः अग्नेः श्वगृध्रयोः।
किम् आत्मनः किं सुहृदाम् इति यः न अवसीयते॥१९॥

तस्मिन् कलेवरे अमेध्ये तुच्छनिष्ठे विषज्जते।
अहो सुभद्रं सुनसं सुस्मितं च मुखं स्त्रियः॥२०॥

त्वङ् मांस रुधिर स्नायु मेदो मज्जा अस्थि संहतौ।
विण्मूत्रपूये रमतां कृमीणां कियत् अन्तरम्॥२१॥

अथ अपि न उपसज्जेत स्त्रीषु स्त्रैणेषु च अर्थवित्।
विषय इन्द्रिय संयोगात् मनः क्षुभ्यति न अन्यथा॥२२॥

अदृष्टात् अश्रुतात् भावात् न भावः उपजायते।
असंप्रयुञ्जतः प्राणान् शाम्यति स्तिमितं मनः॥२३॥

तस्मात् सङ्गः न कर्तव्यः स्त्रीषु स्त्रैणेषु च इन्द्रियैः।
विदुषां च अपि अविश्रब्धः षड्वर्गः किमु मादृशाम्॥२४॥

श्रीभगवान् उवाच।
एवं प्रगायन् नृपदेवदेवः सः उर्वशीलोकम् अथः विहाय।
आत्मानम् आत्मनि अवगम्य मां वै उपारमत् ज्ञानविधूतमोहः॥२५॥

ततः दुःसङ्गम् उत्सृज्य सत्सु सज्जेत बुद्धिमान्।
सन्तः एतस्य छिन्दन्ति मनोव्यासङ्गमुक्तिभिः॥२६॥

सन्तः अनपेक्षाः मच्चित्ताः प्रशान्ताः समदर्शिनः।
निर्ममाः निरहङ्काराः निर्द्वन्द्वाः निष्परिग्रहाः॥२७॥

तेषु नित्यं महाभागः महाभागेषु मत्कथाः।
संभवन्ति हिता नृणां जुषतां प्रपुनन्ति अघम्॥२८॥

ताः ये श्रुण्वन्ति गायन्ति हि अनुमोदन्ति च अदृताः।
मत्पराः श्रद्दधानाः च भक्तिं विन्दन्ति ते मयि॥२९॥

भक्तिं लब्धवतः साधोः किम् अन्यत् अवशिष्यते।
मयि अनन्तगुणे ब्रह्मणि आनन्द अनुभव आत्मनि॥३०॥

यथा उपश्रयमाणस्य भगवन्तं विभावसुम्।
शीतं भयं तमः अपि एति साधून् संसेवतः तथा॥३१॥

निमज्ज्य उन्मज्ज्यतां घोरे भवाब्धौ परम अयनम्।
सन्तः ब्रह्मविदः शान्ताः नौः दृढ इव अप्सु मज्जताम्॥३२॥

अन्नं हि प्राणिनां प्राणः आर्तानां शरणं तु अहम्।
धर्मः वित्तं नृणां प्रेत्य सन्तः अर्वाक् बिभ्यतः अरणम्॥३३॥

सन्तः दिशन्ति चक्षूंषि बहिः अर्कः समुत्थितः।
देवताः बान्धवाः सन्तः सन्तः आत्मा अहम् एव च॥३४॥

वैतसेनः ततः अपि एवम् उर्वश्या लोकनिःस्पृहः।
मुक्तसङ्गः महीम् एताम् आत्मारामः चचार ह॥३५॥

इति श्रीमद्भागवते महापुराणे पारमहंस्यां
संहितायामेकादशस्कन्धे श्रीकृष्णोद्धवसंवादे
ऐलगीतं नाम षड्विंशोऽध्यायः॥२६॥

27 Kriya Yoga Gita

English Rhyme

Uddhav spoke, his voice a gentle hum,
"Dear Lord, your devotees, they've come,

To learn the method, the sacred way,
To worship you, in your Deity's array.

What makes a devotee, what's their test?
On what foundation is their worship best?

The sages declare, with voices clear,
That such worship is the most dear.

Narada, Vyasadeva, and Brihaspati,
All concur, in this they agree,

The process of worship, from your lotus lips,
Is the greatest of all spiritual trips.

From Brahma to Bhrigu, the knowledge flowed,
From Shiva to Parvati, the wisdom showed,

Accepted by all, in society's span,
Even by women and the sudra clan.

Lotus-eyed one, universe's Lord,
Please explain, in clear accord,

The means of liberation, the sacred art,
From the bondage of work, how do we part?

The Lord replied, his voice like a song,
"Dear Uddhav, the path is long,

Innumerable are the Vedic ways,
To execute the Deity's praise.

Worship me with care, choose your path,
Vedic, tantric, or a mix of both hath,

Listen faithfully, understand the rite,
Of the twice-born's worship, in its right.

A twice-born should, with heart so pure,
Worship me, of this be sure,

With appropriate offerings, in devotion true,
In my Deity form, or in nature's view.

Purify the body, cleanse the teeth,
Bathe in water, feel the relief,

Then smear the body with earth so fine,
Chant the mantras, Vedic and tantric line.

Fix the mind on me, let it not waver,
Perform your duties, let your devotion not waiver,

Chant the Gayatri, at the day's three joints,
Such acts the Vedas appoints.

My Deity form, in eight varieties it comes,
Stone, wood, metal, the list runs,

Earth, paint, sand, mind or jewels,
In these forms, the Deity rules.

My Deity form, the living entities' shelter,
Can be established, in ways helter-skelter,

Temporary or permanent, but once called,
The permanent Deity, can never be stalled.

The temporary Deity, can be called and sent,
But these rituals, are always meant,

For the Deity traced on the ground's face,
Bathing should be done, but not always the case.

Worship me in my Deity forms, offer the best,
But a devotee free from desire, faces the test,

He may worship me, with what he can obtain,
Even within his heart, with mental train."

In the temple's sacred space, Uddhav dear,
Bathing, decoration, offerings clear,

For the Deity traced on sacred ground,
Tattva-vinyasa is most profound.

Sesame, barley soaked in ghee,
Offered to the fire, a sight to see,

Upasthana and arghya for the sun,
Worship in water, the holy one.

Even a little water, offered with faith,
Is dear to me, in every case,

Opulent presentations, they may be,
But without devotion, they don't satisfy me.

Cleanse thyself, collect with care,
All the paraphernalia, handle with flair,

Arrange your seat, with kusa grass,
Tips pointing east, let the moments pass.

Sit facing east or north, in quiet contemplation,
Or face the Deity, in divine orientation,

Sanctify your body, touch and chant,
Do the same for my Deity, nothing scant.

Clean the Deity, with hands so pure,
Of old flowers, and offerings of yore,

Prepare the sacred pot, the sprinkling vessel,
In this worship, you must wrestle.

With the proksaniya's water, sprinkle around,
The Deity, the offerings, the ground,

Adorn with auspicious materials, three vessels of water,
In this worship, you're the author.

Purify the vessels, one, two, three,
Chant the mantras, let your spirit free,

Meditate on my subtle form, within you,
The source of all life, eternally true.

Invite the Parmatma, to join the Deity's form,
Worship me, let your heart transform,

Imagine my seat, decorated with deities,
Of religion, knowledge, renunciation, and opieties.

My nine spiritual energies, around me swirl,
In an eight-petaled lotus, with saffron curl,

Offer me water, for feet and mouth,
Arghya and others, from north to south.

By this process, you'll come to see,
Both material enjoyment, and liberation free,

Worship in order, my Sudarsana disc,
My Pancajanya, my club, don't risk.

My sword, my bow, arrows and plow,
My musala weapon, my Kaustubha now,

My flower garland, the Srivatsa on my chest,
In this worship, you'll be blessed.

Worship my associates, Nanda and Sunanda,
Garuda, Pracanda, and Canda,

Mahabala, Bala, in adoration,
Kumuda, Kumudeksana, in veneration.

With proksana offerings, worship begins,
Durga, Vinayaka, Vyasa, sins cleans,

Visvaksena, spiritual masters, gods in line,
All in their places, facing the Divine.

Bathe the Deity, as assets permit,
With waters scented, where fragrances sit,

Sandalwood, usira, camphor's delight,
Kunkuma, aguru, a pleasing sight.

Chant the Vedic hymns, let them ring,
Svarna-gharma, Mahapurusa-vidya sing,

Purusa-sukta, Sama Veda's song,
Rajana, Rohinya, to the Lord belong.

Decorate the Lord, with love and care,
Clothing, Brahmin thread, ornaments wear,

Marks of tilaka, garlands so fine,
Anoint the body, with oils divine.

Present the Lord, with offerings pure,
Water, oils, flowers, grains secure,

Incense, lamps, offerings galore,
In faithful worship, let your heart pour.

Offer the Lord, within your means,
Sugar candy, sweet rice, ghee's sheens,

Saskuli, apupa, modaka sweet,
Samyava, yogurt, soups to eat.

On special occasions, daily if so,
Massage the Deity, let your devotion show,

Mirror, eucalyptus stick, nectar bath,
Opulent foods, singing, dancing's path.

In the sacred arena, fire sacrifice make,
Sacred belt, sacrificial pit, altar take,

Ignite the fire, with wood piled high,
By your own hands, under the sky.

Spread kusa grass, sprinkle with water,
Perform anvadhana, as the scriptures order,

Arrange the oblations, sanctify with care,
Meditate on the Lord, in the fire's glare.

Meditate on the Lord, of molten gold hue,
Four arms resplendent, a vision true,

Conch shell, disc, club, lotus in hand,
Peaceful, dressed in lotus garment grand.

Helmet, bracelets, belt shine bright,
Arm ornaments fine, a splendid sight,

Srivatsa symbol, Kaustubha gem's glow,
Garland of forest flowers, in devotion bestow.

Worship the Lord, with firewood soaked,
In sacrificial ghee, devotion invoked,

Perform aghara, present the oblation,
To sixteen gods, in sacred dedication.

Having worshiped thus, in fire's embrace,
Bow to the Lord's associates, in humble grace,

Present offerings, chant the mula-mantra low,
Remember Narayana, let your devotion flow.

Offer the Deity, water once more,
Give remnants of food, to Visvaksena adore,

Present the Deity, with perfume's scent,
And prepared betel nut, in worship spent.

Sing along with others, chant and dance,
In my transcendental pastimes, take a chance,

Hear and tell stories, in festivity immerse,
In such divine joy, let your heart converse.

Offer homage to the Lord, with hymns and prayers,
From the Puranas, ancient scriptures, and traditional layers,

Pray, "Lord, be merciful to me," with devotion pure,
Fall flat, like a rod, in obeisance sure.

Place your head at the Deity's feet,
Stand with folded hands, the Lord to greet,

Pray, "Lord, protect me, I surrender to you,
In this ocean of existence, be my rescue."

Pray in this way, with respect and grace,
Place the remnants on your head, in a sacred space,

If the Deity is to be sent away, perform the rite,
Place the Deity's light, in your heart's lotus light.

When faith in me develops, in my Deity form,
Worship me, for I am the norm,

I exist within all, and in my original state,
I am the Supreme Atma, the ultimate fate.

Worship me, through methods prescribed,
In Vedas and tantras, as described,

From me, you'll gain your desired perfection,
In this life and the next, in every direction.

Establish my Deity, construct a temple grand,
With beautiful gardens, across the land,

Provide flowers for worship, processions and holidays,
In such divine service, spend your days.

Offer the Deity gifts, of land and more,
So that worship and festivals, can forever pour,

You'll achieve opulence, equal to my own,
In such divine offerings, your devotion is shown.

Install the Deity, become earth's king,
Build a temple, three worlds under your wing,

Worship and serve the Deity, to Brahma ascend,
Perform all three, a transcendental form you'll end.

But one who serves, with no fruitive aim,
Attains me, in my eternal frame,

Worship me as described, with service pure,
You'll attain devotional service, of this be sure.

Steal not the property, of gods or the Brahmins,
Or live as a worm in stool, paying for your sins,

Not just the thief, but all who partake,
Must suffer a consequence, make no mistake.

Sanskrit Text 27

अथ सप्तविंशोऽध्यायः।
उद्धवः उवाच।
क्रियायोगं समाचक्ष्व भवत् आराधनं प्रभो।
यस्मात् त्वां ये यथा अर्चन्ति सात्वताः सात्वतर्षभ॥१॥

एतत् वदन्ति मुनयः मुहुः निःश्रेयसं नृणाम्।
नारदः भगवान् व्यासः आचार्यः अङ्गिरसः सुतः॥२॥

निःसृतं ते मुखाम्भोजाद्यत् आह भगवान् अजः।
पुत्रेभ्यः भृगुमुख्येभ्यः देव्यै च भगवान् भवः॥३॥

एतत् वै सर्ववर्णानाम् आश्रमाणां च संमतम्।
श्रेयसाम् उत्तमं मन्ये स्त्रीशूद्राणां च मानद॥४॥

एतत् कमलपत्राक्ष कर्मबन्धविमोचनम्।
भक्ताय च अनुरक्ताय ब्रूहि विश्वेश्वर ईश्वर॥५॥

श्रीभगवान् उवाच।
नहि अन्तः अनन्तपारस्य कर्मकाण्डस्य च उद्धव।
संक्षिप्तं वर्णयिष्यामि यथावत् अनुपूर्वशः॥६॥

वैदिकः तान्त्रिकः मिश्रः इति मे त्रिविधः मखः।
त्रयाणाम् ईप्सितेन एव विधिना मां समर्चयेत्॥७॥

यदा स्वनिगमेन उक्तं द्विजत्वं प्राप्य पूरुषः।
यथा यजेत मां भक्त्या श्रद्धया तत् निबोध मे॥८॥

अर्चायां स्थण्डिले अग्नौ वा सूर्ये वा अप्सु हृदि द्विजः।
द्रव्येण भक्तियुक्तः अर्चेत् स्वगुरुं माम् अमायया॥९॥

पूर्वं स्नानं प्रकुर्वीत धौतदन्तः अङ्गशुद्धये।
उभयैः अपि च स्नानं मन्त्रैः मृद्ग्रहणादिना॥१०॥

सन्ध्या उपास्ति आदि कर्माणि वेदेन अचोदितानि मे।
पूजां तैः कल्पयेत् सम्यक् संकल्पः कर्मपावनीम्॥११॥

शैली दारुमयी लौही लेप्या लेख्या च सैकती।
मनोमयी मणिमयी प्रतिमा अष्टविधा स्मृता॥१२॥

चल अचल इति द्विविधा प्रतिष्ठा जीवमन्दिरम्।
उद्वास आवाहने न स्तः स्थिरायाम् उद्धव अर्चने॥१३॥

अस्थिरायां विकल्पः स्यात् स्थण्डिले तु भवेत् द्वयम्।
स्नपनं तु अविलेप्यायाम् अन्यत्र परिमार्जनम्॥१४॥

द्रव्यैः प्रसिद्ध्यैः मत् यागः प्रतिमादिषु अमायिनः।
भक्तस्य च यथालब्धैः हृदि भावेन च एव हि॥१५॥

स्नान अलंकरणं प्रेष्ठम् अर्चायाम् एव तु उद्धव।
स्थण्डिले तत्त्वविन्यासः वह्नौ आज्यप्लुतं हविः॥१६॥

सूर्ये च अभ्यर्हणं प्रेष्ठं सलिले सलिल आदिभिः।
श्रद्धया उपाहृतं प्रेष्ठं भक्तेन मम वारि अपि॥१७॥

भूर्यपि अभक्त उपहृतं न मे तोषाय कल्पते।
गन्धः धूपः सुमनसः दीपः अन्न आद्य च किं पुनः॥१८॥

शुचिः संभृतसंभारः प्राक् दर्भैः कल्पित आसनः।
आसीनः प्राक् उदक् वा अर्चेत् अर्चायाम् अथ संमुखः॥१९॥

कृतन्यासः कृतन्यासां मदर्चां पाणिना मृजेत्।
कलशं प्रोक्षणीयं च यथावत् उपसाधयेत्॥२०॥

तत् अद्भिः देवयजनं द्रव्याणि आत्मानम् एव च।
प्रोक्ष्य पात्राणि त्रीणि अद्भिः तैः तैः द्रव्यैः च साधयेत्॥२१॥

पाद्य अर्घ आचमनीयार्थं त्रीणि पात्राणि दैशिकः।
हृदा शीर्ष्णा अथ शिखया गायत्र्या च अभिमन्त्रयेत्॥२२॥

पिण्डे वायु अग्नि संशुद्धे हृत्पद्मस्थां परां मम।
अण्वीं जीवकलां ध्यायेत् नाद अन्ते सिद्धभाविताम्॥२३॥

तया आत्मभूतया पिण्डे व्याप्ते संपूज्य तन्मयः।
आवाह्य अर्च आदिषु स्थाप्य न्यस्त अङ्गं मां प्रपूजयेत्॥२४॥

पाद्य उपस्पर्श अर्हण आदीन् उपचारान् प्रकल्पयेत्।
धर्मादिभिः च नवभिः कल्पयित्वा आसनं मम॥२५॥

पद्मम् अष्टदलं तत्र कर्णिकाकेसर उज्ज्वलम्।
उभाभ्यां वेदतन्त्राभ्यां मह्यं तु उभयसिद्धये॥२६॥

सुदर्शनं पाञ्चजन्यं गदासीषुधनुः हलान्।
मुसलं कौस्तुभं मालां श्रीवत्सं च अनुपूजयेत्॥२७॥

नन्दं सुनन्दं गरुडं प्रचण्डं चण्डम् एव च।
महाबलं बलं च एव कुमुदं कुमुदेक्षणम्॥२८॥

दुर्गां विनायकं व्यासं विष्वक्सेनं गुरून् सुरान्।
स्वे स्वे स्थाने तु अभिमुखान् पूजयेत् प्रोक्षण आदिभिः॥२९॥

चन्दन उशीर कर्पूर कुङ्कुम अगरु वासितैः।
सलिलैः स्नापयेत् मन्त्रैः नित्यदा विभवे सति॥३०॥

स्वर्णघर्म अनुवाकेन महापुरुषविद्यया।
पौरुषेण अपि सूक्तेन सामभीः राजनादिभिः॥३१॥

वस्त्र उपवीत आभरण पत्र स्रक् गन्ध लेपनैः।
अलंकुर्वीत सप्रेम मद्भक्तः मां यथा उचितम्॥३२॥

पाद्यम् आचमनीयं च गन्धं सुमनसः अक्षतान्।
धूप दीप उपहार्याणि दद्यात् मे श्रद्धया अर्चकः॥३३॥

गुडपायससर्पींषि शष्कुलि आपूप मोदकान्।
संयाव दधि सूपां च नैवेद्यं सति कल्पयेत्॥३४॥

अभ्यङ्ग उन्मर्दन आदर्श दन्तधौ अभिषेचनम्।
अन्नद्य गीत नृत्यादि पर्वणि स्युः उतान्वहम्॥३५॥

विधिना विहिते कुण्डे मेखलागर्तवेदिभिः।
अग्निम् आधाय परितः समूहेत् पाणिना उदितम्॥३६॥

परिस्तीर्य अथ पर्युक्षेत् अन्वाधाय यथाविधि।
प्रोक्षण्या आसाद्य द्रव्याणि प्रोक्ष्याग्नौ भावयेत माम्॥३७॥

तप्तजाम्बूनदप्रख्यं शङ्खचक्रगदाम्बुजैः।
लसत् चतुर्भुजं शान्तं पद्मकिञ्जल्कवाससम्॥३८॥

स्फुरत् किरीट कटक कटिसूत्रवर अङ्गदम्।
श्रीवत्सवक्षसं भ्राजत् कौस्तुभं वनमालिनम्॥३९॥

ध्यायन् अभ्यर्च्य दारूणि हविषा अभिघृतानि च।
प्रास्य आज्यभागौ आघारौ दत्त्वा च आज्यप्लुतं हविः॥४०॥

जुहुयात् मूलमन्त्रेण षोडशर्च अवदानतः।
धर्मादिभ्यः यथान्यायं मन्त्रैः स्विष्टिकृतं बुधः॥४१॥

अभ्यर्च्य अथ नमस्कृत्य पार्षदेभ्यः बलिं हरेत्।
मूलमन्त्रं जपेत् ब्रह्म स्मरन् नारायण आत्मकम्॥४२॥

दत्त्वा आचमनम् उच्छेषं विष्वक्सेनाय कल्पयेत्।
मुखवासं सुरभिमत् ताम्बूलाद्यम् अथ अर्हयेत्॥४३॥

उपगायन् गृणन् नृत्यन् कर्माणि अभिनयन् मम।
मत्कथाः श्रावयन् श्रुण्वन् मुहूर्तं क्षणिकः भवेत्॥४४॥

स्तवैः उच्चावचैः स्तोत्रैः पौराणैः प्रकृतैः अपि।
स्तुत्वा प्रसीद भगवन् इति वन्देत दण्डवत्॥४५॥

शिरः मत् पादयोः कृत्वा बाहुभ्यां च परस्परम्।
प्रपन्नं पाहि माम् ईश भीतं मृत्युग्रह अर्णवात्॥४६॥

इति शेषां मया दत्तां शिरसि आधाय सादरम्।
उद्वासयेत् चेत् उद्वास्यं ज्योतिः ज्योतिषि तत् पुनः॥४७॥

अर्चादिषु यदा यत्र श्रद्धा मां तत्र च अर्चयेत्।
सर्वभूतेषु आत्मनि च सर्व आत्मा अहम् अवस्थितः॥४८॥

एवं क्रियायोगपथैः पुमान् वैदिकतान्त्रिकैः।
अर्चन् उभयतः सिद्धिं मत्तः विन्दति अभीप्सिताम्॥४९॥

मदर्चां संप्रतिष्ठाप्य मन्दिरं कारयेत् दृढम्।
पुष्प उद्यानानि रम्याणि पूजा यात्रा उत्सव आश्रितान्॥५०॥

पूजादीनां प्रवाहार्थं महापर्वसु अथ अन्वहम्।
क्षेत्रापणपुरग्रामान् दत्त्वा मत् सार्ष्टिताम् इयात्॥५१॥

प्रतिष्ठया सार्वभौमंसद्मना भुवनत्रयम्।
पूजादिना ब्रह्मलोकं त्रिभिः मत् साम्यताम् इयात्॥५२॥

माम् एव नैरपेक्ष्येण भक्तियोगेन विन्दति।
भक्तियोगं सः लभते एवं यः पूजयेत माम्॥५३॥

यः स्वदत्तां परैः दत्तं हरेत सुरविप्रयोः।
वृत्तिं सः जायते विड्भुक् वर्षाणाम् अयुतायुतम्॥७४॥

कर्तुः च सारथेः हेतोः अनुमोदितुः एव च।
कर्मणां भागिनः प्रेत्य भूयः भूयसि तत्फलम्॥७५॥

इति श्रीमद्भागवते महापुराणे पारमहंस्यां
संहितायामेकादशस्कन्धे श्रीकृष्णोद्धवसंवादे
सप्तविंशोऽध्यायः॥२७॥

28 Gyan Yoga Gita

English Rhyme

The Lord spoke, his voice a gentle breeze,
"Praise not, criticize not, let your judgments cease,

See this world, in its grand design,
As material nature and Atmas divine.

Indulge not in praise or criticism's snare,
For in illusory dualities, you'll lose your share,

Just as the Atma, in sleep or dream,
Loses consciousness, so it may seem.

So too, a person in material duality,
Must encounter illusion, and reality's fatality,

What is expressed by words, or meditated in mind,
Is not ultimate truth, in this world you'll find.

Shadows, echoes, mirages, all,
Are but reflections, however small,

Yet they cause a semblance of perception,
Just as the Atma's false identification.

The Parmatma alone, the ultimate controller,
The creator of this world, and its sole enroller,

The Atma of all existence, maintains and is maintained,
Withdraws and is withdrawn, by him, all is contained.

One who has understood, the process of knowledge,
Does not indulge in criticism, nor in praise's homage,

Like the sun, he wanders freely, without a care,
In this world, with wisdom to share.

By perception, deduction, testimony, realization,
Know this world has a beginning, and an end's station,

It is not the ultimate reality, this truth unmask,
Live in this world, without attachment's task."

Uddhav asked, his voice a curious song,
"Dear Lord, to whom does material existence belong?

The spirit Atma, with perfect knowledge endowed,
And the material body, not conscious, not loud.

The spirit Atma, inexhaustible, pure,
Transcendental, self-luminous, forever secure,

But the material body, like firewood, is dull,
In this world, who experiences the pull?"

The Lord replied, his voice a soothing tide,
"As long as the Atma, in material body resides,

Attracted to senses, and vital force,
His material existence, continues its course.

The living entity, is transcendental, it's true,
But due to his mentality, his material existence ensues,

Just as in a dream, he experiences all,
Upon awakening, he recalls.

Lamentation, elation, fear and anger,
Greed, confusion, hankering, danger,

Birth and death, experiences of the ego,
Not of the pure Atma, this truth we know."

The living entity, in false identification,
With body, senses, mind, in fascination,

Assumes the form, of his own making,
In material existence, he is partaking.

The false ego, though baseless it be,
Is perceived in forms, as many as the sea,

But with the sword of knowledge, sharp and true,
A sage cuts off this false view.

Real spiritual knowledge, a precious gem,
Discriminates spirit from matter, condemns,

Cultivated by evidence, austerity, perception,
Narrations, inference, without deception.

The Absolute Truth, alone and pure,
Before creation, after, and evermore,

Is the time factor, the ultimate cause,
Even in creation's pause.

Gold alone is present, before and after,
In its use, it's gold that we're after,

Similarly, I alone exist, in all time,
Before, after, and in creation's prime.

The material mind, in three phases manifests,
Wakefulness, sleep, deep sleep, in these rests,

Perceiver, perceived, regulator of perception,
In these roles, finds its reflection.

That which did not exist, and will not be,
Has no existence, can't you see?

It's but a superficial designation,
Created, revealed, by another's formation.

Though not existing in reality,
The mode of passion creates a duality,

Appears real, as the Absolute Truth,
Exhibits Himself, in material youth.

Understanding clearly, the Absolute Truth's position,
Refute misidentification, with expert precision,

Cut to pieces, all doubts about the self,
In the Atma's ecstasy, find your wealth.

The material body, of earth made,
Is not the true self, let it fade,

Nor senses, gods, air of life,
Nor external elements, nor mental strife.

For one who has realized, my identity,
As the Supreme Godhead, in entirety,

What credit if his senses, in meditation concentrate?
What blame if they agitate? It's not too late.

Indeed, what does it mean, to the sun so bright,
If the clouds come and go, obscuring light?

The sun shines on, in its radiant glory,
Unaffected, it continues its story.

The sky may display, qualities of air and fire,
Water and earth, heat and cold aspire,

Yet the sky is never entangled, in these qualities' play,
Just as the Supreme Truth, holds contaminations at bay.

Goodness, passion, ignorance, the ego's transformation,
Yet the Supreme Truth, remains in pure isolation,

Until by devotional service, one's mind is free,
From material passion, in its entirety.

Just as a disease, improperly treated,
Repeats its distress, until it's defeated,

So the mind, not purified, will find,
Attachment to material things, of every kind.

Sometimes progress is checked, by attachment's snare,
To family, disciples, others who care,

Sent by envious gods, to halt the stride,
But imperfect transcendentalists, on strength abide.

An ordinary entity, performs material work,
Driven by desires, that in shadows lurk,

But the wise, having tasted bliss so sweet,
Gives up material desires, fruitive work retreat.

The wise man, consciousness fixed in the self,
Does not notice his own actions, as if on a shelf,

Standing, sitting, walking, lying down,
Understands the body acts, in nature's gown.

A self-realized Atma, may sometimes see,
An impure object, an impure decree,

But he does not accept it, as real or true,
Just as a waking man, views a dream's residue.

Material nescience, expands in variety,
Accepted by the conditioned Atma, in anxiety,

But through spiritual knowledge, this nescience fades,
The eternal self, never assumed, never evades.

When the sun rises, it destroys the dark,
But it does not create, the objects that embark,

Similarly, realization of me, will clear,
The darkness covering, a person's true sphere.

The Supreme Lord, self-luminous, unborn,
Pure transcendental consciousness, in the morn,

Perceives everything, one without a second,
Realized only after, ordinary words have reckoned.

Apparent duality, perceived in the self,
Is but the confusion, of the mind's stealth,

Such supposed duality, has no basis, no room,
Apart from one's own Atma, in the cosmic loom.

The duality of elements, in names and forms,
Is perceived by those, who ignore the norms,

Those who say this duality is real,
Are pseudoscholars, in fanciful appeal.

The physical body, of the yogi in practice,
May sometimes be overcome, by disturbances drastic,

Therefore, a process is recommended, to be,
For the yogi, to overcome, and truly see.

Obstructions may arise, in the yogi's path,
Counteracted by meditation, or postures' math,

Concentration on breathing, austerities, mantras, herbs,
Each a tool, in the yogi's reserve.

Inauspicious disturbances, they may be,
But can be removed, gradually,

By remembrance of me, chanting my name,
Or following yoga masters, of great fame.

By various methods, some yogis find,
Freedom from disease, and old age unkind,

Keeping the body youthful, in their quest,
For material mystic perfections, they invest.

But this mystic bodily perfection, so it seems,
Is not valued highly, in transcendental dreams,

For the Atma, like a tree, is permanent, strong,
While the body, like a tree's fruit, does not last long.

Though the physical body, may be improved,
By yoga's processes, as it behooved,

The intelligent person, dedicated to me,
Gives up such procedures, lets them be.

The yogi, who has taken shelter in me,
Remains free from hankering, experiences glee,

Of the Atma within, in yoga's dance,
Never defeated by obstacles, in life's vast expanse.

Sanskrit Text 28

अथ अष्टविंशः अध्यायः।
श्रीभगवान् उवाच।
परस्वभावकर्माणि न प्रशंसेत् न गर्हयेत्।
विश्वम् एकात्मकं पश्यन् प्रकृत्या पुरुषेण च॥१॥

परस्वभावकर्माणि यः प्रशंसति निन्दति।
सः आशु भ्रश्यते स्वार्थात् असत्य अभिनिवेशतः॥२॥

तैजसे निद्रया आपन्ने पिण्डस्थः नष्टचेतनः।
मायां प्राप्नोति मृत्युं वा तद्वत् नानार्थदृक् पुमान्॥३॥

किं भद्रं किम् अभद्रं वा द्वैतस्य अवस्तुनः कियत्।
वाचा उदितं तत् अनृतं मनसा ध्यातम् एव च॥४॥

छायाप्रत्याह्वयाभासा हि असन्तः अपि अर्थकारिणः।
एवं देहादयः भावाः यच्छन्ति आमृत्युतः भयम्॥५॥

आत्मा एव तत् इदं विश्वं सृज्यते सृजति प्रभुः।
त्रायते त्राति विश्वात्मा ह्रियते हरति ईश्वरः॥६॥

तस्मात् नहि आत्मनः अन्यस्मात् अन्यः भावः निरूपितः।
निरूपितेयं त्रिविधा निर्मूला भातिः आत्मनि।
इदं गुणमयं विद्धि त्रिविधं मायया कृतम्॥७॥

एतत् विद्वान् मदुदितं ज्ञानविज्ञाननैपुणम्।
न निन्दति न च स्तौति लोके चरति सूर्यवत्॥८॥

प्रत्यक्षेण अनुमानेन निगमेन आत्मसंविदा।
आदि अन्तवत् असत् ज्ञात्वा निःसङ्गः विचरेत् इह॥९॥

उद्धवः उवाच।
न एव आत्मनः न देहस्य संसृतिः द्रष्टृदृश्ययोः।
अनात्मस्वदृशोः ईश कस्य स्यात् उपलभ्यते॥१०॥

आत्मा अव्ययः अगुणः शुद्धः स्वयंज्योतिः अनावृतः।
अग्निवत् दारुवत् देहः कस्य इह संसृतिः॥११॥

श्रीभगवान् उवाच।
यावत् देह इन्द्रिय प्राणैः आत्मनः संनिकर्षणम्।
संसारः फलवान् तावत् अपार्थः अपि अविवेकिनः॥१२॥

अर्थे हि अविद्यमाने अपि संसृतिः न निवर्तते।
ध्यायतः विषयान् अस्य स्वप्ने अनर्थ आगमः यथा॥१३॥

यथा हि अप्रतिबुद्धस्य प्रस्वापः बहु अनर्थभृत्।
सः एव प्रतिबुद्धस्य न वै मोहाय कल्पते॥१४॥

शोक हर्ष भय क्रोध लोभ मोह स्पृहादयः।
अहंकारस्य दृश्यन्ते जन्म मृत्युः च न आत्मनः॥१५॥

देह इन्द्रिय प्राण मनः अभिमानः जीवः अन्तरात्मा गुणकर्म मूर्तिः।
सूत्रं महान् इति उरुधा इव गीतः संसारः आधावति कालतन्त्रः॥१६॥

अमूलम् एतत् बहुरूप रूपितं मनोवचःप्राणशरीरकर्म।
ज्ञानासिना उपासनया शितेन छित्त्वा मुनिः गां विचरति अतृष्णः॥१७॥

ज्ञानं विवेकः निगमः तपः च प्रत्यक्षम् ऐतिह्यम् अथ अनुमानम्।
आदि अन्तयोः अस्य यत् एव केवलम् कालः च हेतुः च तत् एव
मध्ये॥१८॥

यथा हिरण्यं स्वकृतं पुरस्तात् पश्चात् च सर्वस्य हिरण्मयस्य।
तत् एव मध्ये व्यवहार्यमाणम् नानापदेशैः अहम् अस्य तद्वत्॥१९॥

विज्ञानम् एतत् त्रियवस्तम् अङ्ग गुणत्रयं कारण कार्य कर्तृ।
समन्वयेन व्यतिरिकतः च येन एव तुर्येण तत् एव सत्यम्॥२०॥

न यत् पुरस्तात् उत यत् न पश्चात् मध्ये च तत् न व्यपदेशमात्रम्।
भूतं प्रसिद्धं च परेण यद्यत् तत् एव तत् स्यात् इति मे मनीषा॥२१॥

अविद्यमानः अपि अवभासते यः वैकारिकः राजससर्गः एषः।
ब्रह्म स्वयंज्योतिः अतः विभाति ब्रह्म इन्द्रिय अर्थ आत्म विकार
चित्रम्॥२२॥

एवं स्फुटं ब्रह्मविवेकहेतुभिः परापवादेन विशारदेन।
छित्त्वा आत्मसन्देहम् उपारमेत स्वानन्दतुष्टः अखिल
कामुकेभ्यः॥२३॥

न आत्मा वपुः पार्थिवम् इन्द्रियाणि देवाः हि असुः वायुजलं हुताशः।
मनः अन्नमात्रं धिषणा च सत्त्वम् अहंकृतिः खं क्षितिः
अर्थसाम्यम्॥२४॥

समाहितैः कः करणैः गुणात्मभिः गुणः भवेत् मत्सुविविक्तधाम्नः।
विक्षिप्यमाणैः उत किं न दूषणम् घनैः उपेतैः विगतैः रवेः किम्॥२५॥

यथा नभः वायु अनल अम्बु भू गुणैः गतागतैः वर्तुगुणैः न सज्जते।
तथा अक्षरं सत्त्व रजः तमः मलैः अहंमतेः संसृतिहेतुभिः परम्॥२६॥

तथापि सङ्गः परिवर्जनीयः गुणेषु मायारचितेषु तावत्।
मद्भक्तियोगेन दृढेन यावत् रजः निरस्येत मनःकषायः॥२७॥

यथा आमयः असाधु चिकित्सितः नृणाम् पुनः पुनः सन्तुदति प्ररोहन्।
एवं मनः अपक्व कषय कर्म कुयोगिनं विध्यति सर्वसङ्गम्॥२८॥

कुयोगिनः ये विहित अन्तरायैः मनुष्यभूतैः त्रिदश उपसृष्टैः।
ते प्राक्तन अभ्यासबलेन भूयः युञ्जन्ति योगं न तु कर्मतन्त्रम्॥२९॥

करोति कर्म क्रियते च जन्तुः केनापि असौ चोदितः आनिपातात्।
न तत्र विद्वान्प्रकृतौ स्थितः अपि निवृत्त तृष्णः स्वसुख अनुभूत्या॥३०॥

तिष्ठन्तम् आसीनम् उत व्रजन्तम् शयानम् उक्षन्तम् अदन्तम् अन्नम्।
स्वभावम् अन्यत् किम् अपि इहमानम् आत्मानम् आत्मस्थमतिः न वेद॥३१॥

यदि स्म पश्यति असत् इन्द्रिय अथ नाना अनुमानेन विरुद्धम् अन्यत्।
न मन्यते वस्तुतया मनीषी स्वाप्नं यथा उत्थाय तिरोदधानम्॥३२॥

पूर्वं गृहीतं गुणकर्मचित्रम् अज्ञानम् आत्मनि अविविक्तम् अङ्ग।
निवर्तते तत् पुनः ईक्षया एव न गृह्यते न अपि विसृज्य आत्मा॥३३॥

यथा हि भानोः उदयः नृचक्षुषाम् तमः निहन्यात् न तु सद्विधत्ते।
एवं समीक्षा निपुणा सती मे हन्यात् तमिस्रं पुरुषस्य बुद्धेः॥३४॥

एषः स्वयंज्योतिः अजः अप्रमेयः महानुभूतिः सकलानुभूतिः।
एकः अद्वितीयः वचसां विरामे येन ईशिता वाक् असवः चरन्ति॥३५॥

एतावान् आत्मसंमोहः यत् विकल्पः तु केवले।
आत्मन् नृते स्वमात्मानम् अवलम्बः न यस्य हि॥३६॥

यत् नाम आकृतिभिः ग्राह्यं पञ्चवर्णम् अबाधितम्।
व्यर्थेन अपि अर्थवादः अयं द्वयं पण्डितमानिनाम्॥३७॥

योगिनः अपक्वयोगस्य युञ्जतः कायः उत्थितैः।
उपसर्गैः विहन्येत तत्र अयं विहितः विधिः॥३८॥

योगधारणया कांश्चित् आसनैः धारण अन्वितैः।
तपोमन्त्रौषधैः कांश्चित् उपसर्गान् विनिर्दहेत्॥३९॥

कांश्चित् मम अनुध्यानेन नामसंकीर्तन आदिभिः।
योगेश्वर अनुवृत्त्या वा हन्यात् अशुभदान् शनैः॥४०॥

केचित् देहम् इमं धीराः सुकल्पं वयसि स्थिरम्।
विधाय विविध उपायैः अथ युञ्जन्ति सिद्धये॥४१॥

न हि तत् कुशलात् दृत्यं तत् आयासः हि अपार्थकः।
अन्तवत्त्वात् शरीरस्य फलस्य इव वनस्पतेः॥४२॥

योगं निषेवतः नित्यं कायः चेत् कल्पताम् इयात्।
तत् श्रद्दध्यात् न मतिमान् योगम् उत्सृज्य मत्परः॥४३॥

योगचर्याम् इमां योगी विचरन् मत् व्यपाश्रयः।
न अन्तरायैः विहन्येत निःस्पृहः स्वसुखानुभूः॥४४॥

इति श्रीमद्भागवते महापुराणे पारमहंस्यां
संहितायामेकादशस्कन्धे भगवदुद्धवसंवादे
परमार्थनिर्णयो नाम अष्टाविंशोऽध्यायः॥२८॥

29 Bhakti Yoga Gita

English Rhyme

Uddhav spoke, his voice a gentle plea,
"Dear Acyuta, the yoga you describe, I see,

Is difficult for one, who cannot control his mind,
Please explain to me, a method more kind.

Lotus-eyed Lord, yogis try in vain,
To steady the mind, but find only pain,

Unable to perfect, the state of trance,
In their attempt, they weary in the dance.

Therefore, lotus-eyed Lord, of the universe vast,
Swanlike men take shelter, holding fast,

To your lotus feet, the source of all joy,
While those in pride, your illusory energy employ.

Dear infallible Lord, it's no surprise,
That you approach your servants, under the skies,

During your appearance as Ramacandra, so divine,
You showed affection for Hanuman, a sign.

Who could dare reject you, the Atma so dear,
The object of worship, the Supreme Lord clear,

Who gives all perfections, to devotees in your care,
Who would be so ungrateful, who would dare?

Transcendental poets, experts in spiritual lore,
Could not express their debt, even if they bore,

The lifetime of Brahma, for you appear,
As the Acharya, and Parmatma, ever near.

Sukadeva said, his voice a soothing balm,
Questioned by Uddhav, in affection's calm,

Krishna, the supreme controller, began to reply,
With a loving smile, and a twinkle in his eye.

The Lord said, his voice a gentle song,
I shall describe devotion, to conquer death's wrong,

Always remembering me, perform your duties true,
With mind and intelligence offered, attract my view.

Take shelter of holy places, where my devotees reside,
Be guided by their actions, let them be your guide,

Either alone or in gatherings, with singing and dance,
Celebrate holy days, in devotional trance.

With a pure heart, see me, the Supreme Atma within,
Unblemished by material, free from sin,

Present everywhere, externally, internally,
Just like the sky, eternally, eternally.

Brilliant Uddhav, view all living entities,
With the idea that I am present, in all varieties,

Offer due respect, considered wise,
See equally all, through enlightened eyes.

For him who meditates, on my presence within,
Bad tendencies of rivalry, envy, sin,

Along with false ego, are quickly destroyed,
In constant remembrance, of the Atma's void.

Disregard the ridicule, of companions near,
Give up the bodily conception, and its accompanying fear,

Offer obeisance before all, in humility's thread,
Even dogs, outcastes, cows, asses, let your respect spread.

Until one sees me, in all living beings,
Continue to worship, with mind, words, and feelings,

By such transcendental knowledge, of all-pervading Lord,
One sees the Absolute Truth, in accord.

Freed from doubts, give up fruitive actions,
In this process, find satisfaction,

Using mind, words, and bodily functions,
Realize me within all, without obstructions.

Dear Uddhav, this process, I decree,
Is transcendental, from material motivation free,

A devotee never suffers loss, in this pursuit,
In devotional service, they take root.

Uddhav, greatest of saints, in danger's face,
An ordinary person cries, fears, laments in disgrace,

But activities offered to me, without personal aim,
Even if externally useless, amount to religion's claim.

This process is the supreme intelligence, of the intelligent,
The cleverness of the clever, in life's event,

By following it, one can use the temporary, the unreal,
To achieve me, the eternal reality, the ideal.

Thus have I related, in brief and detail,
The science of the Absolute Truth, without fail,

Even for the gods, this science is a maze,
Difficult to comprehend, in its blaze.

I have spoken this knowledge, with clear reasoning,
Understand it properly, doubts will be easing,

Attain liberation, be free from all doubts,
On these clear answers, fix your thoughts.

One who disseminates this knowledge, among devotees,
Is the bestower of the Absolute Truth, with ease,

To him I give, my very own self,
In the lamp of transcendental knowledge, he finds wealth.

Anyone who listens, with faith and attention,
Engaging in my service, without pretension,

Will never become bound, by material work's chain,
In the reactions of material work, he will not remain.

Dear friend Uddhav, have you understood,
This transcendental knowledge, as you should?

Are confusion and lamentation, now dispelled,
In your mind, has clarity dwelled?

Share not this instruction, with those who are not true,
Hypocritical, atheistic, dishonest, without a clue,

Or with anyone who will not listen faithfully,
Who is not a devotee, or simply not humbly.

This knowledge should be taught, to one who is pure,
Free from bad qualities, with a heart that's sure,

Dedicated to the welfare, of the Brahmins kind,
Kindly disposed, saintly, with a noble mind.

And if common workers, and women too,
Are found to have devotion, for the Supreme Lord true,

They are also to be accepted, as hearers qualified,
In the path of knowledge, they are sanctified.

When an inquisitive person, comes to understand,
This knowledge, he has nothing further to demand,

For one who has drunk, the most palatable nectar,
Cannot remain thirsty, in this life's sector.

Through analytic knowledge, work, and mystic yoga's call,
Mundane business, political rule, people seek to install,

Religiosity, fiscal development, sense gratification, liberation,
But as my devotee, find all these in my adoration.

A person who gives up, all fruitive activities,
Offers himself to me, in service that gives,

Achieves liberation, from birth and death's ties,
And is promoted to share, in my own opulences' rise.

Sukadeva said, his voice a soothing balm,
Hearing Krishna's words, Uddhav felt a calm,

But his throat choked up, with love so deep,
His eyes overflowed with tears, he could not speak.

Steadying his mind, overwhelmed with love,
Uddhav felt grateful, to Krishna above,

Bowed down to touch, the Lord's lotus feet,
Spoke with folded hands, in reverence complete.

Uddhav said, his voice a gentle plea,
Unborn, primeval Lord, your mercy I see,

My ignorance dispelled, by your association kind,
How can cold, darkness, fear, a foothold find?

In return for my surrender, insignificant and small,
You bestowed on me, the torchlight of knowledge, tall,

What devotee of yours, with gratitude in his heart,
Could ever give up your lotus feet, and from you depart?

The rope of my affection, for the families dear,
Dasarhas, Vrsnis, Andhakas, Satvatas, near,

A rope you cast, by your illusory energy's might,
Is now cut off, by transcendental knowledge's light.

Obeisance to you, greatest of yogis, in your feet I find,
Undeviating attachment, to your lotus feet, bind,

Instruct me, surrendered unto you, in your wisdom steep,
How I may have this attachment, deep.

The Lord said, his voice a gentle song,
Dear Uddhav, take my order, to you it belong,

Go to my asrama, called Badarika, in sight,
Purify yourself, in the holy waters, bright.

Shed wrongful deeds weight, by the hallowed river's side,
Don bark attire, feast on nature's gifts, in purity abide,

Joy emerges, chains of longing broken, patience as our light,
Kind-hearted, self-restrained, inner peace, wisdom in sight.

With steadfast gaze, ponder these holy verses,
Inhale their spirit, clutch them tight, like age-old curses,

Voice and ponder the celestial, heighten your understanding,
Surpass the states, welcome infinity's landing.

Sukadeva proclaimed with a voice so clear,
Krishna, the wise, who quells life's fear,

Uddhav, the devotee, circled the Lord in reverence,
Fell at His feet, his heart in severance.

Free from worldly dualities, yet his heart did ache,
At the time of parting, his tears did make,

A river at the Lord's feet, a testament of his love,
His fear of separation, fitting like a glove.

Unable to leave the Lord's side, his heart in strife,
He bowed again and again, as if for life.

Placed his master's slippers on his head, a mark of respect,
And with a heavy heart, he had to accept.

With the Lord in his heart, Uddhav set forth,
To Badarikasrama, he ventured north.

Engaged in austerities, his devotion never swayed,
To the Lord's abode, his path was laid.

Krishna, the divine, served by yogis great,
Spoke to Uddhav, a discourse that would satiate.

The nectar of knowledge, an ocean of bliss,
Assured liberation for those who wouldn't miss.

To that Lord, Krishna, the greatest being,
I offer my obeisance, my heart agreeing.

He, the author of Vedas, the destroyer of fear,
Has given his devotees, the nectar so dear.

Sanskrit Text 29

अथ एकोनत्रिंशः अध्यायः।
सुदुस्तराम् इमां मन्ये योगचर्याम् अनात्मनः।
यथा अञ्जसा पुमान् सिद्ध्येत् तत् मे ब्रूहि अञ्जसा अच्युत॥१॥

प्रायशः पुण्डरीकाक्ष युञ्जन्तः योगिनः मनः।
विषीदन्ति असमाधानात् मनोनिग्रहकर्शिताः॥२॥

अथ अतः आनन्ददुघं पदाम्बुजम् हंसाः श्रयेरन् अरविन्दलोचन।
सुखं नु विश्वेश्वर योगकर्मभिः त्वत् मायया अमी विहताः न मानिनः॥३॥

किं चित्रम् अच्युत तव एतत् अशेषबन्धः दासेषु अनन्यशरणेषु यत् आत्म सात्त्वम्।
यः अरोचयत्सह मृगैः स्वयम् ईश्वराणाम् श्रीमत् किरीट तट पीडित पाद पीठः॥४॥

तं त्वा अखिल आत्मदयित ईश्वरम् आश्रितानाम् सर्व अर्थदं स्वकृतवित् विसृजेत कः नु।
कः वा भजेत् किम् अपि विस्मृतये अनु भूत्यै किं वा भवेत् न तव पादरजोजुषां नः॥५॥

न एव उपयन्ति अपचितिं कवयः तव ईश ब्रह्मायुषा अपि कृतम् ऋधमुदः स्मरन्तः।
यः अन्तर्बहिः तनुभृताम् अशुभं विधुन्वन् आचार्यचैत्यवपुषा स्वगतं व्यनक्ति॥६॥

श्रीशुकः उवाच।
इति उद्धवेन अति अनुरक्त चेतसा पृष्टः जगत्क्रीडनकः स्वशक्तिभिः।
गृहीत मूर्तित्रयः ईश्वर ईश्वरः जगाद सप्रेम मनोहरस्मितः॥७॥

श्रीभगवान् उवाच।
हन्त ते कथयिष्यामि मम धर्मान् सुमङ्गलाम्।
यान् श्रद्धया आचरन् मर्त्यः मृत्युं जयति दुर्जयम्॥८॥

कुर्यात् सर्वाणि कर्माणि मदर्थं शनकैः स्मरन्।
मयि अर्पित मनः चित्तः मत् धर्म आत्ममनोरतिः॥९॥

देशान् पुण्यान् आश्रयेत मद्भक्तैः साधुभिः श्रितान्।
देव आसुर मनुष्येषु मद्भक्त आचरितानि च॥१०॥

पृथक् सत्रेण वा मह्यं पर्वयात्रा महोत्सवान्।
कारयेत् गीतनृत्य आद्यैः महाराज विभूतिभिः॥११॥

माम् एव सर्वभूतेषु बहिः अन्तः अपावृतम्।
ईक्षेत आत्मनि च आत्मानं यथा खम् अमल आशयः॥१२॥

इति सर्वाणि भूतानि मद्भावेन महाद्युते।
सभाजयन् मन्यमानः ज्ञानं केवलम् आश्रितः॥१३॥

ब्राह्मणे पुल्कसे स्तेने ब्रह्मण्ये अर्के स्फुलिङ्गके।
अक्रूरे क्रूरके च एव समदृक् पण्डितः मतः॥१४॥

नरेषु अभीक्ष्णं मद्भावं पुंसः भावयतः अचिरात्।
स्पर्धा असूया तिरस्काराः साहङ्काराः वियन्ति हि॥१५॥

विसृज्य स्मयमानान् स्वान् दृशं व्रीडां च दैहिकीम्।
प्रणमेत् दण्डवत् भूमौ आश्व चाण्डाल गो खरम्॥१६॥

यावत् सर्वेषु भूतेषु मद्भावः न उपजायते।
तावत् एवम् उपासीत वाङ् मन काय वृत्तिभिः॥१७॥

सर्वं ब्रह्मात्मकं तस्य विद्यया आत्म मनीषया।
परिपश्यन् उपरमेत् सर्वतः मुक्त संशयः॥१८॥

अयं हि सर्वकल्पानां सध्रीचीनः मतः मम।
मद्भावः सर्वभूतेषु मनोवाक्कायवृत्तिभिः॥१९॥

न हि अङ्ग उपक्रमे ध्वंसः मद्धर्मस्य उद्धव अणु अपि।
मया व्यवसितः सम्यक् निर्गुणत्वात् अनाशिषः॥२०॥

यः यः मयि परे धर्मः कल्प्यते निष्फलाय चेत्।
तत् आयासः निरर्थः स्यात् भयादेः इव सत्तम॥२१॥

एषा बुद्धिमतां बुद्धिः मनीषा च मनीषिणाम्।
यत् सत्यम् अनृतेन इह मर्त्येन आप्नोति मा अमृतम्॥२२॥

एष ते अभिहितः कृत्स्नः ब्रह्मवादस्य संग्रहः।
समासव्यासविधिना देवानाम् अपि दुर्गमः॥२३॥

अभीक्ष्णशः ते गदितं ज्ञानं विस्पष्टयुक्तिमत्।
एतत् विज्ञाय मुच्येत पुरुषः नष्टसंशयः॥२४॥

सुविविक्तं तव प्रश्नं मया एतत् अपि धारयेत्।
सनातनं ब्रह्मगुह्यं परं ब्रह्म अधिगच्छति॥२५॥

यः एतत् मम भक्तेषु संप्रदद्यात् सुपुष्कलम्।
तस्य अहं ब्रह्मदायस्य ददामि आत्मानम् आत्मना॥२६॥

यः एतत् समधीयीत पवित्रं परमं शुचि।
सः पूयेत अहः अहः मां ज्ञानदीपेन दर्शयन्॥२७॥

यः एतत् श्रद्धया नित्यम् अव्यग्रः श्रृणुयात् नरः।
मयि भक्तिं परां कुर्वन् कर्मभिः न सः बध्यते॥२८॥

अपि उद्धव त्वया ब्रह्म सखे समवधारितम्।
अपि ते विगतः मोहः शोकः च असौ मनोभवः॥२९॥

न एतत् त्वया दाम्भिकाय नास्तिकाय शठाय च।
अशुश्रूषोः अभक्ताय दुर्विनीताय दीयताम्॥३०॥

एतैः दोषैः विहीनाय ब्रह्मण्याय प्रियाय च।
साधवे शुचये ब्रूयात् भक्तिः स्यात् शूद्र योषिताम्॥३१॥

न एतत् विज्ञाय जिज्ञासोः ज्ञातव्यम् अवशिष्यते।
पीत्वा पीयूषम् अमृतं पातव्यं न अवशिष्यते॥३२॥

ज्ञाने कर्मणि योगे च वार्तायां दण्डधारणे।
यावान् अर्थः नृणां तात तावान् ते अहं चतुर्विधः॥३३॥

मर्त्यः यदा त्यक्त समस्तकर्मा निवेदितात्मा विचिकीर्षितः मे।
तदा अमृतत्वं प्रतिपद्यमानः मया आत्मभूयाय च कल्पते वै॥३४॥

श्रीशुकः उवाच।
सः एवम् आदर्शित योगमार्गः तदा उत्तम श्लोकवचः निशम्य।
बद्ध अञ्जलिः प्रीति उपरुद्ध कण्ठः न किंचित् ऊचेः अश्रु परिप्लुत
अक्षः॥३५॥

विष्टभ्य चित्तं प्रणय अवघूर्णम् धैर्येण राजन् बहु मन्यमानः।
कृताञ्जलिः प्राह यदुप्रवीरम् शीर्ष्णा स्पृशन् तत् चरण अरविन्दम्॥३६॥

उद्धवः उवाच।
विद्रावितः मोह महा अन्धकारः यः आश्रितः मे तव सन्निधानात्।
विभावसोः किं नु समीपगस्य शीतं तमः भीः प्रभवन्ति अज अद्य॥३७॥

प्रत्यर्पितः मे भवता अनुकम्पिना भृत्याय विज्ञानमयः प्रदीपः।
हित्वा कृतज्ञः तव पादमूलम् कः अन्यत् समीयात् शरणं
त्वदीयम्॥३८॥

वृक्णः च मे सुदृढः स्नेहपाशः दाशार्ह वृष्णि अन्धक सात्वतेषु।
प्रसारितः सृष्टिविवृद्धये त्वया स्वमायया हि आत्म सुबोध हेतिना॥३९॥

नमः अस्तु ते महायोगिन् प्रपन्नम् अनुशाधि माम्।
यथा त्वत् चरण अम्भोजे रतिः स्यात् अनपायिनी॥४०॥

श्रीभगवान् उवाच।
गच्छ उद्धव मया आदिष्टः बदरि आख्यं मम आश्रमम्।
तत्र मत् पाद तीर्थोदे स्नान उपस्पर्शनैः शुचिः॥४१॥

ईक्षया अलकनन्दाया विधूत अशेष कल्मषः।
वसानः वल्कलानि अङ्ग वन्यभुक् सुख निःस्पृहः॥४२॥

तितिक्षौः द्वन्द्वमात्राणां सुशीलः संयतेन्द्रियः।
शान्तः समाहितधिया ज्ञानविज्ञानसंयुतः॥४३॥

मत्तः अनुशिक्षितं यत् ते विविक्तमनुभावयन्।
मयि आवेशित वाक् चित्तः मद्धर्म निरतः भव।
अतिव्रज्य गतीः तिस्रः माम् एष्यसि ततः परम्॥४४॥

श्रीशुकः उवाच।
सः एवम् उक्तः हरिमेधसा उद्धवः प्रदक्षिणं तं परिसृत्य पादयोः।
शिरः निधाय अश्रुकलाभिः आर्द्रधीः न्यषिञ्चत् अद्वन्द्वपरः अपि
उपक्रमे॥४५॥

सुदुस्त्यज स्नेह वियोग कातरः न शक्नुवन् तं परिहातुम् आतुरः।
कृच्छ्रं ययौ मूर्धनि भर्तृपादुके बिभ्रन् नमस्कृत्य ययौ पुनः पुनः॥४६॥

ततः तम् अन्तर्हृदि संनिवेश्य गतः महाभागवतः विशालाम्।
यथा उपदिष्टां जगत् एकबन्धुना ततः समास्थाय हरेः अगात्
गतिम्॥४७॥

यः एअतत् आनन्द समुद्र संभृतम् ज्ञानामृतं भागवताय भाषितम्।
कृष्णेण योगेश्वर सेविताङ्घ्रिणा सच्छ्रद्धया आसेव्य जगत्
विमुच्यते॥४८॥

भवभय अपहन्तुं ज्ञानविज्ञानसारम् निगमकृत् उपजहे भृङ्गवत् वेदसारम्।
अमृतम् उदधितः च अपाययत् भृत्यवर्गान् पुरुषम् ऋषभम् आद्यं कृष्णसंज्ञं नतः अस्मि॥४९॥

इति श्रीमद्भागवते महापुराणे पारमहंस्यां
संहितायामेकादशस्कन्धे भगवदुद्धवसंवादे
परमार्थप्राप्तिसुगमोपायकथनोद्धवबदरिकाश्रमप्रवेशो
नाम एकोनत्रिंशोऽध्यायः॥२९॥

30. Yadu Dynasty Disappears

Uddhav set forth for Badarikashrama, his journey begun,
Krishna advised the Yadavas, under the setting sun,

To abandon Dwarika, to Prabhasa they must steer,
On Sarasvati's bank, to counteract the looming fear.

Heeding his advice, to Prabhasa they came,
Lost in festivity, they played the fateful game.

Intoxicated, quarreling, they fell one by one,
Till not a man was left standing under the sun.

Bala, Krishna's brother, by yoga, his body he did yield,
At the sight, Krishna sat silently in the field.

A hunter named Jara, in error, let his arrow fly,
Struck Krishna's foot, mistaking it for a deer nearby.

Krishna consoled the repentant hunter, his heart ablaze,
Told him it was his own desire that guided his ways.

Krishna's charioteer, lamenting, came to his side,
Was told to inform Dwarika, of the Yadu's demise.

To leave Dwarika for Indraprastha, was Krishna's advice,
And the charioteer, obeying his Lord, paid the price.

Author

MunindraBooks.blogspot.com

Munindra Misra honoured with a badge & awarded

Top Viewed Author Award

by Knol, a unit of knowledge of Google
Over 108 Published works

The inimitable writings of Munindra Misra in English rhyme on Hinduism and Hindu culture, provides a lucid comprehension of the Sanatan (Eternal) Dharma's path, culture, traditions and practices. His unique and rare works are path breaking, peep into the heart and expression of its spiritual understanding, shedding light, making it easier to comprehend and appreciate. They have not been so exhaustively written in English rhyme previously.

In verses simple, with a rhythmic charm,
Munindra pens Dharma, of Sanatan arm.

Not word for word, but spirit he captures,
In English rhymes, of ancient scriptures.

Upanishads, Gitas and Purans unfold,
Tales of Goddesses, Gods, in rhymes bold.

Prayers, Neeti, Dohe, and Chalisa ring,
In simple verses that dance and sing.

No claim to fullness, just a guiding light,
An introduction to the spiritual height.

The Sanskrit's depth, do not fully bloom,
As words many, minus an English room.

Hidden imports, depths in names reside,
In Misra's work, they're gently implied.

An overview, a map to treasure vast,
Pointing to texts where truth is held fast.

For seekers true, the message is clear,
Original texts, one must hold dear.

For deep meanings and wisdom's root,
Sanskrit scriptures - the absolute pursuit.

Hindu Rhymes: https://hindurhymes.wordpress.com/
Website: https://MunindraBooks.blogspot.com/
Blog: https://MunindraMisra.blogspot.com/

ॐ

Way Beyond the Term 'God'

Sanatan Dharma in English rhyme

In Hindu thought, the term 'God' falls short,
Thus Brahman, Ishwar and Atma, we resort;
Not a being in heaven, but in all we see,
Brahman is the essence, in you and me.

Brahman, pure consciousness, unfathomable, vast,
Always present, the eternal contrast;
Sanatan Dharma, not religion but the way,
Where divinity in every moment does stay.

Seek not the 'God' in realms afar,
Find the divine within, where you truly are;
Transcendent yet imminent, closer than our bones,
Brahman, the reality, in whispers and tones.

The divine is not just a thought to conceive,
But an experience, in each breath we perceive;
Ishwar, Bhagwan, Devata, and more,
Each name a doorway to the divine core.

9 788119 264834

Printed at Repro India Ltd.